AF647439

# Witches, Tea Plantations, and Lives of Migrant Laborers in India

# Witches, Tea Plantations, and Lives of Migrant Laborers in India

Soma Chaudhuri

LEXINGTON BOOKS
*Lanham • Boulder • New York • Toronto • Plymouth, UK*

FOUNDATION® BOOKS

FOUNDATION® BOOKS

Foundation Books is an imprint of Cambridge University Press India Pvt. Ltd.

Cambridge House, 4381/4 Ansari Road, Daryaganj, New Delhi 110 002

www.cambridgeindia.org

Copyright © 2013 by Lexington Books

This edition was published by arrangement with Lexington Books.

This publication is in copyright. Subject to statutory exception and to the provisions of relevant collective licensing agreements, no reproduction of any part may take place without the written permission of Cambridge University Press India Pvt. Ltd.

First South Asia edition 2014

Printed in India at Sanat Printers, Kundli, Haryana

ISBN 978-93-82993-45-2 Hardback

Cambridge University Press India Pvt. Ltd. has no responsibility for the persistence or accuracy of URLs for external or third-party internet websites referred to in this publication, and does not guarantee that any content on such websites is, or will remain, accurate or appropriate.

Photospread images courtesy of Soma Chaudhuri

*To my parents, Susanta and Sukriti Chaudhuri, with love*

# Contents

# Note

North Bengal People's Development Center (NBPDC), the NGO that helped me get access to the field, requested that I use their real name in my book. I previously used the name Dooar's Development League (DDL), a pseudonym, to describe them in some of my earlier academic writings. NPBDC is a grassroots organization that has received no governmental financial aid to fight witch hunts in the region. Academic writings, such as this book, might bring this organization much needed attention and grants for their antiwitch hunt campaigns in the Dooars.

To protect the identity of all participants, I have changed all the names of the participants (unless they wanted their original names to be cited) and used fictitious names of locations (wherever necessary). The pictures used in this book are used with the permission of all the participants in the study.

# Acknowledgments

This book would not have been written without the support and kindness of the women and men who participated in this study. They patiently answered all my questions, knowing perhaps that in the end not much would change—that their lives would continue as before. I was humbled by the warm greetings they gave me every time I went to talk to them, and for their sincerity in answering my questions after their long days at work in the plantation. I am also very grateful to my friends at North Bengal People's Development Center, Jalpaiguri. Thank you Chandana di. Without your support, this project would not have been possible. Thank you, Lobha, Rita, Suchitradi, Bapi da, Manas da, Mashima, and Mitra da for allowing me into your lives wholeheartedly and for all your words of wisdom and friendship. I would also like to thank Shova Lama and her family for giving me a home in Tia Bon, Chalsa. Shova di also accompanied me on numerous trips around the region and helped me translate some of the interviews. Ram Kumar Lama in Central Doors and Balawant da in Falakata helped me arrange numerous trips in the region and accompanied me during all hours of the day to the sites. I am also very grateful to Malati and Jaochim Baxla in Kalchini for giving me access to *Gram Sabha* meetings and documents. Rahul Srivastav, IPS, and Jogesh Chandra Chatterjee, IPS, provided immense help with data from the police archives and ensured that I had the most secure place to stay and to store my data in the city of Jalpaiguri.

This project started as dissertation research at Vanderbilt University. I would like to acknowledge the funding support from two Summer Research Grants and one Dissertation Enhancement Grant from Vanderbilt University. I am very grateful to Gary F Jensen for his foresight and wisdom for supporting this project for the last ten years. He and George Becker foresaw this research as a book project long before I did. I would also like to thank Holly McCammon for her advice on research methods and data collection throughout my tenure at Vanderbilt and beyond. I would also like to thank Laura Carpenter, Dan Cornfield, Thomas Gregor, Ronnie Steinberg, and Larry Isaac for their very useful feedback on my project at various stages.

At Michigan State University, Edmund Mcgarrell (Ed) at the School of Criminal Justice provided me with a much needed semester off from teaching in 2011 so that I could concentrate on writing this manuscript. Ed also provided me with a generous research fund to help with the additional costs associated with book production. I would also like to thank Steven Gold for helping me think through some of the theoretical frameworks and concepts in this book. Lisa Fine helped me with her comments on the theorization of the project. Tia Stevens provided excellent research assistantship for the data set used in this book.

Numerous others helped me with comments on the drafts of chapters, discussions, references and words of support. Adam Ashforth, Nachman Ben Yehuda, Anuradha Chakravarty, Jessica Johnson, Merry Morash, Zachary Neal, Prasanta Ray, Isaac Reed, Xuefei Ren, Paromita Sanyal, Sehjo Singh, and Jaita Talukdar deserve special mention. My graduate students in the Sociological Theory seminar that I taught at MSU for the last four years influenced my writing with their endless questions, perplexities, and admiration for Karl Marx. Additionally, the seminar and conference participants at places where I presented various chapters and findings from this book (American Sociological Association Meeting; Rethinking Development Conference at Cornell University; Moral Panics in the Contemporary World Conference at Brunel University; Center for Gender in the Global Context, MSU) helped shape key arguments in this book.

I would also like to thank the two anonymous reviewers for their in-depth and extensive comments on various versions of the manuscript. The Indian edition for this book would not have been possible without the support and enthusiasm of Suvadip Bhattacharjee at Cambridge University Press for the last two years. Suvadip supported this project at a critical time, when Indian editions of foreign books are becoming increasingly harder to print. Words are not enough to express my gratitude.

Finally I would like to thank my family and my husband Arijit Mukherjee for always supporting my work.

# Prologue: Beech Tea Estate, Central Dooars, March 2005

The Beech Tea Estate in Hatimtala, Central Dooars, is located in the district of Jalpaiguri, in the state of West Bengal, India, at the foothills of Bhutan. Bhutan is barely six kilometers away, and there is an unfenced border between the two countries that makes illegal border crossings between the two nations a daily routine. The area falls under the jurisdiction of the Border Security Force (BSF) of India, and the nearest BSF post is twenty miles away. To get to Hatimtala, one has to cross three dry riverbeds, each of which is five miles wide. The two roads, both of which lead to the tea garden and inside the plantation, are broken, resulting in a very bumpy car ride. The dry riverbeds are a potential source of danger for both motorists and locals during the monsoon season, because of flash floods that come down from the hills of Bhutan. The tea plantation's labor lines are very much isolated from people outside plantation life, and in the three months of the monsoon season, school attendance and travel becomes a problem. There are no health centers in the villages, and electricity and running water are scarce resources. Electricity poles run right through the villages to the management quarters and to the colonial relics of the past: the planter's bungalow.

In early February 2005, towards the end of winter, Nepul Munda's family started "experiencing" bad luck. Nepul's daughter-in-law's feet started swelling, and her infant daughter had constant stomach problems accompanied by fever. Their small collection of livestock, some chickens and a pig, also fell ill. Nepul was also undergoing some additional stress because of the family's financial situation. His son was recently laid off from his job at the plantation, because he was frequently drunk when he showed up for work. Nepul was also frustrated with the loan payments he had to make to the money lender, from whom he had borrowed some money. Weeks passed without any improvement in the condition of the Munda household. Witnessing the family's predicament, Nepul's friend Sushil advised him to consult a *janguru,* the local medicine man. The *janguru* confirmed Nepul's suspicion that his family was under the spell of "dain" (translated as witches and pronounced as "*dy-en*") and advised Nepul to stay away from "old women" in the village.

Upon returning from the visit, Nepul, aided by his son, Benglu, and Sushil, called a meeting in his house. In the meeting, Nepul told his relatives and friends that his current misfortune was caused by witchcraft being practiced against his family. Benglu (who was laid off from work and whose wife and daughter were ill) was the first to support his father. He confirmed Nepul's suspicions by telling people in the room that for months his family had been in misery as a result of constant bad luck. Benglu explained to his audience that he had "a good idea who was causing it." As the evening progressed, the discussion in the room started heating up. Alcohol (*haria*) was served, and Benglu went outside for some time with a few men. The group of six men started visiting homes in the village informing the villagers of the witchcraft against Nepul's family, and the group started growing in numbers. It was during these visits that one of the neighbors offered up the name of two old women in the *para* (neighborhood or community) who could be *dain.*

Later that evening, the family members of Savitri (a widow in her mid-seventies, who lived with her son and his family) were getting ready for dinner. Savitri's daughter-in-law had just served dinner and the old woman had just scooped some rice from her bowl when they heard a commotion outside their house. A friend of the family rushed inside the house and shouted at Savitri to run for cover from the mob [*daini key martey lok ashchey*]. Savitri tried to escape from the back door of the house, but her physical deformity caused by a hunched back made it difficult. Also, there were people waiting for her in the back yard. The mob (around forty, mostly men) grabbed her grandson, who was barely one year old, from his mother, pointed a kukri (small knife) at him, and threatened to kill him if the family resisted Savitri's capture. The mob, led by Nepul Munda and his family, then dragged Savitri to their courtyard where another woman was waiting.

The other woman was Padma (a widow in her eighties), who was also accused by Nepul and his friends of witchcraft against his family. Padma lived with her oldest son's family. Earlier in the evening, a mob led by Nepul Munda went to Padma's house and dragged her out, hurling abuses and hitting her constantly with sticks. The mob, inebriated with *haria,* the local brew, kept on chanting, "Kill the *daini.*" *Daini* is the singular term for witch. A group of villagers surrounded Padma's family members to prevent them from running to get help.

It seemed that the entire village was in a frenzy to kill the witches that evening, and there was a lot of commotion in the courtyard of Nepul Munda. In the commotion, Padma's youngest son Viral escaped. Viral ran to the nearest BSF picket (barely four miles away) and asked the patrol for help. The BSF men scoffed at Viral for being drunk on *haria* and said he must be imagining the attack. Frustrated, Viral went back to the village where the witch hunt had already started.

By this time, an angry crowd of men, women, and children had gathered outside Nepul's house. While the men were more active participants in the hunt and torture, the women stood watching and hurling abuses at the *dains*. The smell of *haria* was overpowering in the area. Nepul and his family members dragged the two traumatized women, who were barely able to walk, inside his house and locked the door. Over the next hour, the villagers heard cries of help from the two women as Nepul and his family thrashed the women with sticks till they nearly passed out. The women were then brought outside the house and handed over to the waiting crowd. The crowd, this time led by Sushil, dragged the women to a spot 500 meters away from Nepul's house and pushed the women into the high drain. The crowd then started hurling huge boulders at the women and stoned them to death.

The Hatimtala incident took place three months before my first trip to the village. The chronology of events that took place during the witch hunt was pieced together with the help of interviews with Nepul's daughter, family members of Savitri and Padma, and villagers who were present during the hunt.

# Chapter 1

# The Politics of Witchcraft Accusations and Witch Hunts: An Introduction

Nepul's house looked like any other house in the labor lines: a simple mud structure with a thatched roof, sparsely furnished with a few plastic chairs and a wooden cot. Nepul's life, which included struggles with money, alcohol, and illness, was the story of every worker in the plantation villages, including the families of Padma and Savitri. So an answer to the question of how Padma and Savitri went from being ordinary women to suddenly being seen as witches who were responsible for the misfortunes of Nepul's family needs careful consideration. Why did the rest of the villagers in the labor lines, who had no interest at stake in the witch hunt against the two old women, join the hunt either actively or passively? What purpose did the witch hunt serve in bringing a change in Nepul's fortunes, and that of the other villagers?[1] In other words, what did Padma and Savitri do (if anything) to provoke the ire of the entire village that resulted in them being labeled as witches?

The answers to the above questions perhaps lie in the broader rhetoric of the tumultuous relationship between the tea plantation management and the *adivasi* (tribal) workers, the relationship between the industrial economy and wage laborer, and the transition from agricultural workers to industrial wage laborers that took place more than a century ago. The tea plantation management refers to the planters and their managerial staff; and by workers, I am referring to only the tribal labor group in these plantations. In a study on spirit possession among Malay women factory workers, Aiwa Ong (1987) argues that spirit attacks relate to the contemporary experiences of Malay women and their families as the country makes the transition from peasant society to industrial production. In this transition, conflicting agencies and the consciousness of Malay women are tied to the new constellation of power relations within the factory. This is further exposed in the nature of cultural change within the Malaysian experience, as the population evolves into not only a classic proletarian class but a complex multiplicity of groups (Ong 1987, xii–xiv). Thus to understand this complex phenomena, I follow Ong's logic in this book, arguing that it is crucial to place the *adivasi* tea plantation workers as historical subjects and to place them in terms of their unique subjective experiences within the tea plantations of Jalpaiguri. This is the best way to understand the witchcraft accusations against *adivasi* women and witch hunts that result from it (xii).

Thus, in *Witches, Tea Plantations, and Lives of Migrant Laborers*, I present a unique group of *adivasi* workers in Jalpaiguri, where witchcraft accusations and witch hunts are taking place. This particular group of *migrant adivasi workers* is unique particularly because of their location as laborers in the tea plantations, a status that assumes their identity as *adivasis* secondary to their status as workers. They are workers first and *adivasis* second. *Adivasi* is an identity that is reflected both in the attitude of the tea industry and in West Bengal's state policies. Second, and perhaps most important for understanding the distinctive nature of witch hunts in the tea plantations, I argue that these witch hunts in Jalpaiguri tea plantations are historically and contextually different compared with the cases that are taking place in other parts of India, such as in Jharkhand, Chhattisgarh, and Bihar. For instance the hunts that are taking place in other *adivasi* communities in India are in communities that have existed in these areas for hundreds of years and are considered indigenous populations for those states. Their identity as *adivasis* is prominent in the respective state politics and feature in the political representations of these states. For instance both Jharkhand and Chhattisgarh are states that emerged as a result of decades of *adivasi* politics. Thus *adivasi* rights and identity are predominant in the everyday political debates and public life of these states. In contrast, the *adivasis* in the tea plantations of Jalpaiguri are in a much different position. It's a position that affects their rights within the plantations, and ultimately the politics of witch hunts that are tied to the West Bengal government's politics of plantation worker management. For one, the tea plantation *adivasis* are outsiders who were brought in from neighboring states when the first plantations were set up more than a century ago. From the very beginning, the plantations were set up so that the *adivasi* workers were kept in isolation. This was accomplished through the coercion and control of garden *sardars* from the outside world. Though the coercive politics to keep the workers isolated has long disappeared, the long-term implications of such policies are felt even today. For instance, the *adivasi* migrant workers in the tea plantations do not identify (and are not indentified) with the indigenous *adivasi* population of Jalpaiguri: the *bhumiputras*. Also, when discussing *adivasi* politics within West Bengal, the tea plantation workers' problems are overlooked, because West Bengal has its own *adivasis* who have their own issues, and these issues have prominence in state politics. West Bengal's state identity and politics are not tied to its tribal/*adivasi* identity, because non-tribals are the majority of the population. This is different from the situation, for example, in *adivasis* states like Jharkhand or Chhattisgarh. Thus within the politics of *adivasi* rights in a non-tribal state, the tea plantation migrant *adivasis* workers' plights and stories of witch hunts get lost. As a result, the witch hunts that are taking place within the labor lines in the tea plantations of Jalpaiguri are contextually different from the witch hunts described by historians and anthropologists elsewhere in India (see, for example, Kelkar and Nathan 1991; Sundar 2001) where, for example, witchcraft accusations are tied to contentious *adivasi* land rights (Kelkar and Nathan 1991). In contrast, in Jalpaiguri, the witchcraft accusations and witch hunts should be addressed within (1) the broader rhetoric of the position of *adivasis* as tea plantation workers, (2) the cultural change from agricultural workers to industrial wage earners, and (3) ongoing conflicts between the management and the workers within the plantations. Let me explain with an example.

One of the popular theoretical explanations for witch hunts given in the sociology and anthropology literature is that by Marvin Harris in *Cows, Pigs, Wars, and Witches: The Riddles of Culture* (1974). Harris argues that there is always a rational, practical explanation for all seemingly irrational cultural practices; for example, pigs are considered impure creatures in Islam, and poor Hindu farmers in India would rather die from starvation than kill their cows for food. The image of a dry barren cow is an image of hope for the poor starving farmer against money lenders; a hope that in the near future, with the coming of monsoons, that the dry barren cow will fatten up and provide milk. The farmer's refusal to sell or kill the cow, which would allow him to earn a few rupees or temporarily feed his family on the cow's meat, is justified by his optimism about the long-term benefits of keeping the cow alive (11–20). Similar to the cow, the pig too echoes symbols of both love and hate among humans. While it is well known that pigs are considered to be unclean creatures among Muslims, Jews, and Christians, in some New Guinea and South Pacific Melanesian tribes, pigs are revered creatures and are important for all ritualistic feasts. Harris argues that it is perhaps competition for food (nuts, fruits, and berries) with man that has made pigs less favorable creatures (41–53). The third example by Harris of how seemingly bizarre practices have deep-rooted explanations that can be justified as rational and practical, is the execution of witches in premodern Europe. In premodern Europe, the witch craze that resulted in hundreds of executions of witches was legitimized by local churches to draw attention away from peasant revolts. As a result, the clergy and nobility emerged as the saviors against the hidden enemy, brought back order, and justified taxes. Thus, Harris argues, all social customs and habits of societies, no matter how illogical they may seem to outsiders, can be explained in terms of deep-rooted explanations that become essential to practitioners.

Harris's explanations about seemingly irrational practices and events provide a useful initial trajectory through which we can understand the Jalpaiguri tea plantation witch hunts. However, situated within the worker-management discourse, these witch hunts need a deeper analysis, beyond the deep-rooted rational explanations type of justification. The complex network of gender relations and village politics situated in the broader context of labor and management relations in the tea plantations of Jalpaiguri might provide clues to understanding this riddle.

*Witches, Tea Plantations, and Lives of Migrant Workers in India* is an attempt to understand the complex network of relationships, ties of friendship, family, politics, and gender that provide legitimacy before the witch hunt takes place. In most cases of witch hunts in this area, seemingly petty conflicts within the villagers often escalate to a hunt. At the center of the conflict leading to the witch hunt, the exploitative basis of the relationship between the plantation management and the *adivasi* migrant workers often gets hidden. However it is within this backdrop of the labor-planters relationship, the consciousness of the *adivasi* workers, that one should study the witch hunts that are taking place. The following story highlights some of the key issues in management-worker conflicts in the tea plantations of Jalpaiguri.

In a story narrated almost fifty years ago in one of the regions in Jalpaiguri (Malbazar) where I conducted the current study, the author, Jeff Tikari, reflects on how a seemingly "good deed" of the planter burdens the poor tribal worker, who is bound by plantation norms of not being able to refuse the planter's offer of giving him a ride. On a heavy monsoon evening, a planter and his wife on their way to a party decides to give a ride to impoverished worker whom they meet on the road. They assume that the man is waiting for a ride and ask him where he wants to go. They think that he wanted to go to Mal, a location where the couple was heading as well. The couple decides to offer the "wretched" man a ride in their car, and they remark that "the ungrateful man" did not look too pleased. Throughout the car ride, the couple makes derogatory and condescending remarks about the man's "dim-witted responses" to their questions. The man gets off at Mal, and the couple continues to the party. On their return home, later that night, the couple notices the same man walking, looking even more tired and haggard than he was earlier that evening. The couple stops and asks him why he came back. The man pleadingly replies that he left for Mal two days ago, and walked all day today to come back home. When he met "sahib" (planter), he had just returned home, but sahib took him back to Mal again. He walked back again to his home all evening, and pleaded the planter to spare him and let him go home to his family (see Jeff Tikari 2012, *Aroma of Orange Pekoe*, 96–101).

The above story highlights the following observations about the relationship between the workers and management in the tea plantations. These observations are central to the arguments of *Witches, Tea Plantations and Lives of Migrant Laborers in India.* First, the arrogant attitude of the planter couple in assuming that the man needed help, to the extent of being oblivious to the man's responses to their question, is symbolic of the feelings of the management and the outside world towards the migrant *adivasi* workers. The uneducated tribal worker here does not know what is good for him, but the kind planter somehow does and offers him a ride he doesn't ask for. Second, the worker is so subservient to the planter that he dare not refuse the ride, even at the cost of his own comfort.

These two observations bring into focus a critical component in the politics of tea plantations that is manifest in witchcraft accusations among the tribal workers: the extreme hierarchical nature of the relationship between workers and management based on rigidity of power and ignorance.

Piya Chatterjee, in *A Time for Tea: Women, Labor, and Post/Colonial Politics on an Indian Plantation*, describes this relationship between the planters and the workers within a culture and politics of patronage, in which the image of the planter is that of a benevolent father figure: *mai-baap* (mother-father). Behind the mask of benevolence and patronage lies a relationship of coercion that is enforced through social distance, hierarchy of orders, and a social structure in which the planter is positioned at the top of the pyramid (Chatterjee 2001, 6). Such relationships of patronage are not peculiar to tea plantations in India, nor did they originate with the establishment of these plantations. Rather, these relationships of patronage existed for a long time in India, starting with caste stratification, in which certain higher castes' positions were based on superiority, patronage, and exploitation over both the lower castes and those people outside the caste positions (*adivasis*). Ajay Skaria also talks about a similar hegemonic stratification that has existed in India since colonial times. In these stratifications, the native population is divided according to various shades of wildness (Skaria 1997b and 1999). Skaria writes: "But what do wildness, ascriptions of and claims to wildness mean? Conventionally, in much mainstream western thought, wildness has been understood in terms of an opposition to civilization. It usually signifies what comes before or lies outside civilization. Civilization is of course valorized, and ascriptions of wildness have justified much violence and oppression . . . two most common ways in which wildness is talked about—wild spaces and wild people" (1999, Preface v–vi).

Skaria does not claim that castes were considered to be "civilized" and that the tribes were considered to be "wild" in British India. He claims instead that the civilizing mission which was the foundation for the belief in colonialism was based on a "rule of difference" (a term borrowed from Partha Chatterjee (1993)), i.e., that the colonizers (civilized) were *fundamentally different* from the colonized (wild). Thus the difference between tribes and castes in British India was not wild versus civilized but rather was based on different shades of wildness; the tribes were considered to be "more wild" than other natives in India (Skaria 1997b, 727). Ashforth (2005) refers to a similar attitude that existed regarding African spirituality among European colonizers. Colonial attitudes toward African spirituality, we might even say obsessions, were a mixture of revulsion and fascination that served to perpetuate stereotypes of African irrationality and grounded colonial claims that Africans were incapable of governing themselves without white overlords, being as the Africans were, wild and uncivilized (Ashforth 2005, xiii).

I refer to the caste-based stratification in precolonial India and the construction of wildness in colonial India to argue how the planters' image of the *adivasi* workers as wild, uncivilized, uncontrollable individuals who are unable to make decisions for their own good, are based on historical assumptions of the *adivasi* image. According to this image, the planters see themselves as benevolent patrons who have a "paternalistic need to civilize" (Skaria 1997b, 736) the wild, incorrigible *adivasi*. Continuing from the British planters, the plantation management of today has a distorted image of the *adivasis* that naturally accommodates witch hunts. To the *adivasis* is attributed the reputation of a wild, aboriginal nature that could be channeled into productive work, and thus they were recruited initially by trickery and later by coercion for the new tea plantations starting in Assam and later in Jalpaiguri. The contracts these indentured *adivasis* worked under obligated them for between three to five years and were enforced by agency houses whose sole purpose was recruiting bound labor with threats of imprisonment and heavy fines against deserters (Liu 2010, 88).

Contemporary plantation managers mostly belong to the mainstream non-*adivasi* population, and their images of the *adivasis*, reflected in their attitudes towards them, are typically based on the colonial images of wildness. The colonial planters themselves are long gone, but what remains is everything else: attitudes, hierarchy of relationships, and politics of patronage that are fundamental to the running of a plantation economy. How does the above story by Tikari and its reflection on the patronizing and paternalistic relationship between the worker and the planter provide lead to understanding and analyzing the implications of witchcraft accusations among the *adivasi* migrant worker population in the tea plantations of Jalpaiguri? For one, a careful examination of the witch hunt incidents in the region reveals that social stress in the worker community exists before the hunts take place. That social stress is often related to plantation management-worker politics connected to issues about wages, job security, and living and working conditions.

Perhaps a major point of conflict in recent times between the *adivasi* migrant workers and the planters is the infrequent payment of wages that are often very low to begin with. Added to this, because the social and economic existence of the workers is tied to the plantation, and that tie is maintained by strict regulations as to social hierarchy and social interaction both within and outside the plantations, the *adivasis* have very few options for finding work outside the tea plantations. Ever since the plantations were set up almost 130 years ago, the economic and social conditions of the workers, and their conflictual relationships with management, have remained unchanged. The Oraon labor agitations in Jalpaiguri in 1915–1916 (see Ranajit Das Gupta 1989)—which were rooted in the rejection of the colonial capitalist economy that had turned the migrant tribal peasants into wage laborers—as well as the contemporary wage conflicts and the closure of tea plantations that resulted in deaths due to starvation all highlight the management-worker conflicts in the tea plantations (see Talwar, Chakraborty and Biswas 2005). For instance in recent times, the wages for the tea industry in North Bengal have been determined through an industry-wide wage negotiation that takes place every few years. In 2005 the minimum wage for a tea plantation worker was Rs 45.90 per day (approximately one US dollar). However, in practice, the workers receive much less, particularly during the lean season, when they receive only 70 percent of the negotiated wages. Similarly according to some contracts, the wages of the workers consisted of subsidized rations and cash, and often they received 50 percent of the promised amount. Additionally a large number of these plantations were closed by the owners in 2000–2009 (at the time of the current study described in the book), and the crisis is mostly described as caused by internal factors. The crisis became particularly acute between 2001 and 2004, when about 22 plantations in the region were closed, affecting 95,000 people. During the crisis, the Payment of the Wages Act and other labor acts were violated. The owners closed the plantations illegally, i.e., without giving the workers any prior notice. With the closure of the plantations, the workers faced starvation and unemployment, because they lacked the necessary skills to run the plantations on their own (see "Public Systems Report on Study of Labor Conditions in Tea Gardens of Jalpaiguri").

In some plantations, the gardens remained open, but payment for wages was irregular. For example, in Kalchini (one of the areas for this study and where the Central Dooars witch hunt incident took place) the workers worked for half wages and half rations for more than a year, from March 2004 to May 2005. In some plantations, a new system of wages was introduced by management to deal with failing tea production. Under this new system, if the worker failed to pluck fewer than 25 kilograms of tea leaves per day, he would have to compensate by giving up a portion of his daily wages. This was an especially a steep target, because the workers can only fulfill this amount during peak seasons (Talwar, Chakraborty, and Biswas 2005, 14). Access to daily life resources such as water and electricity are scarce commodities in the labor lines. Typically there is no running water system in the lines. The companies provide for the tube wells and water tankers, but these supplies are mostly insufficient. The workers often depend on other sources to meet their daily water demands. In the study conducted by Talwar, Chakraborty, and Biswas that covered thirteen plantations, they found only one plantation with sufficient water supply (15). Similar studies have documented the occurrence of repeated strikes by workers in the Dooars region, some of them as long as seven months, over the issue of better medical facilities. More common are smaller scale protests that demand, on the grounds of inefficiency, the replacement of doctors appointed by the plantation or the Government (Chaudhury and Varma 2002, 35). In chapter 3 "Two Leaves and a Bud: The Beginning," I discuss in detail the history of the plantations and the people involved in this history. Behind the conflict between the two classes lies the classic Marxian explanation: the worker (in this case the tea plantation workers) is nothing but a mere commodity in the eyes of the owners (here, the planters and the management). The work that they do is exploitative because they do not enjoy the profits of their labor. The wages that they earn cannot be called "profit" or a true reimbursement of the labor that they invest in (as seen from the previous study), and wages often fluctuate. The misery and the exploitative existence of the workers are tied in inverse proportion to the accumulation of wealth and profits in the hands of the owner; this is a condition necessary for the monopoly of wealth in a plantation economy (see Marx 2005, *Economic and Philosophical Manuscripts*, 85).

To ensure a steady supply of workers for the plantations and because the local population refused to work as wage laborers, *adivasis* from neighboring regions of Chhottanagpur and Santhal Parganas were brought into the newly set up plantations. Family migration, another feature of plantation economy globally, was particularly encouraged through deception and violence perpetrated by the garden *sardars* (Chaudhury and Varma 2002, 21), because this would provide the plantations workers for generations to come. The set-up was as if the migrant *adivasi* workers had no other calling except be "good workers" for the tea plantations. To transform them into good workers, the planters went through great lengths to keep them segregated physically, socially, and economically from the world outside of the plantations, so much so that even today the community remains marginalized from the mainstream population. In the end, the planters succeeded in creating a group of workers who owed their very existence to the plantations, and thus any action that was against the planters/plantation system became an act against the worker's own livelihood. Similar to the relationship between the owners and workers described in the *Economic and Political Manuscripts* by Marx (2005), the very isolation and exploitation of these workers were fundamental to the success of these plantations in bringing increased profit in the pockets of the planters. Like other plantations around the world, the Indian tea plantations relied on cheap migrant labor and a large cooperative infrastructure modeled upon the factory systems of urban production (Liu 2010, 74). For the workers, the feelings of helplessness about their situation were so extreme that the workers became seemingly immobilized to protest against the plantation owners and management, except for occasional strikes that were met with severe repercussions. And this was exactly what the planters wanted to achieve. For instance, from the very beginning, the planters maintained their own coercive machinery, the North Bengal Mounted Rifles (NBMR) to quell all labor discontent in the plantations. Beatings were frequently inflicted upon the laborers, and desertion was severely punished. The entire system discouraged protests, and the leaders of the nationalist movement did not show much interest in linking the laborers to the freedom struggle (Chaudhury and Varma 2002, 21–23). Thus all protests were violently suppressed, the mainstream population continued to disassociate themselves from the workers, and the *adivasi* migrant laborers became isolated in all respects.

This pattern of exploitation and domination of the tea plantation workers in Jalpaiguri is similar to other examples of the manipulation of workers' dependency on wages by the owners, and it has been observed globally (Errington and Gewertz 2004). For instance, a study on textile workers in Thailand observes that feelings of powerlessness over the oppressive conditions, the lack of support from the Thai government, lack of access to labor laws, and fear of speaking out all led to a crippling sense of alienation among the workers. The workers were not just alienated from the work and its product but also from themselves and the community (Pangsapa 2007, 76–77). Observing the spirit possession of Malay women in factories, Aihwa Ong (1987) describes how within the factory working women confront industrial discipline as a diverse and wide ranging network of overt and covert power relations. With the transformation of the agrarian peasant economy to that of industrial wage laborers, the factory system had changed the Malaysian society in fundamental ways. Caught between noncapitalist morality and capitalist discipline, some factory women alternate between states of self-control and spirit possession, and the spirit possession is a reflection of the loss of autonomy and humanity inherent in production work (xiv–xv; 7–8).

Throughout this book, I describe the *adivasi* workers in the plantations as "migrant" workers.[2] My decision to call this group (which migrated almost more than a century ago) a migrant group is a conscious one. First, while all the land in the plantations where the labor lines are housed belongs to the owners of the plantations, the *adivasi* workers described themselves as being aliens in this (meaning Jalpaiguri) land. Historians have commented how the feelings of deep attachment of the migrant *adivasis* workers in Jalpaiguri to their homelands in Chhotanagpur and in Santhal Parganas intersect with feelings of deliverance from the misery caused by the oppression and exploitation (see Das Gupta 1989). Second, as mentioned in previous paragraphs, the very strict class hierarchy in the plantation and restrictive rules of labor, along with the hostility that *adivasis* faced from the local population, made the assimilation of the *adivasis* into the local population very difficult. Thus, even 130 years after their migration to the plantations, the *adivasis* identify themselves as aliens who have very few rights or opportunities for social mobility. The term migrant worker here represents both the conflict and the alienation that the *adivasi* workers face in their daily lives as laborers in the tea plantations and as members of a marginalized and isolated community.

I must also add here a note on the use of the terms "tribals" and "*adivasis*." The very term *adivasi* today brings together two political genealogies: that of the mobilization of *adivasis* within the context of decolonization in India and that of the presence of *adivasis* as indigenous peoples within contemporary globalized economy and politics. Given the heterogeneity of *adivasi* experiences in India as a result of colonial rule, modernization, and now globalization, one may broach these issues by introducing the idea of multiple *adivasi* subjectivities. Very simplistically, the word *adivasi* is a Hindi term that denotes descendents or original inhabitants of a given place. The term is at best uneven and it has "different connotations in terms of people-place relationships, and refers to a wide range of topographies and inhabitants. . . . The *adivasi* concept has gained widespread resonance and currency in contemporary India, but it has yet to supersede the concept of the 'tribe' in nation arenas" (Rycroft and Dasgupta 2011, 1–7).

Thus, while the government officials, the plantation management, NGO activists, and the *adivasi* workers themselves in my study switched between the two terms *adivasi* and tribals to describe the groups, there is a lot of politics behind the use of the two terms in contemporary Indian politics. The colonial policies of constructed categories in British India transformed the relationship between castes and tribes, and with the rise of nationalism, the construction of categories on the basis of wildness began to be questioned. As early as in 1930, terms such as *janglijati* (wild castes) began to be considered derogatory, and the term "*adivasi*" emerged (meaning "inhabitants from the earliest times or autochthonous.") The term emerged in Chhottanagpur and was popularized as being less derogatory by Gandhian nationalists who were concerned with the idea of a united nation. However, despite attempts to avoid derogatory assumptions behind the term "*adivasi*," the idea that *adivasis* were primitive or uncivilized became entrenched in the minds of the dominant Indian groups, where castes are seen as superior. Two images of the *adivasi* emerged: the *adivasi* man was a less-masculine figure compared with the dominant Indian groups (his masculinity was downplayed or was not desired. Contrary to the colonial image of the *adivasi* man, the *adivasi* woman was a very sexualized and erotic being. (Her sexual freedom was more emphasized by the nationalists than by the colonialists.) The *adivasi* man thus once again became primitive and savage compared with the Indian upper and middle castes, where masculinity was defined by parameters of modernity (see Skaria 1997b, 740–43). In this book I use the term "*adivasi*" to describe the migrant worker population, unless the narratives use the term "tribe" or an explanation requires the use of this term.

## *Adivasi* Women Workers, Witches, and Witch Hunts

In almost every society and community around the world and in all time periods, episodes of violence against women are common. Through these acts, men exert power, authority, and control over women's bodies and behavior. Common examples of violence against women include rape, domestic abuse, and sex-trafficking. Witch hunts directed against women can be another example of violence against women, triggered by the ongoing struggle of power between men and women. According to some scholars, the hostility against witches developed during a period of economic, religious, and political transition in *adivasi* communities in central India. During this period, power and order were maintained by legitimizing the use of violence against the accused women resulting in myths that provide clues about how the power over land and politics was taken by women from men (Kelkar and Warrier 1999, 315). Rumor and conspiracy played important roles in identifying credible scapegoats for witch hunts.

In recent times, according to Federici (2010), a United Nations report stated that there were about 25,000 witch killings recorded in India between 1987 and 2003. It is recognized that the actual figure is much higher. Some incidents (such as the ones in the Jalpaiguri plantations) never make it to the Indian statistics on witch hunts, and so this means that many more women have been "tortured, maimed, traumatized for life" than the statistics show. While some states have passed anti-witch-hunt legislation, such as Bihar in 1999, Jharkhand in 2001, and Chhattisgarh in 2005, few of the perpetrators have been brought to justice (Federici 2010, 13–14).

However, to suggest that witch hunts in Jalpaiguri are a form of violence against women provides a one-sided explanation of the problem. It is also important to understand the incidents of hunts in the plantations within the framework of plantation politics, in which witchcraft accusations against *adivasi* women are only one part of the puzzle. As Kiernan (2006) reflects while arguing about the need to rethink theories of witchcraft in contemporary Africa, sometimes witchcraft emerges as the weapon of the strong (Geschiere 1997), i.e., witchcraft accusations are a form of violence against women. At other times witchcraft is located within areas of contested power, where the occult is a weapon of the weak (Niehaus 2001), i.e., witchcraft accusations are a way for the *adivasi* workers to get control over their lives within the exploitative nature of the plantations. Both of these approaches acknowledge the interplay of local contingencies and global forces in contemporary discourses on witchcraft (Kiernan 2006, 12–13). In this context, it is important to talk about the role of *adivasi* women in plantation economy, and the position of these women within the family.

The inclusion of women as workers in tea plantations of India was gradual, particularly in the state of Assam, where the first plantations were set up. In the Jalpaiguri plantations, women (particularly migrant *adivasi* women) were a part of the workforce from the very beginning, and their numbers began to increase when the planters realized that resettlement of whole families as workers guaranteed a stable workforce for the plantation for generations to come. Today, almost 80 percent of the tea-plucking labor is done by women in the plantations (Liu 2010, 87). Work in the plantations was mainly gendered: women were "considered" to be efficient pluckers and men did most of the maintenance work in the plantations. Often, despite the gendered division of labor, men and children also engaged in the work of tea-plucking, along with other kinds of work.[3] Perhaps the rationale for employing a large number of women in these plantations was to keep wages low, a matter of convenience for the owners, and to keep productivity high, i.e., a preference for women may have been based on the idea that women's nimble fingers were more efficient at the plucking job. The women were thus "simultaneously fetishized and pragmatically devalued" through lower wages (Chatterjee 2001, 6). Women constitute more than half of the labor in the plantation economy even today (Sarkar and Bhowmick 1998, 50–51). Until the Equal Remuneration Act was passed in 1975, women workers in the tea plantations of Jalpaiguri were paid less than the male workers. Today, despite the Act, women workers are still paid less than their male counterparts in some plantations in the region. Also, women workers constitute almost 50 percent of the total labor force in the plantation, but they have remained marginalized in trade union representations in the region (51).

The *adivasi* woman worker is perhaps the most vulnerable group within the plantation. She is the lowest and most oppressed category of person within the plantation hierarchy. Scholars have commented on how women in marginalized groups face more oppression than either their marginalized male counterparts or other women in the privileged groups. These women face a sort of double oppression. Their gender and marginalized group status combine to make them susceptible to exploitation from the dominant groups and from the males in their own groups. For instance, research on domestic violence has shown how the gendered expectations for immigrant women from developing countries becomes stricter as immigrant men cope with a devalued status in the new country (Das Dasgupta 2007; Mazumdar 1998). As a result, immigrant women may find themselves deeply entrenched in patriarchal relations and roles in their marital families in the new country (Chaudhuri, Morash, and Yingling forthcoming; Hondagneu-Sotelo 1994; Shankar and Northcott 2009; Ong 1993). Thus patriarchy promotes patriarchy and patronage over women constantly, and women in weaker class positions face threats more often than other women in higher class positions. For the *adivasi* migrant women in Jalpaiguri, the primary job of tea-plucking constitutes the outer perimeter of the plantation, which is sustained by a hierarchy of male supervisors and overseers. The *adivasi* woman worker is an icon of wildness and primitivism, and her very existence requires a civilizing and disciplining mission (Chatterjee 2001, 6–8). This ranges from criticism about how she dresses to criticisms about her conduct (Sundar 2001, 429). There is a contradiction here regarding her position: on one hand, she is viewed as more independent than non-*adivasi* women because she participates in all aspects of labor and supposedly keeps control over her own wages. On the other hand, she is subjected to severe ritual, economic, and political disadvantageous compared to the *adivasi* men. For example, decisions regarding village-level disputes and participation in *panchayat* meetings and rituals are often denied to the women.[4] Also, their image as wild, uncontrolled, promiscuous woman with out-of-control libidos often makes them susceptible to sexual abuse by outsiders and men in positions of power, including traders, contractors, supervisors, and managers (429). In addition, the lack of health care, sanitation, access to clean drinking water, and nutrition affects *adivasi* women and children in the plantation communities more than men, because women are the primary caretakers of families. If the Plantation Labor Act of 1951 had been rigorously enforced, then the lack of access to sanitation, drinking water, and standard housing would not have been an issue in these locations (Bhowmik 2011, 251).

The female *adivasi* migrant workers in the plantations of Jalpaiguri are caught in a web of conspiracy: a conspiracy constructed by their fellow male *adivasi* migrant workers. These men use rumor and gossip to manipulate the emotions of those in the community during periods of social stress, and then they direct these emotions against the women. The *adivasi* migrant labor group is also caught in the bigger conspiracy of the plantation owners and management, who manipulate the witchcraft accusations and witch hunts that follow as means to further isolate the community from the mainstream population with constructed images of primitiveness and wildness that get legitimized by the witchcraft accusations that take place. However, it is also important to note that witchcraft accusations are not exclusive to *adivasi* groups (Sundar 2001, 428). For instance, there are newspaper reports about housewives in an urban metropolis being accused of witchcraft by neighbors who were attempting to get her house so they could expand their business (see "Witch Tag on Neighbor," Telegraph (Kolkata), July 18, 2005).

Similar to other *adivasi* communities in India (for instance, in Bastar, Santhal Parganas, Jharkhand, and Chhattisgarh), within the *adivasi* migrant community, any misfortune or unexplained illness is attributed to the deed of a witch. A witch in this context is primarily constructed as a malicious woman who uses her dark powers to cause harm to individuals who are in some way related to her. These relations aren't necessarily through blood or kinship; rather they could extend to neighbors and fellow villagers. Witchcraft does not harm strangers, and jealousy is an important component for the instigation of witchcraft. Given the limited resources for the workers in plantation, conflicts over drinking water, property, and ailments often manifest as witchcraft accusations. But it is important to note that witchcraft beliefs appear predominantly within the *adivasis* compared with other groups (and I am not denying that other groups do not have witchcraft accusations or beliefs in witches), and while the context within which the accusations take place has changed due to migration of *adivasis* to the plantations, the beliefs have remained.

For instance, writing about witchcraft beliefs in colonial India, Chhotanagpur, Sinha (2006) says: "[B]elief in spirits and witches has long occupied a central phase in *adivasi* cosmology and moral economy." Based on gender conflicts and legitimized by religion, folklore and patriarchal customs, the traditional construction of the image of witches and witchcraft did reflect oppositions to the position of mainly women (127). Thus fear and suspicion of women's sexuality not only influenced the construction of witches, it also played a role in women's invisibility from *adivasi* rituals and religion (131). The further impact of colonial rule and the changes brought about by an alien capitalist economy shaped the continuity and changes in the belief in witches and witchcraft accusations (127). All of this implies the following: that even as the "reasons" behind witchcraft accusations have changed, the tradition of witchcraft accusation has continued within the community, and it has done so by taking on a new shape. Thus the socioeconomic changes caused by the displacements of people and the takeover of traditional *adivasi* lands reinforced and sharpened the impact of social changes and added new dimensions to prevalent notions on witchcraft.

Similarly, according to P. O. Bodding (1986), for the *adivasis*, the invisible world is filled with spirits that cause diseases and illness; these are the darker spirits. The central idea is to seek an alliance with the helpful white spirits, who would then control the evil spirits (Bodding 1986, 38). Thus there is no genuine Santhal, he writes, who does not believe in witches (Sinha 2006: 128–29). The

Santhali myth about the origin of witchcraft traces it to a gender conflict in which women stole knowledge from the men through trickery and manipulation. This access to knowledge was previously denied to women, and there is a reference to a mythical era when there was a change in the order of society by which the authority of men was established (Nathan, Kelkar, and Xiaogang 1998, 59–61).

Nathan, Kelkar and Xiaogang discuss how the authority of men is further established through witchcraft accusations. At the beginning, the woman who is named as a witch may be incented to pay a fine and mend her ways through threats. Simultaneously though, there may be deaths in the village (as a result of unidentified ailments, a common occurrence in regions where medical aid is dismal) and other tragedies that prompt the *ojha* (medicine man) to put the blame back on the accused witch. By this time, there is already a consensus in the village regarding the identity of the witch and the recurrence of the usual tragedies is regarded as proof that the witch is unrelenting. The woman may then be either driven out of the village or killed. Women are viewed as potential sources of evil, and such an ideology is conducive to the social process of controlling women. According to their argument, every Santhal women lives under the threat of being declared a witch; and especially during times of crisis (like epidemics), all the women of a village could be attacked as witches (61).

Similarly in the Jharkhand and Dangs region, witchcraft accusations have been used to dispossess women, often widows, of their lands. Sundar (2001) offers a different argument for the accusations in Bastar. She says that while belief in witchcraft and sorcery is widespread in the region "as a part of a wider cosmology," she observes that in Bastar both men and women are equal targets of witchcraft accusations (Sundar 2001, 426). These targets do not fit into any pattern of gender, age, dependency, or kinship. However, women tend to suffer more during accusations because their honor is at stake (431). "However all accusations appear to follow a series of illnesses. Accusations of occult malpractice therefore, seem to be a way of coping with the uncertainties of human existence and attributing agency to local actors in a context where, in practice, people have little power" (426). Thus Sundar argues that it is perhaps problematic to attempt to understand witchcraft accusations that go beyond traditional remnants of superstitious pasts that disappear with the coming of modern education. Instead, the Bastar witchcraft accusations should be understood "as a quintessentially modern experience, in which people are part of a nation state from which they get little succor in terms of livelihood or health, but which exercises coercive power over them" (426). Taking a cue from Sundar's arguments, I ask how does one place the *adivasi* migrant worker in the tea plantations of Jalpaiguri within the context of plantation politics of patriarchy and patronage? How does one analyze these accusations as different from the accusations that occurred in these workers' homelands of Santhal Parganas and Chhotanagpur prior to their migration to the plantations? How does one explain the witchcraft accusations within the background of the plantation economy?

At the center of witchcraft accusations within the *adivasi* workers group are illness or misfortune in the community that are blamed on the handiwork of the witch. The lack of health care and sanitation, and the irregularity of payment of wages, makes the community and its members regularly susceptible to health issues, starvation, nutritional issues, and water borne ailments. All of these are common within the worker groups. Often the health centers in the plantations are ill-equipped and lack medicines and trained medical personnel. Common ailments, such as diarrhea or malaria, which can be treated with simple precautions, in most cases take a turn to epidemic proportions. The lack of interest from the plantation owners and management in improving the living conditions of these workers does not help, nor does the lack of economic resources that the community faces. This seems to justify a rational exercise the reliance on supernatural explanations for dealing with illness. Further, within the *adivasis* as mentioned before, beliefs in spirits and witches have a long history, and during times of social stress caused by epidemics or deaths, witchcraft is given as the most common explanation.

The actual process of identifying and punishing the witch is a complex one. Local politics, personal conflicts, and the gendered nature of violence play a huge role. In almost all cases, the identity of the witch is that of a local village woman whose reputation can be easily maligned through accusations of witchcraft. In a matter of few hours, through gossip, rumor, and conspiracy, the entire village then blames her for the misfortunes. The role of gossip, rumor, and conspiracy during witch hunts has been analyzed in previous research. Collectively these play an important role both at the beginning of stressful periods in the community and later during accusations and gathering support for the witch hunt (Stewart and Strathern 2003, xi). Rumors and gossip through conspiracies play a crucial role in displacing reality in the minds of the community. We saw this in the Central Dooars case in which the accuser group went all over the village successfully convincing other villagers who had no motive for killing the women to join in their hunt. Rumors and gossip establish a "rationale of how witchcraft works" that becomes the true reality, i.e., is realized (52). There is a power play involved in the displacement and replacement of reality and in its construction. This power is held primarily by the men in the community, who manipulate it for a motive that is profitable to some; the women are mere passive participants or victims in the hunt.

Throughout this process of witchcraft accusation leading to witch hunts, the plantation management maintains a policy of noninterference and does nothing to rescue the accused woman. If they do interfere, their interference is often very late and half hearted. Their aloofness from the lives and daily stresses of the migrant workers serves two political purposes. First, by not interfering in witchcraft accusations, they give their tacit approval for the prevalence of the belief in witches. This is a strategy that well serves their purpose of maintaining a workforce that is *jungli*. This noninterference attitude also helps in displacing the blame. Instead of blaming the plantation management for the poor conditions that led to the ailments in the first place, the workers blame the witches, as an outcome of false consciousness. Second, the incidents of witch hunts further establish the image of the *adivasis* as "primitive" and "violent" in the eyes of the mainstream population, and this keeps the *adivasis* isolated and marginalized for generations. Consequently, this helps in maintaining the lack of interest on the parts of both government and the mainstream population in improving the lives of the *adivasi* migrant workers in the plantations, because these workers are perceived to be "incurable from their traditional practices." This strategy has paid off. Newspapers often do not report incidents of witch hunts in the region, and even if they do, the incidents are reported in the ninth or the tenth page as a 100-word report. For example, the recent crisis at the Jalpaiguri tea plantations which led to catastrophic starvation deaths within the community was reported in the newspapers within the state rather infrequently. It did not receive the attention it should have had (Chatterjee 2008, 499).

From the perspective of the *adivasi* workers in the plantations, feelings of alienation from the plantations and from the outside world lead to feelings of submission; they feel they have no way out of the plantations and no recourse but to let things continue. As a result, the planters get access to a workforce that is so tied to the plantation economy that they have become powerless to protest and to de-stress look for enemies within their own group. The witch hunts become a double conspiracy: (1) against the accused women by the men in the *adivasi* migrant worker community who take advantage of social stress and instigate an accusation often for a motive other than eradication of the witchcraft and (2) by the planters who manipulate the emotions of the workers by not stopping the hunts. The *adivasi* women workers become scapegoats in this double conspiracy.

## Organization and Scope

In Chapter 2, "Theory and Literature on Witchcraft Accusations and Witch Hunts," I trace gendered explanations of witch hunts, from patrilinieal laws on property inheritance, from local politics to scapegoats, covering the various disciplinary approaches towards understanding the accusations. Reviewing the literature in history, anthropology and in sociology, I explore whether the witchcraft accusations among the *adivasi* migrant workers are indeed an expression of gendered conflicts, or whether the *adivasi* workers should be treated as historical subjects with unique subjective experiences within the tea plantation economy. As a consequence, witchcraft accusations adapt, change, and reemerge in conjunction within modern plantation economy, as a manifestation of worker management conflict.

Chapter 3, "Two Leaves and a Bud: The Beginning," discusses the history of the tea plantations in Dooars. The chapter traces the roots of the oppressive relationship between the management and the workers and sets the stage for the need for a sensitive research to study witch hunts. In the process, I discuss the nature of spirits and beliefs within the tribal spiritual framework. I conclude the chapter with a discussion on the methods used for the study.

In Chapter 4, "Categorization of Witch Hunts," in an attempt to explain why witch hunts takes place in the Dooars region, I classify the incidents into two categories of witch hunts: surprise and calculated hunts. Through these categories I explain the motivations behind the accusers and the characteristics of the accused witches, who are often women. Categories provide the first step for an explanation why witch hunts are common incidents among the migrant tribal plantation workers. While the motivations behind witchcraft accusations vary (from sudden impulses to calculated acts), the immediate cause is always some sort of illness. Women are typically blamed for causing illness and misfortune within the community. Chapters 4 and 5, by giving readers a look at village politics, gender relationships, and witchcraft accusations within the worker communities, provide a microcontext to witch hunts.

In Chapter 5, "Women, Moral Boundaries, Gossip in the Plantations," I take a closer look at the accused women in witch hunts. I explain why women are blamed as witches during times of misfortune, and how this blaming links to the construction of power through moral boundaries. I argue that the patriarchal nature of the plantation, which is built on politics of coercion and patronage over the *adivasi* workers, trickles down to the patriarchal nature of relationships between men and women within the migrant tribal worker community. Within the plantations, the *adivasi* woman worker occupies the lowest position both economically and socially. This makes them the most vulnerable social group. Patriarchy promotes patriarchy; and through coercion, gossip and control, women are controlled. The blaming of illness and social stress on the accused women serves two important functions in the communities. First, it helps the *adivasi* migrant workers community find a scapegoat who can take the blame for misfortunes over which the workers have no control. Second, the accusations provide a way for accusers to fulfill their personal interests, settle debts, or execute revenge against the woman or her family.

In Chapter 6, "Tea Plantation Politics, Oppression, and Protest," I trace the politics of witch hunts, a seemingly microconflict between men and women, as it becomes a macrolevel conflict that is the outcome of oppressive relations between the plantation management and workers. I argue that the alienation experienced by the workers, who have no opportunities for social mobility or protest, is the dominant cause behind witch hunts. As seen in similar situations, the workers deal with stress caused by economic, social, and medical factors by looking for a scapegoat. As protest against the real causes of misfortune is not possible because of their alienation, the *adivasi* women provide the perfect scapegoat for witchcraft accusations. The chapter also explains the attitude of the police and plantation management towards the migrant tribal workers. This attitude reflects the view that witch hunts are a necessary way for the workers to alleviate stress.

In Chapter 7, "Towards a New Direction: Activism and Protests," I show how a community that has no avenues for protest and that is alienated in all senses of the term gradually learns to combat witchcraft accusations. Here, the focus is on the how activist interprets witchcraft accusations in order to attract the migrant *adivasi* women to anti-witch-hunt campaigns. While witch hunts are interpreted as superstitious practice, through the campaign, the women are given avenues to combat the accusers, and the campaigns create opportunities for mobility in the lives of the workers. I end the chapter with reflections on future directions for mobilization of *adivasi* migrant workers against the plantation economies.

## Notes

1. I use the term witch hunt here instead of using the term that is more among anthropologists, "witchcraft accusations." The term "witch hunt" is the preferred term among sociologists and is particularly relevant for my research, which focuses on the brutal nature of the attack against the accused women. In this book, I use both terms but in temporal sequence: the witch hunts typically follow witchcraft accusations.

2. The term "migrant" refers to someone who moves from his/her place of origin to another place (this could be in the same or different country or state or from a rural to an urban area) mainly for work. The term has often been used to describe labor migrants.

3. Employment of children in the tea plantations was legally permitted by the Plantation Labor Act of 1951.

4. While *adivasi* women may be formal members of the *panchayats* as a result of reservation policies by the Indian government, women (both *adivasi* and non-adivasi) often are figurehead participants. Their decisions are controlled by the men in their family. Narratives of women *panchayats* in this study point to how their powers are controlled by other male members of the *panchayat* in the village.

# Chapter 2

# Theory and Literature on Witchcraft Accusations and Witch Hunts

Although the panic outbreak of executions of women as witches in Europe and the American colonies, commonly referred to as "the early modern witch craze," ended in the 1700s, some women are still being labeled and accused of being witches in some communities in India and other developing nations in Africa, Asia, and South America.[1] Over the past few decades, local newspapers in India have reported incidents of witch hunting at a fluctuating pace. These reports are usually printed on the fifth page in a small corner under "other news." And although the idea of witch hunts seems shocking to most urban educated Indians, the phenomenon is common among the *adivasi* population of India (Bhil, Ho, Munda, Oraon, and Santhal, to name a few), and it occurs among non-*adivasi* populations less commonly. The study of contemporary witch hunts in the tea plantations of Jalpaiguri India has been largely ignored in sociology and anthropology, and the research literature on the pursuit of women as witches, particularly in the state of West Bengal, is scarce and anecdotal (for instance, see Barman 2002; Mishra 2003; Chaudhuri 1987) compared with research on other parts of India. For instance, one of the more recent global works to discuss witch hunts in India (Behringer 2004) includes no cases from contemporary *adivasi* settings, despite the fact that there have been hundreds of documented murders (as well as unrecorded ones).[2] There is a huge and growing body of research on historical witch hunts in early modern Europe and the American colonies and occasional "extensions" of the patterns found to more contemporary episodes, but those extensions are "metaphorical" rather than empirical; that is, they draw general parallels but do not gather any new data.

Traditionally, the study of witch hunts has not been a popular topic for sociologists, perhaps because of the highly specialized nature of the discipline.

Thus, the topic of witch hunts has been left to historians and those anthropologists who have traditionally worked with indigenous populations. There are of course a few exceptions to this neglect in sociology (see Ben-Yehuda 1980, 1981, 1987, and 1990), including *The Path of the Devil* (Jensen 2007), a sociological analysis of the colonial witch hunts in America. Jensen argues that witches and witch hunts can be studied under the rubrics of deviance, social control, and/or collective behavior in sociology. The selection of the area of specialization in sociology, under which one can study witchcraft accusations and witch hunts, can be dependent on the scholar's research focus: witchcraft as a form of deviant behavior, witch hunt as a form of social control, or witch hunt as a panic reaction in the form of collective behavior (Jensen 2007, vi–33).

Even though one does notice a small but detailed body of literature on witchcraft accusations in some parts of India (mainly Jharkhand, Bastar, Bihar and Chhattisgarh), the topic of witch hunts has been largely ignored by researchers. Studies on Indian witch hunts have been neglected by Indian sociologists and anthropologists in favor of research on caste or caste-based conflicts. There are perhaps two reasons for this. First, because it is assumed that most witchcraft accusations take place within *adivasi* communities, it is not recognized as a problem of much importance for mainstream India, unlike caste, religious conflicts, and dowry. At best, most witchcraft studies in India seem to fall under what Skaria terms as a celebration of wildness, a "call for a recuperation by civilized man of the wild man within. . . . These celebrations of wildness may seem innocent, but they are not. They are part of an ethnocentrism, thinking itself an anti-ethnocentrism" (Skaria 1999, vi–vii). Such a celebration of wildness can be traced back to the colonial times in India when belief in witchcraft was also widespread. Yet historians have completed neglected this important area of popular belief and practice, and this neglect may have implications as to the way witchcraft beliefs among *adivasis* is currently addressed in India (Skaria 1997, 109–110).

Second, also related to the first point on celebration of wildness, the neglect of the topic is also a result of the marginalization of *adivasis* and *adivasi* issues/problems from the rest of the mainstream population. Scholars who work in the area of *adivasi* research tend to focus on education, fundamental rights, and political issues among the community rather than on the issue of witch hunts. For example, a cursory glance at any popular undergraduate sociology textbook and other research books on social problems in India would reveal no sections on witch hunts, despite the fact that the hunts affect quite a large number of India's population. Perhaps this disinterest is motivated by the lack of research grants to study witchcraft accusations compared with the availability of grants for attractive and "safer" topics, such as education, women's rights, and political rights. Similarly, researchers who work on topics of violence against women in India tend to focus on domestic violence, honor killings, and dowry-related homicide rather than on witch hunts among the *adivasis*. Witchcraft beliefs, accusations, and witch hunts are a much neglected research and social issue in India, both among domestic and international scholars.

## Property Disputes, Epidemics, and Gendered Conflict

In the few studies there are on contemporary witchcraft accusations and witch hunts in India, the bulk of research is conducted by social anthropologists (Bailey 1992; Bosu Mullick 2000; Carstairs 1983; Desai 2008; Kelkar and Nathan 1991; Nathan, Kelkar, and Xiaogang 1998; Sundar 2001). Despite having a limited but rich literature, the research on witchcraft accusations among *adivasis* mostly deals with regions in central India, particularly Madhya Pradesh, Chhattisgarh, Jharkhand, Bastar, and Bihar. None of these studies (cited above) focus on the witch hunts among the *adivasi* migrant communities of tea plantation workers in Jalpaiguri or on witchcraft accusations among the local tribes (Santhals) of West Bengal.

Scholars studying witch hunts in contemporary India situate gendered conflict, based on myths and folklore (as mentioned in the section "Women *Adivasi* Workers, Witches and Witch Hunts" in chapter 1), as the dominant reason for witchcraft accusation taking place within *adivasi* communities. This gendered conflict is then placed within property disputes, epidemics, and local politics that erupt into witchcraft accusations against local women. For instance, Barman (2002), one of the few anthropologists studying witch hunts in contemporary West Bengal, argues that witch hunts are a form of "persecution" towards widows, who face "a condition of marginality culminating in total exclusion from society" (1). Her analysis, based on a case study of the Malda district in West Bengal confirms the findings of previous work on the subject: witch hunts in India are an outcome of property disputes involving widows and husbands' kin (Chaudhuri 1987; Kelkar and Nathan 1991; Kelkar and Warrier 1997; Nathan, Kelkar, and Xioagang 1998; Singh 1990). The accused women are mostly childless widows who have a life interest in lands (i.e., a right to control the land and its production that will, after their death, pass on to their nearest male relative). By accusing these women of practicing witchcraft, those male relatives inherit the land immediately. This persecution, according to Barman (2002), is part of a calculated assault on women's traditional rights. This assault results in the successful establishment of a patriarchal order, and it forces widows into a particular gender role—that of being subordinate to the men—that is considered appropriate.

Kelkar and Nathan (1991) similarly link witch hunts in the *adivasi* regions of Jharkhand and West Bengal (this does not include the *adivasi* migrant labor community in tea plantations) to the land rights of the widow. The right of a widow to the property of her husband is denied, according to the *adivasi* laws, if her husband's kin are able to prove that she is a witch. Kelkar and Nathan write that *adivasi* women have limited rights over land. In the *adivasi* community of Jharkhand, land is inherited through the male lineage, but women have some, though limited rights over land. Rights over the land for the women can be broadly divided into two categories: a life interest in land, i.e., the right to manage land and its produce, and the right to a share of the produce of the land. The right to a share of the produce is further divided into two kinds. The first is *kharposh*, or a maintenance right. The second is the right to a share of the produce which may be over and above the *kharposh*, for example, an unmarried daughter may have a share of the crop that she has helped to harvest. This second right is very important for the daughters in poor families (Kelkar and Nathan 1991, 88). Kelkar and Nathan observe that the "right to a share of the produce of the land" becomes very crucial during witchcraft accusations, because, since the land belongs to the woman, it and can be transferred to her husband's home. Over the years, for widows this right has changed from "rights to land" to a mere "right to be maintained." This reduced what is provided to widows to the barest minimum possible.

The limited rights over land for *adivasi* women together with the deterioration of land rights for them has also given rise to a slight trend to increase their rights in recent times. For instance, those who do not have sons among the Santhals, Ho, or Munda groups insist on the transfer of land rights to daughters, whether living with the widows or elsewhere (92). Despite this trend, there is a resistance to women's having rights to land. This resistance comes from both women and men, who find it difficult to break away from traditional patrilineal lineage (92–93). This struggle over land inheritance has been one of the primary causes for witchcraft accusations against women in the region. The studies by Barman (2002) and Kelkar and Nathan (1991) note the immense pressure that *adivasi* widows face from the male heirs of the husband's family to give up their land in exchange for maintenance.

In addition to widows, *adivasi* women with absentee husbands are also vulnerable to accusations of witchcraft. The threat of such a "witch" label increases when the woman suddenly has an increase in economic status. Typically the labeling comes from neighbors or kin. Mishra (2003) finds that family and village politics play a role in depriving a woman of her economic assets through witchcraft accusations. Fines are imposed on the woman accused of practicing witchcraft. These fines take the form of goods (holding a banquet for the village), money, or giving up of some fixed asset such as land. Sometimes the punishment may be banishment from the village or even murder.

Some scholars studying witch hunts in India find that the gendered nature of the conflict leading to witchcraft accusations can be linked to epidemics. Major diseases such as malaria, cholera, small pox, and the resultant death of family members or livestock, might all be blamed on the witch. For instance, in Alipurduar, one of the subdivisions in Jalpaiguri where witchcraft accusations are frequent among the plantation workers, approximately 61 people died and about 3,000 people were affected by malaria in 2006 (see "Malaria Claims 61 Lives in West Bengal," *Times of India*, July 3, 2006). A major part of Mishra's (2003) study links health conditions and witchcraft accusations in the *adivasi* regions of India. The *adivasi* belts of India have some of the worst health facilities in the country. There are very few, if any, modern medical facilities available in these areas, and as a result people consult traditional healers and midwives (*dhais*) during illness. Marginalization of the *adivasi* community, illiteracy, lack of proper health facilities, and governmental corruption all contribute towards the reliance of *jangurus* and *ojhas* (traditional healers/medicine men). There are a few women medicine healers,[3] but they are exceptions; men dominate the profession. These *ojhas* serve both as the medicine man and as a mediator in the daily troubles of the people. They are also viewed as religious ministers or religious priests, the ones next to God, who play an active role in saving the people from epidemics with the help of special knowledge or skills that they posses. They are thus important religious, political, and social figures in the tribal community. These *ojhas* play a crucial rôle in legitimizing witch hunts (as we saw in the Central Dooars case) by confirming the presence of witchcraft, identifying the accused witch, and then justifying a hunt against her. Village-level politics further contribute to the villagers in the hunt. Typically, women from a rival feuding family are labeled as witches, and they are then held responsible for accidents or deaths (Mishra 2003).

The analyses I have considered so far have situated witch hunts in India within property conflicts against either widows or women with absentee husbands and within the need of a troubled community to find a suitable scape-goat on whom to blame its epidemics. But how does one connect these to the broader argument of the literature on Indian witchcraft accusations to gendered conflict? There are two ways that witch hunts can be interpreted as a form of gendered conflict: (1) the "witchcraft" (i.e., women's acting outside of established norms) that fuels the hunts can be seen as a rebellion against an established order of society and (2) the witch hunts are attempts by men to denounce the ritual knowledge of women and link it to evil. Thus, witch hunts become a part of the process by which men establish their societal dominance over women, either by dismissing women from higher positions in society or by demeaning their knowledge and labeling it as malicious. Kelkar and Nathan (1991) would perhaps argue that witch hunts are more likely to occur in situations where women have relatively high status and that status is under threat. For example: in cases of widows who possess rights over lands (98–100). Further, Kelkar and Nathan (1993) argue that the dismissal of women by men is aided and accomplished by witch hunts in two ways, both of which demonstrate gendered conflict. First, as observed among the *adivasis* of Jharkhand, witch hunts provide a convenient opportunity for the men from dominant lineage to get rid of any women who oppose them politically. Second, witch hunts get rid of "unwanted females," such as widows and women who have become pregnant outside of marriage, and in this way they eliminate potential sources of social scandals (Kellar and Nathan 1993, 113).

Nathan, Kelkar, and Xiaogang (1998) link witch hunts to a "patriarchal dispute." Specifically, the authors take another look at some events that seem to provide evidence of the struggle between women and men in the course of establishing men's domination. The phenomena that they analyze are those of *dain* among the Santhal and Munda in Jharkhand (Nathan, Kelkar, and Xiaogang 1998, 58). The focal point of their study is the notion of witchcraft as peripheral, marginal, and as nonstructured cults. They propose that there could have been a period in history when there was female domination and that conflicts related to witchcraft can be viewed from this perspective. These cults, once dominant, are now peripheral, underground, and marginal as a result of persecution that led to the diminution of women's power (59). They write: "Another way is to see the denunciation of ritual knowledge by women as evil as an attempt of the denouncers (men) to change the established order (which may have been one of the authorities of women alone, or one of the joint authorities of women and men) and set up in its place an order based on the authority of men. Witch hunting is, in this analysis, not the suppression of a rebellion; it is itself a rebellion, not by women, but by men in the process of establishing the authority of men. . . . And in the case of the Santhal we will see that witch hunting was related to a change in women's land rights. In each case, it is the men, who, in their attempt to change an established order, denounce women, or certain types of women, as witches" (59).

In furthering the gendered conflict argument, Nathan, Kelkar and Xiaogang discuss the Santhal myth of the origin of witchcraft and connect it to the "struggle between the genders, between men and women, in the family and in Santhal society as a whole" (59). The Santhal myth mentions that the men did not steal something (implying ritual knowledge) from the women that perhaps under the control of the women. On the contrary, the myth suggests that it was the women, who through trickery, acquired knowledge that they had no right to.

But despite the fact that the roots of gendered conflict within Santhal society is mythical and not based on reality, what is perhaps important is that in all these myths there is a reference to a change in the order of society, a change that establishes the authority of men. Thus, though these myths are not historically based, they do refer to an era when women ruled. So, what becomes important is the reason behind the existence of these myths (60). The authors conclude that witch hunts are, by this logic, a way that men, by evoking these myths, establish authority over women. Through the use of myths, women are transformed into sources of evil; this view supports the ideology that women must be socially controlled. The threat a woman might be declared a witch at anytime will prevent her from deviating from or not conforming to established patriarchal rules that have been established to benefit men and to preserve their status in society. The presence of this threat at all times is a powerful tool that can be used by men to change the old order and establish a new one, which will further disadvantage the women in Santhali community. In using the above logic, the authors infer the following about Santhali women:

> (1) [A]t some time Santhal women did function in being spiritual mediators; this is not inferred from the myths, though the myths corroborate it; but from the independent evidence of women' s ritual practices; (2) subsequently men established a monopoly over the higher ritual sphere; (3) women's participation

in these higher rituals then became a sign of their possessing evil powers, being witches; but (4) women continued ill some of the functions connected with these tabooed rituals, like preparing the sacrificial materials (61).

However, other literature on witchcraft accusations in India points to factors other than the gendered nature of conflict. For instance, as mentioned above, Sundar (2011) argues that in Bastar the accused witches do not fit any pattern of gender, age, dependency, or kinship. Thus, attempts to understand these hunts should be placed within the context of the contemporary changes that these communities are facing. Sundar's arguments are similar to Federici's (2010), namely, that to understand contemporary witch hunts in India one has to understand how the social crisis caused by economic liberalism has transformed, uprooted, and plundered communities, forcing people to compete for limited resources. Thus, while one should not underestimate the misogyny that these hunts reveal, government bodies and international financial institutions are equally responsible for witchcraft accusations in contemporary India (11).

Some researchers findings reveal that the victims were not just women and that accusations were also directed against the old and the unprotected. For instance Chaudhuri (1987) writes about how the point of similarity between the victims of witchcraft accusations in Malda: "Most of [them] . . . were widows and aged . . . the significant thing had been the lack of protection or coverage from powerful relatives" (Chaudhuri 1987, 156). Witch hunts and witchcraft accusations then become a sort of class struggle. For others, witchcraft accusations are important in making sense of unexplained events. F. G. Bailey (1994) writes about a witch hunt that took place in the 1950s in Bisipara, Orissa. He comments that witchcraft accusations help in making sense of events in a location where illness, death, and misery "balance out the good . . . if any" (Bailey 1994, 1). When Sushila, a young girl, died suddenly of fever, the villagers of Bisipara identified seven culprits. Among these, one (a man) was identified as the main culprit, and he was accused of engaging in black magic to cause Sushila's death. The villagers extracted a big fine from him as punishment for Sushila's death. The entire process of events (identification of potential culprits, pinpointing of one main culprit, and administration of fine) was carried on rather hurriedly and haphazardly so that the villagers would not face any disruption in the oncoming religious celebrations. To Bailey, this event was much larger and complicated than just the paying of a fine to amend for a witchcraft-related death. Bailey's argument was that the offender's conduct was a threat to people in power, and his punishment was necessary to protect the position of those powerful people. For the people who survived, blaming the culprit made sense: they were making sense of what happened (the death of Sushila), which was more important than the prevention of witchcraft.

## Some Problems With the Application of the Existing Literature to Jalpaiguri

The literature on Indian witch hunts primarily identifies as the leading causes for witchcraft accusations (1) gendered conflict related to the struggle over land inheritance, (2) village-level conflicts between two parties that escalates into a hunt, and (3) making sense of unexplained illnesses and sudden deaths (Barman 2002; Chaudhuri 1987; Kelkar and Nathan, 1991; Mishra 2003; Nathan, Kelkar, and Xiaogang 1998). Though the literature suggests both micro- (family disputes) and macrofactors (gender issues and diseases) as prompting hunts, it is difficult to apply these analyses to the witchcraft accusations in the tea plantations of Jalpaiguri. For one thing, the *adivasi* worker communities in the tea plantations are made up of migrant laborers, unlike the other regions of India, where the people involved are the original inhabitants of the land. For instance, research on witch hunts in the Jharkhand and Bihar states of India focuses on the agricultural land struggles between the *adivasi* widows and their kin as the leading cause of witch hunts. This analysis does not apply to the plantation workers, because the *adivasi* migrant workers do not own any agricultural land in the area. Thus, for example, the struggle between men and women over the inheritance of land that culminates into witchcraft accusations in Jharkhand does not make sense in the plantation worker community. All land in the plantations that the tea plantation workers live and work on belong to the plantation owners. Also, given that the workers work in the plantation as wage laborers, they go not engage in agriculture and thus do not have agricultural lands.

Second, the geographical location of the plantations, the economic conditions of the tea plantation community, and the place of the *adivasi* migrant workers within it make them a distinctive case, different from other the *adivasi* communities in India. The migrant labor community in the plantations is a unique community with social, political, economic, and historical conditions that differ from those of the *adivasis* in the rest of India. To further elaborate on this point, while the research of witchcraft accusations in the places of origin of these groups found gender and economic conflicts to be significant indicators for witch hunts, the migration to the tea plantations and the adjustment of life from agricultural laborers to wage workers considerably impacted the daily lives of the *adivasi* migrant workers. Thus, while the practice of witchcraft accusation (and the witch hunts that follow) has continued over the years, it has changed in form. Geschire (1997) argues similarly that traditional beliefs in witchcraft in postcolonial Africa turn up in a globalized "modern" context with surprising force (Geschire 1997, 8). Explaining with numerous examples, he argues that witchcraft beliefs do not diminish with modernization. Evidence from postcolonial Africa suggests that newer forms of sorcery emerge to cope with ongoing changes (166). "In Africa they are the subject of constant reformulations and re-creations, which often express a determined effort for signifying politicoeconomic changes, or even gaining control over them. In many respects, then, one can speak of the modernity of witchcraft" (2–3).

Thus, while I am not suggesting that previous studies on witch hunts in India are of little use, I argue that, given the unique position of the *adivasi* migrant worker communities in the tea plantations, it is difficult to analyze the phenomenon from the previous studies on India. The context is different here, because these accusations are taking place within a migrant community. In contrast, the witchcraft accusations in Bastar, Jharkhand, or Chhattisgarh are taking place in indigenous communities. A study specifically focusing on the hunts in the tea plantations promises to contribute towards a deeper understanding of witch hunts in that region.

The literature on witchcraft accusations in India identifies a number of factors that prompt a hunt (primarily gender conflict and related conflict over inheritance). Yet, on closer analysis, many of the factors do not seem to be directly relevant to the analysis of the cases in the tea plantations of Jalpaiguri. Additionally, loose use of concepts and weak analysis are some of the problems one finds with the scant literature on witch hunts in Jalpaiguri or in other parts of West Bengal. These problems arise out of the tendency of some scholars to "model" their analysis in the mold of the western hunts (see, for example, Barman 2002; Baruya 2005; Chaudhuri 1987). In the following paragraphs, I elaborate on the problems of existing research in the area and I explain why contemporary witch hunts in the tea plantations of Jalpaiguri are unique.

Let me first discuss the use of the term "persecution" to describe the witchcraft accusations in India. Some theorists have used this term to describe the persecution of women, particularly in positions of authority, through witchcraft accusations during the European witch craze (see, for example, Larner 1984). And some have also used it in characterizing the Indian hunts in Malda district in West Bengal, (see Barman 2002). But the term "scapegoat" is perhaps more applicable to the witchcraft accusations in India. "Persecution" related to religious groups is understood to mean harassment used to afflict or injure because of a group's beliefs or characteristics. Acts committed against a religious group may be deemed persecution by observers or by believers; people committing those acts may see them as being necessary to preserve social order and safety (Jensen 2007). However, witch hunts in contemporary India do not seem to be a structured group activity.[4] Most of the cases reported here are individual instances of witch hunts; the witch craze of early premodern Europe or colonial New England occurred in panic waves. Cases of witch hunts in India rarely lead to an escalating hunt for more witches. Sometimes the accused are forced to pay a fine and/or are asked to leave the community. These punishments are similar to cases in early modern witch hunts that resulted in banishment of witches from villages. Such cases might also involve a hunt for the witch that leads to a trial. In other instances the witches either flee from the village or are lynched.

Second, as mentioned above, while the research on witch hunts in the tea plantations of Jalpaiguri is virtually nonexistent, most scholars, when referring to the Indian context generally, either resort to archaic data or questionable samples. For instance, in his most recent book on the topic of global witch hunts, Behringer (2004) makes no reference to witch hunts in contemporary *adivasi* areas in India, especially after the 1990s, even though he refers to cases after the 1990s in other countries. While this may be an oversight, the implication of this omission is that witchcraft accusations and witch hunts are nonexistent in India after the 1990s. Thus, direct application of previous theoretical models to the cases of witchcraft accusations is perhaps problematic, because models that work in other parts of India might not work in the tea plantations. While previous theoretical models might provide some initial answers or insights into the riddle of Jalpaiguri witch hunts, it is crucial that one understands the context in which the hunts are taking place. With this perspective, I focus on the literature of witch hunts in Europe and Africa with the hope that, while this literature might not provide direct answers in understanding the accusations that are taking place in Jalpaiguri, they might provide some clues.

## Heretics, Changing Economic Climate and Threats to Male Power

In sociology, much of the literature on the European and American witch hunts in the sixteenth and seventeenth centuries that were primarily directed against women set the tone for witchcraft and witch hunt studies in the discipline (Sundar 2001, 425). Although the ideas of witchcraft and malicious witches go back to ancient times, the notion of the heretic witch (one who makes a pact with the Devil) has dominated historical and sociological research on witch hunts in premodern Europe and colonial America. Here, the literature is heavily concentrated on explaining why historically women constituted more than 80 percent of the victims. One type of explanation focuses on witch hunts to be male hegemonic expressions of power and authority reactions against female symbols of power (such as female cults, midwives, and women healers). For example, the literature on the colonial hunts in America (especially the hunts in Salem), identifies religious rebellion in the context of ideal female behavior and inheritance conflicts between men and women as the two central explanations for witch hunts. These explanations refer to the scapegoat (in this case the female witch) who is the victim of conflicts over property, religion, social status, or social stress caused by epidemics or wars. The literature on both the New England witch hunts in America (late seventeenth century) and the premodern witch craze in Europe attribute witch hunts to gender conflict, decline or increase in individual or social economic conditions, and the search for a suitable scapegoat (Barstow 1995; Behringer 2004; Briggs 1996; Godbeer 1994; Hill 1997; Harley 1990; Karlsen 1998; Reis 1997). For instance, Karlsen (1998) argues that economic considerations, especially New England's system of inheritance, provides clues about the special positions of most accused witches vis-à-vis their society's rules for transferring wealth from one generation to another. Most accused women had no legitimate male heirs in their immediate families and therefore stood to inherit or did inherit the property left by their father or husband. These women were aberrations in a Puritan society that had an inheritance system designed to keep property in the hands of men. This situation is particularly relevant in the context of witchcraft accusations among the *adivasis* in Jharkhand, where the hunts have been motivated by intents to deny widows' inheritance.

Continuing the gendered frame of analysis on witch hunts, Barstow (1994) explains witch hunts as an outcome of competition between men and women for power during changing economic and political conditions in premodern Europe. The witch hunts she studied took place at the same time as colonization and the slave trade, and according to Barstow all three were made possible by the legal and political climate that perceived women, slaves, and natives as objects to be exploited. As a result, the witch craze in Europe helped reinforce traditions of misogyny and patriarchal control, as it demonized the image of the woman (Barstow 1994, 13). For instance, Barstow, in discussing why women were attacked in the sixteenth century, explains that in most European cases the accused were very poor compared with their accusers. The witch was typically the poorest of the poor and depended on her neighbors for food:

> The poor were becoming poorer; more peasants were forced to beg or steal in order to survive. Old, single women, especially vulnerable to this economic crunch, came to be seen as nuisances. When they turned them down, people felt guilt. . . . Then when misfortune occurred, people turned on the beggars, a classic example of blaming the victim (26).

In some instances wealthy women were attacked, and Barstow explains that this was typical in the later years of the witch hunt—a time when poor women victims were depleted or when the poor women sought revenge by naming well-to-do women. This pattern was also observed during the Salem witch trials (26–27).

In addition to gender and a changing economic climate, Karlsen (1998) brings in a third factor, religion, and ties it to the previous two. In other words, Karlsen links gender (in the way of sexual terrorism) and religion in explaining witch hunts. As seen in the previous explanations of witch hunts, some theories refer to witch hunts as a form of sexual terrorism—as a system by which males frighten, dominate, and control females. In Puritan New England society, equality of the sexes was seen as a threat to the foundations of social hierarchy. Puritans argued that even though men and women were spiritually equal, this equality did not extend to earthly relations, such as the relationship of the women to the church. Women were expected to identify with the needs, goals, and interest of the men in their families. Any impulses that women had to speak and act on their own behalf had to be stifled. According to Karlsen, witches were not only threats to their neighbors' physical and economic well-being; they were heretics. Witchcraft was viewed as rebellion against God, and the constant fear was that the Devil would be successful in recruiting women and that that would result in the destruction of Puritan churches.

Karlsen further argues that the New England witch trials revealed that the women who resisted the "new truths" of Puritan beliefs on gender roles either symbolically or in fact, were the ones who got accused of witchcraft. In being so identified, they were visible reminders of the potential resistance in all women. The witch in New England was a human with superhuman powers. Foremost among these was her ability to perform "maleficium," that is, to cause harm to others by supernatural means. The motive most commonly ascribed was malice, stimulated by pride, discontent, greed, or envy. Although the witch's power could bring harm to anyone, her victims tended to be close neighbors or other people who knew her well enough to anger her.

Similar to Karlsen's argument, Reed (2007) argues that the Salem hunts were a reflection of the crisis between gender relations and maintenance of social order. The Salem hunts were a necessary reaction of the Puritan culture towards "meddlesome" women who dared to interfere in the affairs of the world (and thus defied societal norms). Reed finds witch hunts to be functional in a society where social actions are structured to maintain social order. The hunts were necessary because they supported the goal of establishing the Puritans as God's chosen people, and they clarified the position of women in relationship to men, God, and the Devil. The witches put both of these goals at risk (Reed 2007, 211).

Who were the other common female targets of witch hunts, particularly when the authority of patriarchal societies and the preservation of social order seemed to be under threat? Women healers, who aided during illnesses and childbirth procedures, were just such targets, particularly during the European witch craze. Barstow (1994) writes that a typical witch in Europe was a woman who possessed the power of healing, which, ironically, also gave her the power to kill. In other words, a witch was typically a woman who had some kind of a power that was perceived to be a threat to the male-dominated society. This power could lie within her real skills to heal, or sometimes her personal characteristics could be interpreted or perceived to be a threat. For instance, women who were considered to be outspoken or shrewish could also be accused of witchcraft. Bever (2002) has an interesting theory as to why women were more likely than men to act out their aggression in ways associated with witchcraft. His argument is that women are naturally less physically aggressive and therefore more likely to engage in indirect or covert aggression, the expression of which may be seen as witchcraft. This is turn gave rise to stereotypes of the female witch as ill-tempered shrew.

From the above discussions, the theoretical implications about witch hunts are, as Kai Erickson said in his 1966 piece in *Social Problems*, "Notes on the Sociology of Deviance," a normal response to abnormal social conditions. Economic disruption and religious chaos led the Puritans to believe that the Devil had "given up his familiar disguises" and instead was to be found at the very heart of the Puritan colony (Erikson 1966, 158). The witches provided the perfect scapegoats for the insoluble problems of the isolated Massachusetts community, a community that was

> alone in the world, bewildered by the loss of their old destiny but are not yet aware of their new one, and during this fateful interval they tried to discover some images of themselves by listening to a chorus of voices that whispered to them from the depths of an invisible wilderness (159).

During periods of illness, death, or economic upheavals leading to social stress (as experienced by the *adivasi* communities in India), the solutions and control of which were out of reach, witches and witchcraft accusations provided the perfect release. Witch hunts serve to maintain social order in periods of conflict, and witches are the perfect scapegoats for upheavals that lead to disruptions of social order.

## From Magic to Modernity: Witchcraft Accusations in Postcolonial Africa

Witchcraft and witch hunts are among the most well-researched topics in anthropology. These topics used to fall under the study of religion and magic among folk or traditional societies (Bailey 1994; Douglas 1970; Mair 1969; Fortune 1932). However, older anthropological works on witchcraft and witch hunts have often been criticized by sociologists, particularly on the context of ignoring sociological variables of gender, class, and kinship in the study of the exotic folk society (Kennedy 1967).[5] In the 1960s there arose a need to advocate a global perspective in the study of witchcraft and witch hunts. European historians, especially, acknowledged the importance of research on witch hunts in the developing world, particularly within the context of postcolonial/modern societies. Hutton (2002) writes that in the last three decades of the twentieth century, most of the research on witch hunts was carried out in the African societies and communities by white western historians and was motivated by a need to understand the newly independent modern states (Hutton 2002, 16). He then goes on to argue that towards the end of the twentieth century, the focus on African communities in witch hunt research was reversed. There arose an abundance of scholarly work on the European witch craze and the colonial American witch hunts by historians who focused primarily on a close study of a single case or community. Hutton is critical of this research, because it rarely studies data outside the western world. According to him, the colonial American and the premodern European witch persecutions are "trivial affairs," particularly when the duration and number of victims is considered, when compared with the hunts in the nonwestern world (16–17).

Hutton's reflections are perhaps not completely accurate. While research on the European and colonial American hunts did increase after the 1960s, research, particularly on postcolonial African witch hunts, has made a strong theoretical, methodological comeback (Moore and Sanders 2001, 10). The contrast between the colonial and postcolonial anthropological accounts of African witch hunts lies in the way the phenomena were viewed. Previously the hunts were studied in isolation: an exotic ritual that was studied in alienation to the sociopolitical events concurrent to the period. For instance, the entire purpose of Evans Pritchard's work on witchcraft among Azande was to demonstrate through functionalist reasoning how witchcraft beliefs led to a stabilizing influence on the moral and social system: a form of control system with a negative impact (Evans-Pritchard 1976, xxii–xxiii). In contrast, postcolonial accounts of witchcraft beliefs treat them as a reaction of traditional societies towards a changing moral, economic, and social order. Witchcraft beliefs do not disappear with the advent of modernization; they adapt, change, and reemerge in newer forms.

The divisions of disciplines, geographical areas of research, and different theoretical strands dominate the current field of witch hunts. Each perspective adds an important piece of the puzzle as to why witch hunts occur, but there is lack of interdisciplinary conversation on the topic. As a result, scholars and researchers are left with a one-sided view of the phenomena, and it's a view that is blurred by the theoretical framework dominant in their respective disciplines. Despite the criticism, some scholars have been able to transcend disciplinary boundaries through historical perspectives (see, for example, Comaroff and Comaroff 1993; Geschire 1997; Skaria 1999) to gain a better understanding of how witchcraft beliefs are constructed. For instance, Frankfurter (2006), in his book *Evil Incarnate*, traces the construction of evil throughout history and in different contexts leading to the late-twentieth century. He argues that evil, which is manifest in moral panic that takes the form of witch hunts and even genocide, is, ironically, based on an impulse to expunge perceived or targeted evil (and its embodiments—its followers) from society. In other words, moral panics arise as a reaction to getting rid of malevolence and its followers.

The present book, *Witches, Tea Plantations, and Lives of Migrant Laborers in India*, is unique in that it takes a holistic theoretical approach to the subject of witchcraft accusations and witch hunts. While explanations of witch hunts as an expression of gender conflicts against feminine cults and women's political, social, and economic power are a useful tool of analysis, witch hunts are also a "normal" reaction of a society under social stress; in that context, the weak and powerless become scapegoats for restoring social order. In other words, every society has the potential to develop witch hunts and select targets during periods of social stress. What is fascinating in the context of the Jalpaiguri tea plantation witchcraft accusations is that they seem to contain elements of the western premodern hunts of Europe, the colonial hunts of America, and the postcolonial African witch hunts (which are taking place within traditional contemporary societies). For instance, the bulk of the literature on India (particularly in the states where the migrant *adivasi* workers originated from) talks about gender conflicts, economic upheavals, and inheritance struggles between widows and their male relatives as contributing factors in witchcraft beliefs (for example, Nathan, Kelkar, and Xiaogang 1998; Sundar 2001). That is how village-level micropolitics are manipulated to select women as targets for scapegoats. On the other hand, the literature on the postcolonial African witchcraft accusations seems particularly relevant, especially when one tries to place the accusations within the plantation economy and within the plantation class conflict. In the following paragraphs of this section, I elaborate as to how the literature on post-colonial African witchcraft beliefs provides a theoretical framework for the broader conflict between the plantation owners and the laborers in the tea plantations, where the macroprocesses at work provides a sense of control to the workers, who are dealing with oppressive life and work circumstances.

The term "witchcraft" in contemporary research on Africa has been used to cover a wide variety of activities such as occult, magic, and enchantment. However, anthropologists (like Geschiere 1997, 13–15) are critical of the use of the term because it ignores "complex, on the ground realities" (Moore and Sanders 2001, 3). In the 1980s a decisive revival in the study of witchcraft occurred (beginning with Geschiere 1988; Rowlands and Warnier 1988; Warnier 1988; Comaroff and Comaroff 1993). Along with innovations in theory and methods, the literature also sought to "unsettle western teleology of social change." Recent scholars claim that witchcraft is modern not traditional, wide ranging not local, historical and not static. For example, in stressing that witchcraft is modern, scholars note that modernities are multiple (Comaroff and Comaroff 1993) and that there are multiple trajectories of modernity; there is no single path to modernity and human lives are never homogeneous (Moore and Sanders 2001, 10–12). For other scholars on postcolonial Africa, witchcraft beliefs arise during periods of change brought about by the development of modern statehood. Brinkman (2003) describes witchcraft accusations in Angola (1966–1975) during its war for independence. Specifically focusing on the Movimento Popular de Libertacao de Angola (MPLA)'s Eastern Front, Brinkman studies the relationship between nationalism and witchcraft; he contrasts accusations of treason with accusations of witchcraft. The theme of witchcraft accusations here was linked to treason and to wider debates over coercion and consent and brutality and legitimacy in times of guerrilla warfare (Brinkman 2003, 305).

In a pioneering account of the role of rituals in everyday lives in postcolonial Africa, Jean and John Comaroff argue that in postcolonial Africa rituals serve as a form of control for the locals that helps them make sense of a world that is changing as a result of the effect of modernity on local customs, life-styles, and social structure (Comaroff and Comaroff 1993, xiv). Rituals are connected to everyday social acts and are not limited to being understood only as arising out of precolonial traditional communities and their tensions. Instead, rituals are very much a part of changing moral discourses, state-building, and conquest and colonialism in these communities. Particularly in the context of postcolonial contemporary Africa, Comaroff and Comaroff argue that rituals, such as ones that involve witchcraft, are integral to the experiences of modernity and that they are called upon to "counter the magic of modernity" (xxv). Witchcraft rituals are representative of the impact of the globalized economy on the local traditions of these communities. These communities are often alienated in today's world, and witches embody modernity's malcontent (xxix).

In a similar explanation, Michael Taussig talks about the reemergence of the Devil in indigenous communities that are experiencing socioeconomic changes as a result of the introduction of European capitalist economics (1980). Taussig looks at the two locations in South America: Bolivian tin mines and the sugar plantations of Columbia. Both of these industries experienced Spanish-led capitalist development in which the local population was drawn into the rank of the workers, or the proletariat. As also observed in the examples of witchcraft-led rituals in postcolonial Africa (Comaroff and Comaroff), the Devil (a western European character) played an important role in mediating socioeconomic tensions brought about by the new imperialism in the mining and sugar plantation worker communities in South America. The once land-owning peasants in the areas, reduced to proletariats, wage-laborers in the new economic structure, believed that the Devil was summoned every time production was maintained or increased. As a result, an increase in wages as a result of increase in production is considered to be unproductive in the long run. Taussig, applying a Marxian interpretation to the emergence of the Devil in these South American communities, argues that the new mode of production alienated the workers from the product and made them subordinate to their wages. In contrast, in the precapitalist system that existed in the same communities, the product and individuals that produced and exchanged the product were not alien to each other. The Devil represents a protest against the new mode of production and an adherence to the old precapitalist agricultural economy (Taussig 1980, 36–38).

Both Comaroff and Comaroff (1993) and Taussig (1980) view the witchcraft and devil believing community as a community in transition where the rituals are used to moderate and intervene during changes in social and moral order. The displacement of the traditional actor from his/her universe has taken place over and over again in Africa, Asia, and South America. Kiernan (2006) writes about the power of the occult in modern Africa and the displacement of traditional actors. He explains how modernity, having roots in the Enlightenment and colonial ideals, first got transported to Africa by explorers, traders, and missionaries. Heavily influenced by individualism, scientific rationalization, and capitalism, modernization introduced Africans to occupational migration, cash crop economy, and taxation. With postcolonization, during the second wave of change, Africans were introduced to nationalism, the formation of postcolonial states, and new political and economic elites among their indigenous groups. Finally, in the last decade of the twentieth century, Africans were introduced to global markets through globalization. Suddenly Africans were facing two contradictory (but often compatible) forces in the contemporary world: (1) the increasing dependence, indebtedness, and marginalization of African countries and (2) an increasing division between the rich and poor, despite the rhetoric of democracy, transparency, and accountability (Kiernan 2006, 3–4).

Magic, occult, and witchcraft accusations can be modernized to such an extent that they can be used as counterpoints to liberal understandings of modernity's transparency and rational progress. Modernity not only constitutes magic as its counterpoint but also develops its own forms of magic. To understand the relationship between magic and modernity, we have to look at how different forms of publicity and secrecy and revelation and concealment complement or supplement each other. How can magic be reinvented in modernity? What are the enchantments that are specific to modernity? How can the need to understand secrecy versus publicity, concealment versus revelation help us understand contemporary society? (Meyer and Pels 2003, 6) It is with these questions in the background that I situate the witchcraft accusations in Jalpaiguri plantations. First, I view the accusations specifically in the context of the plantation economy and not within the context of existing beliefs towards witchcraft that exist within the *adivasi* community. Second, I explore how the witchcraft accusations that evolve into full-fledged hunts reveal the inner tensions within the plantation workers and management. Third, I situate witchcraft within the context of the *adivasi* migrant workers and their lives on the plantations. Finally, I explore how seemingly petty village conflicts, gossip, and rumor can escalate into social protest against the plantation wage economy.

In *Witches, Tea Plantations and Lives of Migrant Workers in India*, I explore how a community that is socially, economically, and politically oppressed uses witchcraft accusations that culminate in witch hunts to deal with stress. It is the argument of this book that the witchcraft accusations are a sporadic reaction of the community against their oppressors, who in this context are the plantation management, against whom they are powerless. The incidents of witch hunts are a discourse, a thought similar to what Frankfurter described when he talked about the representation of evil and myth and the role of that representation in shaping lives and experiences (Frankfurter 2006, 11). It is within this discourse that witch hunts are not to be viewed as exotic/primitive rituals of a backward community but as a powerful protest by a community against its oppressors.

## Notes

1. There have been some exceptions to this, though not these are not as frequent as the incidents in countries in Asia and Africa. For instance, Jeanne Favret Saada's work in Bocage talks about witchcraft beliefs in rural west France. See Jeanne Favret-Saada, *Deadly Words: Witchcraft in the Bocage* (Cambridge: Cambridge University Press, 1980).

2. Apart from documented cases of witch hunts, there are some cases of witch hunts that do not get reported in the police files or in the media. This is because some of

the villages where the hunts take place are in isolated areas where there are no police stations or newspaper offices. These cases have no written documentation (in the form of reports or interviews) and remain "unrecorded." Existence of such cases can be found through the "word of mouth."

3. Though it is not common for women to be *ojhas*, some of the literature on witch hunts has reported the presence of female medicine healers (see Mishra, 2003).

4. One can argue that there is some structure in the Indian hunts. But there are two characteristics in the Indian hunts that can work against it being categorized as persecution. One, the Indian hunts seem to be motivated by individual interests rather than social causes. That is, these acts are not explicitly conducted to preserve social order, but they seem to be directed to achieve personal interests of the accuser, who is typically seeking revenge for ailments or deaths. In the process of a witchcraft accusation that leads to a hunt, the accuser gathers support from the villagers against accused witch, and the villagers then join in to provide support to the accuser's family. Second, and related to the first, because these hunts are individually motivated and not structured group activities towards other groups, they do not result in panic waves in the Indian context. Thus, a single case of witch hunt does not lead to a series of hunts, as witnessed, for example, during the witch craze era in premodern Europe.

5. For detailed reference on the criticisms against previous anthropological works on witchcraft, see G. John Kennedy, "Psychological and Social Explanations of Witchcraft," *Man, New Series* 2, no. 2 (1967): 216–25; and Max Gluckman, "Psychological, Sociological and Anthropological Explanations of Witchcraft and Gossip: A Clarification," *Man, New Series* 3, no. 1 (1967): 20–34.

# Chapter 3

# Two Leaves and a Bud: The Beginning

"How can an avid tea drinker today sympathize with the predicament of pahalwan Ramsuk Tewari, an inhabitant of Bundi. . . . As was the tradition, he migrated to Bengal, seeking his fortune. But, alas within two monsoons Ramsuk turned into a tea addict. It so happened that he began to suffer from dyspepsia and to lose weight daily. In a humorous poem . . . Kumudranjan Mallick, a well known Bengali poet of the 1930s, described his subsequent fate:

> At last hearing the news of his illness, a man from his native village came rushing and gave Ramsuk an earful of the choicest in his local dialect and at the very first instance stopped him from drinking tea.

Following his country-cousin's diktat, Ramsuk Tewari regained his health and life returned to its familiar ways: Tulsi's Ramayana, a regular diet of dal-roti and, of course, no tea" (Excerpt from *From an Imperial Product to a National Drink: The Culture of Tea Consumption in Modern India*, Gautam Bhadra 2005, 1).

The above narrative highlights how tea, now a popular drink in India, was an alien brew that caused ill health to the native drinker when it was first introduced by the British. Though the story describes the plight of a simple village man (Ramsuk), it brings out the hostility of the natives towards the colonial product, a product that is associated with vice. The history of plantations everywhere is the history of a colonial production house where the products are produced primarily for western consumption and profit. The development of plantations required large areas of land and a large labor force, and the production of tea was made possible by the spatial integration of capitalism in Asia. Spatial integration refers to the linkages of commodity production in different locations around the world through exchange (Liu 2010, 75). The political economy of tea in the colonial period aimed to extract the value of various objects, which then could be united in a land hitherto considered a wasteland. Thus, plants, soil, and labor were all viewed as isolatable things whose values were objective and calculable. The colonial trade made it possible to gather and transport labor, capital, and tea bushes across the vast unevenly developed regions of Asia, and ultimately tea came to be promoted and packaged as a breakfast drink commodity that was enjoyed worldwide (73). As a result, to set up the tea plantations in India, the British planters required both a large labor force that would be present to work over generations and vast areas of land. The location of Dooars in Jalpaiguri provided all the requirements needed to establish the plantation economy. The tea plantation industry in India was set up on the basis of coercion, low wages, and an immigrant labor force. Added to this was political support which was given by the British government in India to the planters. The planters' coercive methods of securing labor largely went unchecked and were in violation of labor rights (Bhowmik 1981; Bhowmik, Xaxa, and Kalam 1996). For the British capitalists, tea was a lucrative cash crop, but for the main actors in the tea plantation—the migrant *adivasi* laborers—it was a "tragedy of great dimension" (Jha 1996, 16).

## History of the Tea Plantations in Dooars: Tea Industry, Workers and Tea Bushes

India is ranked among the top tea-producing nations in the world, with an annual production of 750 million kilograms of tea. Today India is both the largest consumer and exporter of tea. Tea production is confined within the four states of India: Assam, West Bengal, Kerala, and Tamil Nadu. West Bengal has two tea-producing districts: Darjeeling and Jalpaiguri. (Jalpaiguri is the location of the current study.) Tea plantations are the largest employers of workers in the organized sector in India; they employ almost 1.5 million workers (Bhowmik 2011; Bhowmik, Xaxa, and Kalam 1996).

The geographical location of this study covers the district of Jalpaiguri in the state of West Bengal. The district of Jalpaiguri is known primarily for its tea plantations, which provide the main source of income for the region. According to the Tea Board Statistics of India, the total current area of land for the production of tea in India is 89,025 hectares, and the district of Jalpaiguri covers approximately two-thirds of this area for tea production (Bhowmik 1981, 2011). The tea-growing area in Jalpaiguri is a part of the Dooars region.[1] Geographically, the Dooars region consists of the area that runs along the foothills of Bhutan, with the river Teesta on the west and the river Sankos in the east. The Dooars region, or the tea-growing area of Jalpaiguri, is a flat strip of land about 22 miles wide and nearly 200 miles long. The area is surrounded by the country of Bhutan and the Darjeeling district in the north, and the Cooch Behar district in the south (ibid.). The region is perfect for growing tea because of its high rainfall and its red loamy clay soil, which is very porous. There are approximately 300 tea plantations in the Dooars region, and they vary from 200 to 1,000 hectares of land (Bhowmik 1981).

The history of tea plantations in India starts in the late nineteenth century, when the first tea bush was brought to this region by an anonymous colonial planter. The first tea plantation was established by a British planter named Dr. Brougham at Gazelduba in the Dooars in 1874 (Chaudhury and Varma 2002). During the establishment of the tea plantations, the British planters faced two hurdles: the area for the plantation land had to be cleared of forests, and there was an inadequate supply of laborers. The indigenous population of the region (the *bhumiputras*:[2] Bhutias, Rajbansis, Mechs, and Totos) was reluctant to join the plantation as laborers. As a cultivating community, they were traditionally resistant to join as industrial wage laborers, and the plantation offered wages that were lower compared to agricultural wages (Chaudhury and Varma 2002, 21–22). The migration of workers that occurred in connection with the tea plantations was very similar to that which occurred in connection with plantations in South America, Africa, and the Caribbean: local populations refused to join the labor force and demanded higher wages to work in the plantations, and so workers had to be brought in from elsewhere. During the time that the plantations were being set up in Jalpaiguri, the *adivasi* regions in the neighboring states of Bengal, especially in the Chotanagpur and Santhal Parganas regions, were experiencing political and economic crisis as a result of the British Permanent Settlement Act.[3] This population of *adivasi*, who were displaced from their lands, provided the much needed labor force for the tea plantations in the Dooars (Bhowmik 1981; Bhowmik, Xaxa, and Kalam 1996; Chaudhury and Varma 2002). Traditionally, and continuing to this day, the bulk of the workforce in the plantations is composed of a number of *adivasi* groups, such as Oraon, Munda, Kharia, Kharowar, Mahali, Santhal, and Gond. Oraon comprise the largest population of *adivasis* working on the tea plantations. This migrant *adivasi* population known as the *Madesia* (people from the middle country) and their descendants, constitutes about 90 percent of the total workforce in the Dooars tea region, and were contrasted with the Nepali workforce known as Paharis (Bhowmik 1981; Chatterjee 2001; Dasgupta and Khan 1983).

In the years prior to Indian independence (1947), no laws regulated the work hours, conditions of work, or living conditions of plantation laborers. Although the tea plantations were recognized as an industry, the relation between the planters and the workers was that of master and servant rather than of employer and employee (Bhowmik 1981). Prior to independence, the British owned the bulk of the plantations in the Dooars, but there were Indian owners as well; and in both groups, the conditions for the migrant *adivasi* workers were dismal. A few years after the launch of the first garden, a few Indian (mainly Bengali) entrepreneurs started investing in gardens in the area. However, despite the presence of Indian planters, the plantation economy manifested all the signs of colonial investment. The most important of these was support of the British government for the European planters in establishing their "planter's raj." The planters' control of the labor supply, rail, and coal fell under special laws that gave the British planters unlimited power (Chaudhury and Varma 2002, 20–21).

The Plantation Labor Act of 1951, a landmark act in the history of labor, laid down rules for the welfare of labor and conditions of work. However, the tea plantations of India, particularly those in the Dooars region, function with disregard of the laws that were enacted. The Dooars plantations practice "the family system of employment." This system implies that adult males, adult females, and young adults are employed in the plantations but are paid wages on scales different from those mandated by the Plantation Labor Act. The bulk of the plantation workforce consists of *adivasi* migrants who, as a result of their marginalization, are largely unaware of labor policies. The result is that they experience a high degree of exploitation through low wages, long hours of work, strenuous working environment, and poor or almost nonexistent medical facilities. Also, a major drawback to the workers in the Dooars plantations is that there is little or no unionization. The problems of these migrant *adivasi* in the tea plantations workers are rarely focused in the local newspapers or journals, and they are rarely discussed at workers' forums (Bhowmik, Xaxa, and Kalam 1996).

Most workers in tea plantations reside within the plantation area. They are housed in rows of huts that are called "labor lines." Almost all tea gardens in the Dooars area have tea-processing factories. The labor force in the tea gardens is therefore of two types: workers in the fields and workers in the factories. Most factory workers are males; women work in the fields as "tea-leaf pickers" because women are considered to be better pickers than men (Bhowmik 1981). Women's work on the plantations is simultaneously fetishized, romanticized (nimble fingers suitable for plucking), and devalued (Chatterjee 2001, 6, 8, 26–27), and this attitude toward women's work is similar to what we find in wage production everywhere—from plantations to factories (for example, Aiwa Ong refers to this in *Spirits of Resistance* (1987) while referring to the attitudes of male supervisors and employers toward women workers). Men are typically employed to hoe, clean the bases of tea bushes, spray pesticides, and occasionally pluck tea leaves. Women and men are segregated in the plantations, and each group has separate zones in which to work. Occupational mobility is almost exclusively limited to men, who can move up the ranks to become factory workers, mechanics, and watchmen. Women have limited mobility within the plantation work.

The plucking season in the Dooars begins with the early rains in March and ends in late November or early December. It reaches its peak during the monsoons (July and August). The first crop of leaves (known as the first flush) in the early monsoon showers is supposed to produce the best quality of tea. The average life span of a tea bush is six years, and it can grow up to a height of 18 feet. The bushes in the plantation are trimmed to maintain a height of three feet for two main reasons. First, the bush spreads out best at that height, and this produces the maximum number of plucking points. Second, because plucking is done by hand, it is convenient to pluck at that height. The tea bush is covered with dark- and light-green leaves. The leaves that are plucked consist of a bud and two light-green leaves on either side. It takes about five kilograms of plucked tea leaves to make one kilogram of processed tea leaves in the factory (Bhowmik 1981).

Today, these plantations in Dooars are owned by both multinational and Indian companies, such as Lipton, Duncan, and Tata. The industry in Dooars went through a crisis from 1999–2007 that intensified during 2002–2004. There are a number of speculations as to why the crisis happened, but bad management that contributed to the fall in quality and price of tea emerged as one of the factors. A number of plantations were closed at that time, and reports of death as a result of starvation rose in numbers among the workers. On both the closed and open plantations, with the exception of a few, workers are housed in structures that are dilapidated. House repairs and compensation for house collapse are unavailable, as are medical facilities. Latrines and urinals are nonexistent, and drinking water, electricity, and transportation for children to go to high and secondary school (15 to 20 kilometers away) are not provided by the plantations (Talwar, Chakraborty, and Biswas 2005). Some of the closed plantations reopened after 2004, but the tea industry in the Dooars continues to be in a crisis even today. Starvation deaths, suicides among the workers due to rising debts, and nonpayment of the workers by the management continue to be problems, and strikes that arise out of disputes over minimum daily wages continue (See "Tea Workers Union Threatens Fresh Strike," *The Indian Express*, August 12, 2011).

## Migration of the Laborers, Life in the Plantation and Class Hierarchy

The recruitment of migrant workers in the initial stages was family-based, and the *adivasis* were encouraged to migrate to the plantations with their families. This strategy served two purposes: first, the planters wanted cheap laborers who would be permanently settled in the plantations, and this could only be achieved by encouraging families rather than individuals to migrate. The entire family then (males, females, children) worked on the plantations at wages determined by the planters. Second, family migration ensured that labor could be reproduced; this would ease the problem of further recruitment in the future (Bhowmik, Xaxa, and Kalam 1996).

The most popular method of recruiting labor for plantations in India during the colonial period was through *arkatis* or recruiting agents who made regular rounds in the drought-stricken *adivasi* areas of central India. *Arkatis* were mainly employed by the tea plantations in Assam. They earned a lot of notoriety in the *adivasi* region, particularly because of their heinous methods of recruitment. They were described in colonial texts as the "scum of the earth," "heartless scoundrels," and they were feared as much as a "man-eating tiger" (Bhowmik 2011, 23; Chatterjee and Dasgupta 1981, 1862). They deceived potential recruits, for example, by calling the tea plantations a part of the government enterprise or promising better marriage prospects and by "dressing" themselves in clothes that gave the impression that they were official government representatives. The *arkatis* used every known trick to recruit the *adivasis* to the plantations in Assam. The plantations in Jalpaiguri and other regions of the Dooars used similar methods—*sardars* or labor headmen—to recruit labor for the plantations, for a commission (two to five rupees per worker). As an incentive for work in the plantations, the potential recruit was also paid an advance, in the range of ten rupees. However, like the *arkatis*, the *sardars* also used every form of abuse and villainy known to them to recruit the workers, including violence and abduction (Bates 2000; Bhowmik 2011). Chaudhary and Varma explain:

> Though the indenture system was not used, the method of recruitment through a garden *sardar* could hardly have been free of unscrupulous methods, deception and even outright violence against men, women and children. The recruits were kept in prison like transit depots, and sent to the tea gardens under heavy guard (Chaudhary and Varma 2002, 22).

Deserters were imprisoned and heavily fined. The poor treatment of the workers was, however, recorded by the British in the nineteenth century and the *sardars* were subject to official investigations (Liu 2010).

The migration of the *adivasis* from central India (Chotanagpur) to the Dooars for employment by the plantations was not documented in written records by the *adivasi* themselves. Folklore and oral traditions of the *adivasis* and some colonial accounts do mention the tremendous hardship and torture that the migrants had to undergo under the "garden *sardars*"[4] or the middlemen that were employed by the colonial planters to recruit the laborers and keep them under control. The *adivasis*, who were initially attracted to the plantation jobs with promises of a better life, firewood rations and work, found themselves under indirect rule of the *sardars* who manipulated considerable power over them (Chatterjee 2001, 73–75).

The laborers were kept in labor lines on the plantations, and these areas initially were not much different from the slave quarters in nineteenth century America. The lack of modern drainage systems, poor hygiene conditions, controls over drinking water and food rations by the planters, badly constructed huts for the laborers, and overcrowding in the labor lines made living conditions very hard for the plantation workers. Added to this, the poor state of living and work conditions made the laborers susceptible to a number of diseases, such as cholera, malaria, black fever, and dysentery, which also resulted in high infant mortality rates (Chaudhury and Varma 2002). The colonial planters had complete control over the labor force. The planters were supported by the British Government and given free rein to do what they wished. While the planters had trade bodies that represented their interests, the plantation workers were prevented from unionizing. For instance, a report from the Commission of Inquiry on the Conditions of Tea Plantation Labor in India and Ceylon, set up in 1944 writes: "[T]he employers are highly organized and powerful whereas the workers are all unorganized and helpless." This implies that, while it was necessary for trade unions to operate in the tea plantations, it was unlikely that they would be allowed to operate, because access to the plantation workers was restricted by the management. At this time the tea plantations employed 1.25 million workers (Bhowmik 2011, 240–41).

Little has changed for these laborers over these last 150 years. After the independence of India from the British in 1947, there seemed to be some changes in the attitude towards the tea plantation workers. For instance, the Minimum Wages Act of 1948 mandated that the plantations establish standard minimum wages for the laborers; wage rates had previously been variable and based only on the planters' whims and fancies. However, the enforcement of such acts was arbitrary, and the condition of workers stayed the same as before (Bhowmik 2011, 242). A survey conducted with a sample of 182 households in the labor lines of Jalpaiguri (initially in 1995, and later updated in 2011 (see Bhowmik 2011)), described the continuing miserable conditions of work and life among the *adivasi* migrant workers. For instance, the labor lines even today have no electricity or running water, and the health conditions are very poor. The labor communities have very high rates of infant mortality, anemia, cholera, endemic fever, black fever, diarrhea, and malaria. Lack of "modern" health facilities and government health aid make these communities dependent on local alternative medicine, which is mostly administered by people in the community with little or no formal training in modern medicine (Bhadra 1997; Chaudhury and Varma 2002). Perhaps the situation after 2001 is even worse compared with the previous decades, because a large number of plantations in Dooars shut operations, leaving their workers destitute (Bhowmik 2011, 244).

Today, as in colonial times and the decades after independence, the plantation system has a very strict class hierarchy that maintains structure between management and the workers: management, staff, substaff, and workers. The management consists of the manager, assistant managers, and the factory manager. The staff is composed mainly of white collar and middle management personnel, and the substaff make up the lower-level supervisors. The *adivasi* workers comprise the bulk of the population in the plantation, and they hold the lowest status in the plantation hierarchy (Bhowmik, Xaxa, and Kalam 1996).

As mentioned in previous chapters, the categorization of the migrant *adivasi* workers as "wild," "primitive" beings somehow justifies (to some) the extreme prejudice that the workers face within the plantations. The construction of the *adivasis* as a wild and primitive group goes back to Hindu notions of pollution-purity and the colonial decision of dividing labor to suit colonial interests (Chatterjee 2001, 8). The hierarchy in the work organization within the plantation is fairly elaborate, and it's built on the system of patronage and discipline that trickles down to the workers through overseers and supervisors (all of whom are men). Several intermediaries exist between the manager and the *adivasi* workers, and in fact many of these strata exist only to relay orders from the top and to widen the social distance between management and the *adivasi* migrant workers. It is a system that is based on fear and maintenance of social distance, and it is not unlike the system that operated in the plantations during the colonial period (Bhowmik, Xaxa, and Kalam 1996). In addition, the constant patronizing and patriarchal surveillance and discipline of the workers by the "higher status men" in the plantation labor lines "resonates within the immediacy of a community-rooted in customary norms of village patriarchy. Patriarchies rest within patriarchies" (Chatterjee 2001, 6–7). Such relationships, based on fear, exploitation, and social distance are not unique to Indian plantations. In the global political economy, plantations have become a metaphor for power and exploitation that is based on feelings of resonance and ambivalence associated with the plantation's past. Arguing how culture and history (such as forced migration and trauma) influence discourses in memory, Khan (2010) argues that interpretations of the past are made meaningful in current social relations of power. Khan calls this "historical consciousness"; it is a sensitive process whereby the past is constructed and interpreted through memories, and it has relevance in the current framework.

For the migrant *adivasi* workers in Jalpaiguri, the trauma and exploitation that existed from the beginning of their forced migrations, and the scheme of the planters to trick them into signing contracts, is reflected in their collective memories even today. For the planters, the goal was to create a steady work force, and they achieved this by creating a "captive work force" in the plantations. The constant vigil of the *sardars* and the forcible prevention of alternative employment for the workers in the tea regions worked towards meeting this goal and resulted in the ongoing abuse of the workers, particularly after independence, when there was no shortage of labor for industries in the nation. However, the *adivasi* migrant worker population, already crippled for generations by the exploitative regulations imposed on them by the colonial planters, found limited opportunities for work for themselves or for their family members outside of the plantations. Once again they turned to the plantations for employment, and today one-third of all plantation workers work as casual or temporary workers. The availability of a large pool of unemployed people on the plantation has placed the employers in an advantageous position, because now plantation management can, by employing casual workers at lower wages, both lower its costs and depress demands by regular workers for higher wages. The *adivasi* migrant worker now has two choices: negotiate for a higher wage and get the number of casual workers reduced; or continue the employment of casual workers and get paid in lower wages. In both cases the workers loose; either way the result is a decrease in household income and no improvement in workers' status (Bhowmik 2011, 247).

For Bhowmik (2011) the suppression of wages in the tea plantations is a form of bondage, He demonstrates how the workers, despite getting unionized after independence, are in a weaker position while bargaining with the plantation owners and management (Bhowmik 2011, 247–50). For instance, in 2005 the workers union, supported by the state government, demanded an increase in the daily minimum wages from 49 rupees and 90 paise to 88 rupees, based on needs-based minimum wages as outline by labor acts. During that time, and despite a 20-day strike by the 300,000 workers in the tea plantations over refusal by the owners to increase wages, the planters prevailed in their argument that the workers were being overpaid and that there could be no increase in wages without increase in productivity. After the final wage negotiations, the minimum daily wage was increased by one rupee, and the productivity clause was passed. There had always been an "incentive wage" (known as *thika*) for the plantation workers to pluck tea leaves above a fixed quota (around 24 kilograms). Typically during the peak seasons, which last maybe a couple of months, the workers have an opportunity to earn twice the amount in daily wages. With the passage of the new clause, the *thika* remained at 24 kilograms, and the worker will get the extra wages only after picking 30 kilograms of leaves. This implies that the worker has to pluck a minimum of six kilograms of tea leaves extra per day during the peak season to receive *thika* (249).

The above discussion on the history of recruitment, conditions of work, and lack of power during negotiations, points to the ongoing marginalization of the *adivasi* migrant workers in the plantations. The social status of these workers as migrants kept them out of mainstream politics and made them further dependent on the non-tea-plantation worker trade union leaders (typically non-*adivasis*) who make decisions on behalf on them. This has in turn contributed to further isolation and marginalization of this group (Bhowmik 2011, 250).

In this context, witchcraft accusations and witch hunts become representative of the tenuous relationships in the plantation among the class hierarchies, through which an oppressed community struggles to maintain order. The collective consciousness of the *adivasi* workers as both *adivasis* and migrants reflects their conscious memories of the past, their present exploited status, and their feelings of alienation in the plantation land. The workers feel alienated from the land, the production, and from the locals. Their identity is based on oppression and subordination. This is an identity that comes across in relationships both within and outside of the members of the migrant *adivasi* worker community. As one elderly worker said in response to my question about whether an improvement in the tea industry in the region might bring a change in their lives: "How would an improvement in the production in this plantation relate to our lives? Good tea? But we will continue to get *guro chaa* (dust tea or the lowest quality of tea)."

# *Adivasis*, Scheduled Tribes of India, Spirits, and the Status of Women

Research on *adivasis* (tribes) represents a major area of focus among sociologists and anthropologists in India.[5] Though there was a lot of ambiguity among researchers on the description of tribes, "the study of groups that subsequently came to be described as tribal studies, began with the establishment of the Asiatic Society of Bengal in 1874" (Xaxa 2004, 245). Phrases such as "groups that practiced animism or tribal religion" were used for a long time by the colonial government census to describe this category of people. Later, in addition to the religious criteria, categories such as "geographical isolation" and "pre-modern conditions of living" were added to the list of descriptions of the *adivasis* in subsequent census enumerations (346). It was not until 1950, when the constitution of the new Republic of India was constituted, that tribals (now constitutionally categorized as "scheduled tribes") were recognized by the government of India as a special category that was eligible for affirmative action policies.

According to L .P .Vidyarthi (1982), an anthropologist who has spent considerable time studying Indian tribes, *adivasi* research has gone through three stages in India: 1874–1919 (the formative period), 1920–1949 (the constructive period), and 1950 onwards (the analytical period). In the first two stages, the focus was on anthropological methods and analysis to study the social structure of the different tribes in India. In the post-independence period (after 1950), academic research on the tribes began to be focused with the view of formulating and implementing developmental policies in the community (Xaxa 2004, 346). In spite of much research on the various tribal groups all over India, research on the tribal migrant labor community of the Jalpaiguri has been much neglected. Perhaps this neglect occurred because the focus of research on this geographical area often shifts to the tea industry and to the laborers as employees of the organized sector. Although some scholars have attempted to study this community and its problems, such attempts have been half hearted and have often lacked in-depth analysis. Thus the study of incidents of witchcraft accusations among the migrant *adivasi* plantation workers demand a careful study of the *adivasis* social structure, the status of women, and the myths within the context of plantation economy. Past and recent studies of the problem of witch hunts among the *adivasi* migrant workers in the Dooars (for example, see Barman 2002; Baruya 2005; Gupta 1979) have operated under the assumption that because the tribals are "primitive" and "backward," practices such as witch hunts are expected behavior from the community. Situating incidents of witch hunts within the larger politics of the plantation economy provides an alternative and lends a nuanced perspective to the incidents. This is because *adivasi* communities are changing in India, even if there are confusions regarding the direction of that change, i.e., whether the movement is towards "modernity" and its different forms, and how this impacts the status of *adivasi* women. For instance, factors have given rise to economic and social structural changes among *adivasis*. These include the introduction of land as private property, the growth of trade and the market economy, the encroachment of nontribals in search of land and employment in *adivasi* areas, the spread of modern education, and the opening up of new occupations. *Adivasis* have lost their land and have been compelled either to take up employment as laborers in nearby quarries, coal fields, and emerging towns as un-skilled or semiskilled workers or to permanently relocate elsewhere for work (for example, to work in the plantations that were opened up in Bengal and Assam). Only a small percentage of the *adivasis* have been able to take advantage of the market forces leading to differentiations among and within the *adivasis* based on criteria such as education, occupation, income, and wealth. Xaxa (2004, 248–52) writes that the *adivasis* today can be categorized as rich, middle income, and poor (besides the landless), and this gives rise to a new type of class relations. Despite heterogeneity among and within the *adivasis*, they seem to share one point in common, that they are different from the dominant community of the region. The non-*adivasis*, or the *bhikus*, are seen as aliens and outsiders, and there have often been situations of intense intercommunity conflict between the two groups.

As mentioned above, in the tea plantations of Jalpaiguri, the *adivasi* migrant worker communities where incidents of witchcraft accusations are frequently taking place belong primarily to Oraon, Munda, and Santhal groups. These three *adivasi* groups have distinct sociocultural structures, along with different legends about the origin of witchcraft that influence their construction of the female witch. For instance, the Oraons were mainly cultivators back in Chotanagpur. They practiced totemism and are divided into a number of subgroups such as *Berga*, *Dhanka*, *Kharia*, and *Khendo*. The Supreme Being, according to the Oraons, is *Dharmi* or *Dharmesh*, the creator and the preserver. In contrast, all misfortunes are attributed to demons. The spiritual lives of the Oraons consist of constant reference to malevolent spirits, nature spirits, and ancestor spirits; and the medicine man has power to cure misfortunes. Oraon women are believed to have greater sexual freedom compared with women in mainstream Hindu society. Sex before marriage and widow remarriage are permitted within the community, in contrast to mainstream Hindu community, where both practices are traditionally looked down upon (Sinha 2007). Similarly, the main occupation of the Mundas was agriculture in their *adivasi* lands, and the villages are governed by the headman. Mundas are nature worshipers and have multiple deities representing the sun, the rain, and rivers. All ailments such as skin diseases, mental illness, and stomach or digestive are caused by the spirit Nasan Bonga.

In contrast to the Mundas and the Oraons, the Santhals have a specific explanation for the origin of witchcraft. The Santhal myth for the origin of the witches is the story of how *Maran Baru* (the creator) taught the Santhal men how to detect witches and hunt them. His teaching was an act of revenge against women, because they had tricked *Maran Baru* and gotten access to knowledge they were not entitled to. The Santhal explanation of witchcraft is based on gendered conflict; it demonstrates how access to knowledge is gendered, and it further establishes and justifies the exclusion of women from rituals. Men's participation in rituals of healing and spirituality signifies their authority in the community. Similarly, women's participation in rituals is perceived to be a challenge to male authority and thereby to social order, because women have evil powers (Kelkar and Nathan 1991; Sinha 2006). The antithesis to *jangurus* and *bhagats* are the *dainis*: mysterious creatures with supernatural powers who have the potential to cause harm to humans, crops, and livestock. In other words, *dainis* are "human embodiments of the evil eye" who can cause harm to human by casting the evil or charms (Sinha 2007).

The *adivasi* construction of the witch is very much related to their belief structure, particularly their beliefs in witchcraft. All diseases in humans or animals are attributed to either one of two causes: the wrath of some evil spirit who has to be appeased, or the spell of some witch who has to be driven out. Though the appeasement of angry spirits could be accomplished by animal sacrifices (mainly of fowls or goats), the evil influence of the witch could only be countered by the physical elimination of the witch (Bodding 1986; Dalton 1960; Man 1983; Sinha 2007). The *jangurus*, the diviner or the medicine man in *adivasi* communities, uses his powers to counteract the powers of the *dain*, or the witch. He is the only one who can control *Obha*, the dreaded wind of misfortune. Also known as *bhagats*, the *janguru* are the ritual masters of healing. They have knowledge of medicinal herbs and roots and prescribe these medicines as supplements to chants, divinations, and amulets that are necessary to get rid of evil spirits (Sinha 2007).

For a long time, the research on *adivasi* women was neglected and/or filled with assumptions. Contemporary scholars (Chauhan 1990; Mann 1987; Zehol 1998) on *adivasi* women consider the perspective that *adivasi* women enjoy greater sexual and economic freedom compared with other communities to be a myth. Additionally, these studies have also been inconsistent in their findings. (See, for instance, Xaxa (2004)'s criticism of Verrier Elwin's works on Naga and Baigas.)[6] Instead, studies by sociologists and social anthropologists at some of India's leading universities argue that *adivasi* women are at a disadvantage vis-à-vis men in their respective society's property, marriage, and inheritance laws. For instance, Xaxa (2004) argues that "the very practices that are indicative of high status in one society can turn out to be in-built depressors in other settings" (Xaxa 2004, 355). Another excellent case point would be the study by Tiplut Nongbri (1998) on the practice of bride price among several *adivasi* groups in Arunachal Pradesh.[7] Nongbri argues that the practice of bride price was originally intended to compensate the bride's family for the loss of an economic asset (the woman). However, with the passage of time, bride price became a practice whereby men could purchase women as mere commodities. The system of bride price thus became a cause for the proliferation of polygamy among the *adivasis* in Arunachal Pradesh, because wealthy men could take in a number of wives by paying the bride price (Nongbri 1998).

## *Adivasi* Research in India: The Case for Sensitive Research

Many scholars, including Farberow (1963) and the often-cited Sieber and Stanley (1988), have defined what constitutes sensitive research, but these definitions have been criticized on the grounds that they are either unclear as to the nature of consequences or too narrow (Lee 1993). Lee (1993), in what is considered to be one of the classics on sensitive research, proposed a "simple" definition of sensitive research as "research which potentially poses a substantial threat to those who are or have been involved in it" (Lee 1993, 4).

Lee's definition includes all of the components that previous researchers excluded in their attempts to define sensitive research. Additionally Lee provides a broader definition, that includes a list of potential consequences towards the researcher, the respondents, or anyone involved in the subject area. Lee argues that the kind of threat posed by a particular research project depends on the relationship between the subject matter of the research and the social context within which the research is conducted. In other words, the focus is on "the conditions under which sensitivity arises within the research process" (5).

The study of *adivasi* communities is a popular topic among anthropologists and sociologists in India, and much has been written about the *adivasis*' social structure, customs, social stratification, and gender relations. As mentioned in the previous chapter, there has also been some research on witchcraft accusations and witch hunts among the *adivasis*. The focus has mostly been on the practice and belief in witchcraft, specifically within the context of *adivasi* communities, and few studies have concentrated on the analysis of incidents of witch hunts within the context of the broader social and economic environments surrounding these communities. But incidents of witchcraft accusations and witch hunts are not a common occurrence of *adivasi* communities. For example, on average, the *adivasi* migrant worker communities in Jalpaiguri might experience two to three cases of witch hunt or witchcraft accusation every year.[8] However, the community takes a long time to recover from the social impact of each incident, because a witchcraft accusation or a witch hunt goes far beyond getting rid of the witch and healing the community. The impacts are much deeper. It is within this perspective that I turn to the need for studying witch hunts in the context of a community that is located within a modern economy. Going back to concerns raised by Comaroff and Comaroff (1993) in *Modernity and Its Malcontents*, perhaps there is a theoretical need to understand how traditional customs are adapted in reaction to changes wrought by modernity; the assumption is always that local cultural traditions get eroded upon contact with modernization. According to this perspective, how does a community reinterpret its traditional beliefs and customs to cope with an economic and social world that is different?

*Adivasi* migrant workers in the tea plantations of Jalpaiguri provide a perfect social location to study incidents of witch hunts. As discussed earlier, it is the very social isolation of this wage labor community within a plantation economy that makes it an interesting case study for witch hunts. Problems within the tea industry, marginalization of the *adivasi* workers, conditions of life and work of the *adivasis*, along with a strong belief in witchcraft, all provide useful clues to an in-depth understanding of the phenomenon. However, the topic of witch hunts is very sensitive from the points of view of the researcher, the participants in the research, the *adivasi* community, the tea industry, and the people outside the *adivasi* community. The very issue of sensitivity of this particular research is tied to spiritual beliefs in the power of the malevolent witch. This belief is so strong and logical that cases have been reported cases in newspapers and in scholarly publications about how individuals frequently and willingly give themselves up to the police after murdering the witch and how individuals sometimes murder their own loved ones based on a suspicion of witchcraft. For example, a story published in an Indian newspaper in 2008 reported on a man who beheaded a woman he thought was responsible for killing his parents and walked with the severed head for five miles to the nearest police station (see "Woman Branded Witch, Beheaded," *Daily News and Analysis*, April 21, 2008). There have been other cases in which the community prevented outside forces (mainly the police) from stopping a witch hunt.

Apart from the very nature of the research topic, the project is "sensitive" because it can create a potential threat to the researcher's emotional and physical safety and to the participant's emotional and physical security, especially the security of living victims of witch hunts. The risks involved in such projects are thus high. Other potential costs include spending time with the researcher and possibly experiencing unpleasant and uncomfortable thoughts and memories that the interviews and narratives might evoke among participants. This discomfort might be especially relevant during interviews with participants who were present during the hunts as victims or relatives of victims or who were a part of the conflict.

I approached every stage of data collection (methods of data collection, sampling techniques, questionnaires) for this project with caution. The need for caution on my part (as a researcher) was particularly important because *adivasi* research in India has often been conducted in the context of a lot of assumptions that have contributed towards the perpetuation of stereotypes, neglect, and bias. Research on incidents of witchcraft accusations and witch hunts should call for a deeper understanding of *adivasi* life in relation to the background of the tea industry, the role of laborers in the industry, gender relations, and relationship between the workers, planters, and men and women in the migrant labor community.

## Methods

The data used in *Witches, Tea Plantation, and Lives of Migrant Laborers* is part of a bigger project on the study of witch hunts among plantation workers in the area. I used a combination of methods: archival methods (police and newspaper archives), qualitative methods of interviewing, and ethnography. The data collection took place over a total of seven months between 2005 and 2007.

Getting access to the research site and to the participants in the study was extremely difficult, partly because of the reluctance of the district administration, police, and tea plantation owners to bring to light cases of witch hunts to the outside world. Apart from the geographical isolation of these sites, the social isolation of the *adivasi* workers made it initially difficult for me to get easy access to the research area. Because this is a sensitive research project, certain strategic steps were taken to get access to the sites and get a sample frame.

One of the first steps to gain entry into the site was to get familiarity and access to a number of nongovernmental organizations (NGOs) working in that area. The rationale for using an NGO to enter in the field was a practical decision. Being an outsider to the migrant *adivasi* worker community because of my caste, class status, and gender, I needed the help of the NGO that was familiar with the community and its challenges and had gained its trust. It was also important to get access to the field without the help of any governmental organization, because governmental organizations have been much criticized for being largely ineffective in providing social care and services in this region. In contrast, NGOs have gained the confidence and trust of the *adivasis* in this area through various economic and social programs, like childcare services, health camps, microcredit banking schemes for women, education, and awareness programs. I looked at the Jalpaiguri district office to get a list of NGOs who operated in the area, and out of the 52 NGOs that operated in Jalpaiguri, only one (North Bengal People's Development Center or NBPDC) listed witch hunts as social problem in the region on Jalpaiguri. But prior to my entering the field in the summer of 2005, I was not aware that, even though NBPDC did mention witch hunts as a social problem, it was engaged in the anti-witch-hunt campaigns. At that point my focus was on locating an NGO that worked in the region and was aware of the incidents of witchcraft accusations among the *adivasi* migrant workers. Apart from NBPDC, 12 other NGO's listed that they were interested in working on problems associated with the *adivasi* tea plantation workers in the region. However, upon further inquiries over phone and emails with these 12 NGOs, I realized that, while they were interested in *adivasi* workers problems in the Dooars tea plantations, they were not interested in working on the issue of witch hunts. Prejudices and stereotypes against the *adivasis*, the sensitive nature of the issue, and a lack of funding have been major factors in the indifference of other agencies, both governmental and nongovernmental.

Thus I decided to enter the field in the summer of 2005 with the help of NBPDC, as it seemed to be the only organization that was interested in the issue of witchcraft accusations among the *adivasi* workers. NBPDC was instrumental in helping me get access to the plantation workers, and it was also crucial for my introduction to the future participants of the research, the district administration, and the plantation management. Because NBPDC was an influential NGO in the region that was interested in economic, education, nutrition, and health services in the region, because it was in close contact with the *adivasi* plantation workers through their local chapters, NBPDC also helped me to get access to a list of cases that did not make it into police records or newspaper reports.

Over the next few trips, I gradually gained the trust and confidence of the local population through frequent trips to the villages, living on site, and being a participant observer in the daily lives of the *adivasi* migrant workers. I observed NBPDC activists working in the areas of children's education, health, and poverty alleviation in Jalpaiguri Sadar, Alipurduar, and Malbazar.

## Archives

The lack of formal governmental records for the total number of witchcraft accusations or witch hunts in West Bengal is perhaps related to the fact that West Bengal has no laws against witch hunts.[9] Despite this, I traced all records of witch hunt incidents in police and local newspaper archives from 1980–2005 for the three subdivisions in Jalpaiguri district (Jalpaiguri Sadar, Alipurduar, and Malbazar) using keyword searches (for the online archives) and by personally examining year-to-year records of police cases. The newspapers were *The Telegraph* (English), *The Statesman* (English), *Ananda Bazar Patrika* (Ben-gali), and *Uttar Banga Sambad* (Bengali). These newspapers were selected based on their wide circulation in North Bengal and their coverage of incidents in the tea industry. While *The Telegraph*, *The Statesman*, and *Ananda Bajar Patrika* are the leading newspapers with a wide circulation in the state of West Bengal, *Uttar Banga Patrika* is the largest daily in Bengali in north Bengal. For the cases recorded in the newspapers, I made use of both online archives and visits to the newspaper archives located in Calcutta and Jalpaiguri. Rigorous Internet searches and trips to the archives offices of three local newspapers produced records of all witch hunt incidents that took place in Jalpaiguri tea plantations that were reported in the newspapers.

For the police records, I looked through the details of cases recorded under homicide, assault (both physical and sexual), and rape; and I recorded all the cases that included witchcraft accusations in the case descriptions. These categories were selected after long conversations with the district police and NBPDC about the charges under which witchcraft accusers are booked by the police. To get access to the police case archive, I traveled to the District Police Headquarters Record Room located in the district capital of Jalpaiguri, and I made several trips to the records room in the summer months of 2005.

While there was no problem in getting access to the newspaper archives, there were some problems associated with the police records room. The police records archive was not available to the public, and special permission was required to get access to witch hunt records. Even with permission, I could not enter the records room and look through the files myself. Instead, a clerk went through the records and typed out the entries on a spreadsheet. There are obvious problems with the way the police archival data was obtained. First, there was little control over the data that was provided from the records room, and so the data provided might not have been a complete list of cases over the years. Second, there was no way to crosscheck the data and check for errors made during the entering of the cases in the spreadsheet.

To verify the data from the police archive and to ensure against obvious bias, cases were crosschecked with the data from the newspaper archives. Duplicate cases from the two sources were deleted to prevent double counting of cases. In addition, NBPDC provided information that allowed for verification of some of the cases from the police archive. All cases from the newspaper and police archives were recorded in a data set. In addition, I added (through newspaper reports) cases that followed the years after the data collection was over. Each case had details such as: year of the witch hunt incident, gender, age, religion/tribe, marital status, occupation of the victim/accused. The records also indicated the following:

- Whether the accused was a midwife
- Whether there were any previous family or village conflicts between the accused and the individual who had accused him/her of practicing witchcraft
- Whether there was any presence of illness or disease in the "victim" of the witch
- The characteristics of the "victim" of the witchcraft
- The characteristic/gender of the accuser
- The relationship between the accused and the accuser
- If there was any involvement of the janguru during the witch hunt
- Whether there was a witch trial prior to the hunt
- The method of the hunt
- The characteristics of the "witch"
- The characteristics of the village
- Whether there was any legal action; and if so, what kind of legal action was taken

Overall there were 362 cases of witchcraft accusations that had taken place in Jalpaiguri in the data set. Out of these, I studied in great detail four cases that took place from 2002 onwards: the Central Dooars case, the Chandmoni tea estate incident, cases of witchcraft accusations against Basanti, and the ongoing accusations against Dulari. All four cases are referenced throughout the discussions in this book.

The following graph presents the spread of the recorded cases in the district of Jalpaiguri in the data set from 1990 onwards. I did not include the cases before 1990 in this graph. I also added the cases from 2006–2010 after the data collection was over. The graph, though not representative of all the cases of witch hunts in the tea plantation of Jalpaiguri (as not all cases of witch hunts makes it to police or newspaper records), is useful in presenting how the data is spread in the district.

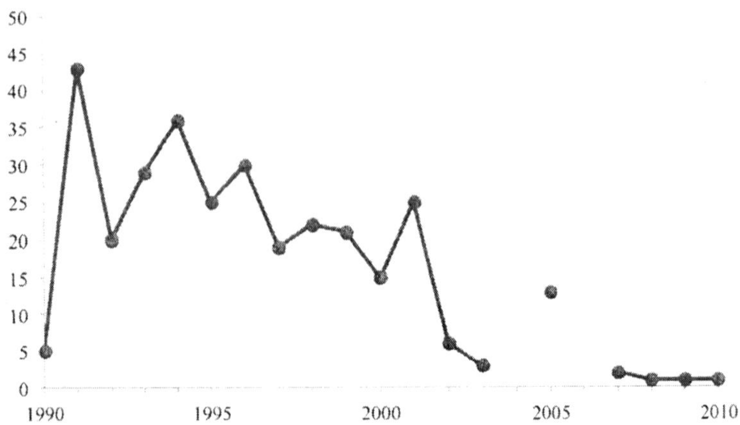


FIGURE 3.1 Recorded Cases of Witch Hunts in Jalpaiguri 1990-2010

## Sampling and Qualitative Methods

Snowball or network sampling methods were used to select the sample for the in-depth interviews. In spite of much criticism initially, especially from survey methods scholars, network sampling found much favor later on in the study of deviant or controversial groups (See Baker 1994; Becker 1998; Lee 1993; Lofland, Snow, and Anderson 2006). Network sampling represents logistically the preferred method of gathering data for sensitive topics. As the name suggests, network sampling relies on social ties to get access to a group of participants, who then refer to another group and so on. Contacts are thus crucial for sampling in this method. One of the limitations of this method is bias. This may arise because the researcher might have a sample that is homogenous in its characteristics. One of the ways to avoid this bias, is to sample "from different directions," meaning having access to socially diverse contacts that will help the researcher to get access to different networks.

Contacts in the police and district administration, along with contacts from NBPDC, allowed me access to an initial pool of participants in the research. After access to the initial pool of participants for the interview was established, I could get access to other interviewees and entry into the *adivasi* villages in the tea plantation. In addition, all members of NBPDC, lawyers, and police personnel who had been involved in the witch hunt incidents in any way (providing support, legal aid and protection to the victims) were considered for the study. In the villages, participants were selected from the villagers who were present at the time of the incident and villagers who were involved in the incident. Relatives of the accused or accuser were also included.

## Interviews

A substantial part of the data came from face-to-face interviews, a method that is useful in understanding the perceptions and interpretations of participants through experiences (Weiss 1994, 1). The face-to-face interview method is an advantage over survey questionnaires, in which answers to categories are fixed or limited. In contrast, in the in-depth interview method, there is likelihood for self-generated response. This advantage, along with the basic nature of in-depth interviews, i.e., they require trust and rapport to be established between the participants and the researcher, are particularly useful for exploring a sensitive topic like witch hunts (Shuy 2003).

I interviewed a total of 80 participants for the project. Apart from the 25 activists and 10 members from various self-help groups, I interviewed another 45 individuals. These individuals were villagers who participated in the hunt, the accused witches and their relatives, plantation managers and policemen, and others. I was accompanied by a translator who intervened, if required, to translate some words from Sadri to Bengali. The interviews were conducted in a mix of Bengali and Sadri (the *adivasi* dialect that is similar to Bengali). The participants, who are Sadri speakers, understood Bengali and Hindi without much difficulty. If there was confusion over words, sentences, or phrases the translator would help. I used two translators for interviews: one male and one female. My male translator accompanied me during interviews with my male participants, and my female translator travelled with me when I interviewed female participants.

The interviews required travel to villages in the district of Jalpaiguri. The villages were selected on the basis of whether there were any incidents of witch hunts over the last three years. All interviews lasted anywhere between two to three hours each. All interviews were tape-recorded and were conducted in a private location of the participant's choosing (mostly at a school compound or home). The interviews were confidential, and the names of the participants were changed to protect their identities. Since maintaining confidentiality of participants, especially the participants who were directly involved during the witch hunt incidents, is the core criteria of any sensitive research, real names did not appear at any stage of the interview. No records of real names were kept, and participants were referred to by their pseudonyms in field notes, tapes, and transcription of the tapes. Location of the villages was kept confidential as well.

## Analysis of the Data

I used a grounded theory inductive logic during the analysis of the data set, interviews, and field notes by identifying recurring themes and patterns in transcripts, field notes, and analytic memos (see Charmaz 1983; Glaser and Strauss 1967). Thus, concepts and theoretical generalizations are "grounded" in the data for inductive analysis, whereby analytic codes and categories are developed from the data, not from preconceived hypotheses (Charmaz 2001). After the conclusion of each interview, I translated and transcribed that particular interview in full. However, coding and analysis of data were performed after a phase of data collection was completed. This procedure was in contrast to the usual grounded theory method, in which data collection and analysis take place simultaneously. Because of the intensive traveling involved each day and time constraints, it was not possible for me to code the data immediately. Instead, after the initial phase of data collection, transcription of interviews, and supportive field notes, I entered the data into a qualitative data analysis package for coding and further analysis. In the following four chapters I present the findings of my research and answer my broader research question as to how the witchcraft accusations in Jalpaiguri plantations are a manifestation of the worker-management conflict.

# Notes

1. The term "Dooars" comes from the English word "door," and the name Dooars implies "door to Bhutan." Jalpaiguri was a strategic location for the British to get access to trade in Bhutan, and it was not until 1864 that the district was annexed by the British from Bhutan.

2. *Bhumiputras* means sons of the soil.

3. The Permanent Settlement Act passed in 1793 was an agreement between The East India Company and the native nontribal landlords (*Zamindars*) to have fixed revenue for the land that the *Zamindars* controlled. The Act prevented small landholders from selling their land. In addition, the Company officials and Indian landlords forced their tenants to grow cash crops such as indigo and cotton rather than rice and wheat. The Permanent Settlement Act was one of the primary causes of the worst famines of the nineteenth century. In addition, tribal society was going through a state of unrest, and Hinduism was slowly making its presence felt in the community. The community was growing through a process of Sanskritization, which was creating divisions within the tribal social structure. This, along with the changes brought about by the Permanent set-

tlement act of 1793 and the infiltration of nontribals (*Dikhus*) and the British in the tribal lands, resulted in the displacement of the lands for the tribals, leading to their migration towards the Dooars.

4. Tea plantations are referred as "tea gardens" in the plantation terminology, and the term "garden *sardar*" is used to refer to the middlemen who were crucial in the recruitment and transfer of the tribals from the neighboring states to the Dooars.

5. The "Scheduled Tribes," also referred to as "*adivasis*" (original inhabitants), are spread across the central, northeast, and southern regions of India. The various tribes resided in India long before the Aryans who arrived around 1500 BC. The tribals were socially and geographically isolated following the entry of the Aryans and then subsequently the Muslims and the British. The more than 50 tribes that constitute the Scheduled Tribes speak a multitude of languages. They are also religiously diverse. Some follow animism, and others have adopted Hinduism, Islam, or Christianity in recent years. The social customs of most tribals distinguish them from the country's majority Hindu population. The category of Scheduled Tribes was established in 1950, three years after India's independence. It sought to encompass the country's diverse tribal groups under a common banner in an effort to help address the disadvantages the tribes encountered and to integrate them into the mainstream of Indian society. Along with being geographically and socially isolated, the tribals have historically been politically underrepresented, and their regions of residence have been economically underdeveloped.

6. Virginus Xaxa writes that while Elwin comments on the Naga woman as being in a subordinate position to the men, elsewhere he writes that Naga women have a higher position in Naga society compared with Naga men. See Xaxa (2004): 349–47.

7. Bride price, also known as bride wealth, is an amount of money or property or wealth paid to the parents of a woman for the right to marry their daughter. In the anthropological literature, bride price has often been explained in market terms as payment made in exchange for the bride's family's loss of her labor and fertility within her kin group.

8. I am using the data on the tea plantation communities here instead of data in other parts of India, because statistics on other parts are not available. For the Jalpaiguri region, the data is based on my research. For details see chapter 3.

9. Bihar, Jharkhand, and Chhattisgarh are the only states in India that have laws against witch hunts.

# Chapter 4

# Categorization of Witch Hunts

## Five Witches and a Jackfruit Tree: Chandmoni Tea Estate, 2002

Chandmoni tea garden is located almost 50 miles from the local police station and about 200 miles from the district capital. The plantation is located in the belt of two national parks and is composed of workers from the Munda, Santhal, and Oraon tribes. In April 2002, the labor lines were experiencing malaria and diarrhea epidemics, the two diseases that are not uncommon in these areas. Chandmoni plantation has a resident *janguru*, who is both the local priest and medicine man for the labor lines. The plantation has a government health center that is dysfunctional, and the nearest health center that has a doctor is 100 miles away.

Toward the end of July 2002, a driver in the tea estate, 30-year-old Anil, complained of stomach illness. Anil's family, led by his brother (Suresh), consulted the local *janguru* (Hariram) to find a cure for his illness. Hariram prescribed some herbs to calm the stomach pains. When the pains became severe and the *janguru* (male, mid fifties, plantation worker) was unable to cure him, Anil was sent to the hospital. Anil died the next day of an undiagnosed illness. After his death, his family members, headed by his brother, went to the local governing body in the village and expressed concern that Anil could have died from witchcraft. The meeting was attended by almost all the villagers in the labor lines (around 250 people). In the meeting, Suresh expressed concern that there was more to Anil's illness than "natural causes." The meeting with the *gram panchayat* was crucial in getting the entire village involved. The village was already going through some stress caused by the malaria and diarrhea epidemics, and it was easy to get the support of the villagers for a witch hunt. Hariram was present at the village meeting.

At the village meeting it was decided that the local *janguru* would use his powers to uncover what was behind the death of Anil. Suresh decided to pay for the rituals. After a day of rituals that involved animal sacrifice (fowl) and feasting, the *janguru* declared that five women (all between the ages of 40 and 75 years) had used witchcraft and that they were not only behind the unusual death of Anil but also the rise in the malaria and diarrhea epidemics in the village. The accused women were: Atashi, Binshu, Dhanni, Sanchari, and Manshi. These five women, identified by the *janguru* as "witches," were married, widowed with families that consisted of husbands, sons, daughters-in-law and grandchildren. Thus they were not destitute women without families. The accused women were employed in the tea plantations as workers and were former employees of the plantation, and all of them lived in the village. They were all neighbors, acquaintances, and friends of Anil and his family. They were not random strangers who were accused.

The witch hunt of the five women took place in the week following Anil's death on a late Friday afternoon, after the tea plantation was closed for the weekend and the managers and supervisors had left for the city. At around 10 p.m. in the evening, a group of 30 people, mostly men, went to the houses of these five women and dragged the women out. This group of 30 was led by two men: Lakhan and Buddhiram. Buddhiram had a dispute with one of the accused women's husband. This group was supported by the rest of the village (around 200 people), who prevented the families of the accused women from resisting the attackers. The women were dragged and taken to a small open courtyard that had a jackfruit tree right in the middle of it. Children used this area as a playground, and the courtyard was surrounded by huts on all sides. The accused women were tied to the tree one at a time. Their ordeal would continue over the next two days. The rest of the villagers kept a strong vigil over the family members of the accused women. When some of the family members of the accused women tried to escape from the village so that they could inform the police, the rest of the villagers prevented them from doing so by using threats and physical assault.

Hariram, Suresh, Lakhan, and Buddhiram supervised the witch hunt. The women were first beaten and hit with stones. The first to die was Dhanni (midseventies, survived by husband, children, and grandchildren). For the remaining four women, the torture continued till late Sunday evening. To drive out the spirits from the entire village, the women had nails driven into their foreheads. They were stripped and beaten with *lathis* and iron rods at regular intervals. The *janguru* who was at the center of the "witch hunt ritual" held *pujas* in front of the jackfruit tree throughout the day on Saturday and Sunday. At one point, one of the women had a "crucifixion" ceremony to "please" the Christians among the villagers. Throughout the weekend, the villagers kept a tight vigil over the families of the accused women.

On Sunday evening, the murders started taking place. The surviving women had their limbs severed before finally succumbing to the injuries. The bodies of five women were then hacked into several pieces before being thrown in the nearby river. On Monday, the villagers returned to their work at the plantation as if nothing had happened. The families of the murdered women were scared to report the witch hunt to the plantation management or to the police. By Wednesday, people from the neighboring villages began to find pieces of human limbs and torsos in the river. The police were informed, and by the end of Thursday over 40 people were arrested on charges of murder, physical assault, and torture of the five women. The management of the tea plantation at Chandmoni was unaware of the witch hunt until the police informed it.

## Comments on the Incident

In the Chandmoni incident, the *janguru* was involved in the hunt from the very beginning. He was involved in the identification of the witches through rituals, and he presided over the trials. The rituals were based on what the *janguru* claimed to be "the ancient texts" of hunting witches in the *adivasi* community. The Chandmoni incident is very similar to the European and colonial American witch hunts in which the accused women were searched for physical evidence regarding their pact with the Devil. Though the concept of Satan is part of Christianity, some of the *adivasis* in the village were Christians, and they were the ones who suggested during the trials to look for evidence of the "pact." The women were searched for horns on their head and the hammering of their forehead with nails was done to drive the Devil away. Also, the idea of having an authoritative text that gives instructions on how to search for witches is similar to "The Witches Hammer" or "The Malleus Maleficarum" document in the fifteenth century. These were used to expose the heresy of the witches in Europe. Extreme violence that involved torture, such as trial by the use of red-hot iron, shaving of the witch's body, and the search for marks, tokens, and amulets (including those sewn under the skin); were all used to identify and get rid of the accused witches (Summers 1971).

Three years after the incident at Chandmoni, the courtyard with the jackfruit tree looks like any other village playground area where children play football with gourds and women dry pickles and pulses in the sun. There is no visible evidence of the horrific torture and murders that took place under the shade of the jackfruit tree. However, the scars of the witch hunt of April 2002 remain. Almost all the people in the village refuse to talk about the incident. They either evaded the topic or avoided discussion of it by telling me that they were away from the village during the weekend of torture and murder. The only people who were willing to talk were the relatives of the victims, who are still waiting for justice after three years. They were the only ones who talked to me about the incident at Chandmoni. Most of the people who were arrested by the police after the incident were let off on minor bails. These people included the *janguru*, who continues to command much power in the village. There have been almost no court dates for the murders, and the relatives of the murdered women are still waiting for the justice that may never come; theirs has been a long and tedious struggle.

When I visited Chandmoni Tea Estate, the village looked deserted. Although three years had passed, people stayed indoors and the air was tense. Most of the villagers refused to talk to me, and they were very suspicious of all outsiders. It was very frustrating for me as a researcher, because every person that I requested an interview of turned me down for weeks. The common excuses were that they were not present during the witch hunt or that they did not know anything about the incident. Typical reactions were: "I was not at home. It was *fagun masher purnima* (day of festival). I was not at home . . . I went to visit a friend." Or "There is no one at home. . . . They have arrested the male members. The wife is living somewhere else." The local *panchayat* head also refused to talk about the incident. Shanti Devi, the *panchayat* leader told me that she was not at home. "I had gone to see my daughter. . . I was away for 15 days. When I came back the incident was over." Pointing to her main gate that had an iron cross, she said, "[S]ee . . . I am a Christian tribal. We do not have these witch hunts among us. It is the uneducated tribals who believe in witches." I asked her what she intends to do next to protect her people. She replied, "What can I do? I get only five rupees a month and tea for this post. I am a poor woman. I cannot do anything." I did meet Hariram, the *janguru* who told me that he was a poor old man and commented that he was framed in the incident. He denied that he was the village *janguru*, and he blamed local politics for his arrest.

I must also note that, after their initial hostility towards me and my translator, the villagers became less hostile upon subsequent visit. However, repeated requests to recruit participants for the project were turned down again and again. From this research site, I was only able to talk to the relatives of the murdered women, who were eager to share their stories.

## Categorizing Witch Hunts

To explain how witchcraft accusations within the *adivasi* migrant worker community are a manifestation of the conflict between the *adivasis* and plantation management, I looked at the incidents of witch hunts through the theoretical tool of categorizing phenomena (see Chaudhuri 2012). Specifically, the aim is to deduce the incidents that led to the witchcraft accusations and to the events that occurred during and after the witch hunts, particularly within the setting of the plantations. In doing so, I revisit the question (later in this chapter and in detail in chapter six) as to whether there are any trends (and Sundar 2001 does mention that there are no trends for the type of individuals who are accused) that can be used to explain the connection between witchcraft accusations and conflict between workers and management.

Any attempt to explain examples of brutal violence such as witch hunts, riots, or genocides would start with efforts at looking at the participants involved in the incidents. In explaining why witch hunts are both a form of protest against and representations of oppression in the lives of the *adivasi* migrant workers, I take a few steps backwards in this analytical exercise. I begin by categorizing witch hunts, before looking at the key actors in the hunts.

Categorizing in theory-building has been under much criticism, because categories, like idea types, are static entities and not dynamic or fluid as reality. For instance, while witches are the targets during witch hunts, individuals who are accusers in one incident could be victims (or relatives of victims) in another incident. Thus categorizations of the phenomena do not address all the complexities involved and are at best oversimplification of events. Such oversimplifications smooth over tensions that exist both within and between categories (Fuji 2009, 7–9). What is needed is an approach that addresses the complexities in phenomena directly. Fuji suggests an alternative dynamic approach—violence as a process—that focuses on the dynamism of actors and the acts of violence. For example, to understand witch hunts as a process, the actors can move between multiple categories or occupy multiple categories at the same time. Fuji argues that such an approach helps in understanding a broad range of individuals' behavior during acts of violence without placing them into predetermined categories. This supports the objective of seeing how actors do not fit categories (10–11).

While the problem of categorization and oversimplification remains, I argue that to understand a complex incident such as witchcraft accusations and witch hunts within the context of workers' emotions of conflict directed against the employers, it is important to break up the episodes into broad categories so that we can understand the logic of operation. To avoid the problem of overgeneralization of categories, I avoided creating the categories prior to entering the field. Instead, I organized the themes that the participants used to respond to questions based on what provoked the witchcraft accusations. In doing so, I hoped to capture the local microdynamics in the migrant worker community and to connect this to the larger context of the plantation within which the community is embedded. Much like Niehaus (2001, 7–9) and his aim to treat people as subjects of their own history, I aim to show how the witchcraft accusations were interpreted by the participants and how the phenomena connected to the broader conflict between the workers and the management of the plantations.

These themes as narrated by the participants were then arranged into categories in order to describe the witchcraft accusations. Categorization helps give us a picture of the key actors and their roles in witch hunts, and this will help in explaining the complex function of this violence within the plantation community. Additionally, I will also refer to the data set on witch hunts that I created for the purpose of the study for descriptive statistics on the characteristics, particularly those of the accusers and accused, in the witchcraft accusations. After the key players and the components of witch hunts are explained, definitions of concepts and connections to profit, protest, and reaction within the plantation worker community can be explained in the following chapters.

I began my interviews with accused women, relatives of witches, and social activists by asking the question: "So tell me why the incident of witch hunt occurred in this village? In other words, what instigated the accusation of witchcraft against the accused?" The answers to this question, based on the responses of the participants, could be organized into two categories of witch hunts: First, one theme emerged that explained the events leading to the accusations and hunts as a complex conspiracy of actors, events, and calculation of profits, i.e., calculated attacks. The second theme that emerged had a surprise element to it: the hunts were described as "sudden" reactions to an otherwise normal day in plantation life, i.e., surprise attacks. As I mentioned above, the names for the two categories of hunts came up during the interviews of the participants when they were asked to describe particular incidents of witch hunt.

## Calculated Attacks of Witch Hunts

In calculated attacks, witch hunts were preceded by clearly defined motives on the part of the accusers; these motives went beyond getting rid of the witch who was responsible for the curse in the community. These motives on the part of the accusers could be anything from maligning the reputation of the accused individual to serving personal motive, from revenge to settle disputes over property to settling a personal score against the accused and her family. In this category of witch hunts, attacking the witch to get rid of witchcraft satisfies a smaller agenda. The real cause for the hunt is a preexisting conflict that has nothing to do with witchcraft. For instance, of the five women who were accused of being witches in the Chandmoni Tea Estate, four had prior conflicts with some of the villagers. These conflicts had nothing to do with Anil's illness but were related to unpaid debts. Ramlal, a plantation worker, explained how the witches were selected:

> It seemed very random . . . the selection of the women . . . but you know that nothing is random. The names [of witches] that Hariram called out were all predecided. Suresh's friend, Lakhan, had paid an additional five hundred rupees to the *janguru* to call out Sanchari's name. Lakhan and Sanchari's husband had a dispute over money. Sanchari's husband accused Lakhan of stealing money from him. So Sanchari's accusation was not random. Same with Atashi, Binshu and Dhanshi . . . their accusations were related to disputes that they had. Manshi's accusation however was random. She was an old woman . . . maybe that is why she was selected.

Similarly, Basanti (whose case I will be discussing in chapter 5) had a preexisting conflict with her in-laws, and her husband was in conflict with the neighbor over property. Basanti's mother Smita explained the conflicts against her daughter that led to the accusations against her.

> My daughter's mother-in-law and sister-in-law could not stand her. They were after her life, her husband's job, and Lekha wanted the land. They started spreading rumors about my daughter . . . of course they gave money to the villagers. . . . My daughter was alone at the meeting. If she did not confess they would have killed her and the baby. The money from the fine went in paying those men to attack her and support the accusations against her.

In both these cases, there is a preexisting conflict between two parties in which the appearance of an illness, either in members of the accuser group or within their family or friendship networks, provides the necessary legitimacy to start the accusation process required before the hunt. Most of the accused are women, and frequently the accusation initially comes from a group smaller in number (maybe even just one individual) than the group that is involved in organizing and conducting the witch hunt. In the Chandmoni Tea Estate case and in Basanti's case, the initial and perhaps the most relevant conflicts that justified the rest of the community to join the accusers were arguments over resources (money, job security, or property). The role of the witchcraft accusation, after the initial contentious relationship was already established, was that it provided an instigation that would give the others an opportunity to organize an attack against the accused women.

Balwant, a male *adivasi* activist who also lived and worked in the plantations, explained how the process of witchcraft accusation starts with a motive and an illness: "Whenever such [illnesses arise] there are always some people [men] in the village who look to get something out of this. They are the ones that start the *chakranto* [conspiracy]." The key strategy for the initial group of accusers is to convince the rest of the community that the illness is caused by witchcraft and that the accused woman is responsible for it. Here, alcohol and money play important roles in persuasion, whereby personal troubles translate into a public concern.

The psychological torture for the accused witch starts almost immediately after the conspirators target their victim. Balwant, continuing his narrative explains: "[A]s you saw [referring to the interview I had conducted days before] in the previous case, first they cut off her banana tree . . . next they threw garbage in her yard." Alcohol or *haria* (local brew) is used as bait to attract more people to support the accusation against the witch. He continues:

> Using haria...they [the conspirators] attract people in their group. From two to four people now ten people are a part of the group. Then the entire *para* [community], next the village . . . everyone is now against the accused woman. They start *phish-phish* [whispering] against her. The witch now only has her husband

> as her support . . . everyone else is against her. Now she is really *beshahara* [vulnerable and without support]. There is no help for her and no one will listen to her. She might to go the *panchayat* for help, but it is best for her to accept the claims and accept whatever fines they may impose on her. But if she does not listen to the *panchayat* and *jid dhorey thakkey* [becomes stubborn] then she may face physical threats and even life threats from the villagers. So ultimately the conspirators win: money, property . . . whatever they had in mind.

Balwant's comments about how the witch accusation develops into a full-fledged attack outline a pattern. The witch hunt begins with an illness in the village that triggers the preexisting misogyny in the community. The illness accompanies the suspicion of witchcraft, and it is at this phase that the conspirators, the key components in a calculated attack, step in. Taking advantage of the situation, the conspirators, who have some ulterior motive behind witch hunt, start gathering support against the accused witch. They accomplish this through a whisper campaign accompanied by the accused woman being isolated from the entire village. The psychological torture often pressures the accused woman into a forced confession, thereby convincing the villagers and the members of the *panchayat* of her guilt.

Thus, in cases of calculated attacks of witch hunts, one can identify the following patterns leading to a witch hunt. The initial step involves either some prior conflict between the accuser and the accused or some "vested" interest on the part of the accuser, who stands to gain something out of the hunt. For instance, Suresh, Anil's brother, was joined in the accusations by Buddhiram, who wanted to settle a score with one of the accused women's husband. Similarly for Hariram, the accusation was an opportunity to establish his authority and credibility in the community, by identifying the witches who were responsible for Anil's death. By identifying the witchcraft that was responsible for Anil's unexplained illness, Hariram justified his inability to cure Anil. The reasoning is this: if you kill the witches, others in the community, who could have fallen to the witchcraft curse, can be saved. It was also an economic transaction for Hariram. It is important to note that during this stage, particularly during calculated attacks, the accused women and their families are aware of their conflict with the other group, even though the other group might not yet have formed into an accuser group.

The next stage following the initial conflict, and what seems to be the most crucial stage in the transformation of the conflict from a personal to a community concern, is the occurrence of an illness in the accused or within his circle of relatives or friends. This illness provides the necessary evidence of witchcraft against the accused group. After the illness sets in, it is necessary for the community to identify the witch who is causing it. The accuser group then goes on to gather support against the accused woman. This leads to a whispering campaign against her. A trial, which could be formal (one that involves the entire village and the community leaders) or informal (one that just involves the accuser group and its supporters), follows the identification of the witch. During this stage, the witch is formally accused of witchcraft, and she is tried before the village. In most cases, the accused women confess to witchcraft because of threats on their lives or to their families. In some cases, the women are let off after payment of fines. However, typically after the trial, if the community does not feel the fines are adequate atonement for witchcraft, a witch hunt occurs in which the entire village attacks the accused woman. In most cases, the witch is beaten to death.

## Surprise Attacks of Witch Hunts

In the surprise attack category of witch hunts, the victims (the accused) and their families were unaware of the witchcraft accusations against the accused women prior to the attack. The attack takes place without any apparent preparation on the part of the accused. The lack of preparation could be because the accused and her family did not have a prior conflict or because they were had no history of witchcraft accusation. In other words, the surprise element comes from the accused and her family not being able to foresee the witchcraft accusations. Almost all of the participants I interviewed for this study informed me, in response to my question on what instigated a particular hunt, "*Ki jani*?!" [who knows]. Lali Oraon, a 40-year-old female tea plantation worker whose mother-in-law was dragged out in the middle of the night by a village mob led by her neighbor, explained: "There was no reason/cause (*karon*) of accusing her [the mother-in-law] of witchcraft. We had no quarrels with anyone in the village. Why did they take her? Before this (incident) no one in the village had accused her of witchcraft or called her a *daini*." Sumitra Oraon is a woman in her 50s who also lived with her mother-in-law. Her mother-in-law was in her 80s, and Sumitra and she did not have a good relationship. The accusation against Sumitra's mother-in-law came from their neighbor, whose child fell ill one day. When I asked Sumitra the question, Sumitra became angry and shouted: "Who knows?! Who knows what the old hag (*buria*) did! I do not know." Sumitra did not conspire with her neighbor against the old woman, and there was no evidence to support the view that the families were in conflict with each other. The above two examples suggest some interesting features about the perception of conflict within the community. In a community that has very few resources, conflicts are an everyday feature of village life, in which the jealousies and stresses of daily lives play an important role. Petty conflicts that involve women quarrelling over household issues are a part of daily existence, and within the verbal exchange, name-calling (that is calling each other a *dain*) is widespread. What is fascinating is how these petty conflicts evolve into witchcraft accusations. According to Lali and Sumitra, their families were not involved in "real" conflicts, i.e., conflicts that would justify witchcraft accusations against their family members. As they perceived the incident, the witch hunt happened without any provocation on their part. Their relatives did not have a history of being labeled by the others, and their families were not engaged in any serious conflicts with others that could have provoked the witch hunt.

Similarly, Pokua, a 45-year-old male plantation worker, whose mother was murdered during a witch hunt said: "We did not know anything about this [accusation of witchcraft] beforehand. A group of people came at night, mostly men, armed with kukri and took my mother away. They were all from this village. We were all at home.... Around ten thirty at night.... They took her then."

Sumitra, Pokua, and Lali's responses to being surprised at the witch hunt are also echoed in Bila, a 33-year-old female: "Why they took her . . . *kya malum* [Who knows]? We never fought with them [the family of accusers] and neither did my mother-in-law. I do not understand why this happened. Does having white hair make one a witch? How do I know? They killed her." [Starts crying softly]

Bila's description of her mother-in-law as an old woman with white hair and Sumitra's description of her mother-in-law as an old hag resonate with the image the community might have had that caused the community to label these old women as witches. It is also interesting to mention that, in spite of the fact that in cases of surprise attacks the participants argue that there were no prior warning signals, there was always an immediate cause that instigates the attack. The cause in most cases was an ailment; in a few cases it was a prior quarrel or a verbal exchange. In both the cases at Central Dooars and at Chandmoni Tea estate (where one out of the five women targeted could be categorized as having come under surprise attack), ailments in the accuser group led to witchcraft accusations. Perhaps the accusations against that woman in the Chandmoni tea estate witch hunt were made to provide evidence that there was no conspiracy in the witchcraft accusations: the five women were selected because they were guilty of witchcraft. The ailment argument leading to witchcraft accusations, similar to the arguments in the cases of calculated attacks, are very crucial in convincing the community to join the hunt.

However, not all villagers wanted to join the hunt. The refusal to join mainly comes from the relatives of the accused women. As we saw in the Chandmoni incident, these relatives were overpowered by the rest of community so that they could not prevent the witch hunt. In addition, as in the calculated hunts, some of the villagers had to be offered enticements to join the accusers. Here alcohol, money, and ailments played important roles in mobilizing the community against the witch. The performance of witch hunts depends on actors (Straus 2006, 120). For recruitment of actors in any violent act, shared knowledge and regular face-to-face interactions are important (Fuji 2009, 128). Shared knowledge may consist of the belief in and the fear of the powers of the witch. This shared knowledge can be vital in legitimizing and exe-cuting the hunt. For instance, not all people in these communities were offered incentives to join the hunt. A core group was identified, and it was this core group that was persuaded with alcohol and money to join in the witchcraft accusations. In the Central Dooars case, the core group was Sushil's friends. In the Chandmoni incident, Hariram, Lakhan, and Buddhiram used Suresh's money to persuade their friends to join. After the core group of people has been convinced of the need for the witch hunt, the rest of the villagers join in with little consideration. The rest of the villagers' feelings against the accused woman become so strong that they become crucial in keeping a watch on the relatives of accused woman during the witch hunt. As Bhutiya, whose mother-in-law was killed in the Central Dooar's incident explains: "More than money and *haria*, the fear of *dain's* eye works. People change when they hear that a *dain* is responsible. Then they do not remember that we are friends . . . companions of good and bad days. All they want is to kill the *dain*."

For the relatives of the "victims of witchcraft," the fear of the *dain* is a real threat. It is a threat that becomes so severe that they are willing to get rid of the witch at any cost. For instance, in the case of the women killed in Central Dooars, Nepul's daughter Duli was so convinced of the power of the witches against her family that she refused to agree that her father and brother had committed murder (see narratives in the following chapters). To her, the murder was justice against the witches, and the fact that her nephew and sister-in-law became well after the women were killed was proof of the witchcraft. Similar themes echo in other incidents of witchcraft accusations leading to murder, in which murderers kill their loved ones and surrender willingly to the police (see chapter 1). Thus, shared activities, knowledge, and daily interactions that involved gossip, greeting, and working in the same wage economy became ties that brought the community together during the hunt (Fuji 2009, 128).

## Differences Between Calculated and Surprise Categories of Witchcraft Accusations

Despite problems with categorization as a theoretical tool, the two types of witchcraft accusations are different in terms of the events that lead to the witch hunts. One must, of course, approach categories with caution, because categories are ideal types, and in actual incidents of witch hunts in the plantations, there may be overlapping of features. The goal here is to understand, solely from the point of the view of the participants, the events leading to the hunt.

A key difference between calculated and surprise attacks is the fact that a trial may take place during a calculated attack. These trials are important for the constructions of guilt (and in rare cases, constructions of innocence) of the accused woman. In cases of surprise attacks, trials are usually absent, because the accusers and their supporters do not see a need to give the woman an opportunity to prove her innocence. Here, the Central Dooars case and its events can be considered a classic case of surprise attack, where trials were not necessary before the two women were murdered. The trial leading to a witch hunt could be anything from an informal group meeting consisting of only the accusers, to a more formalized meeting in which the entire village and the local governing body are present. During calculated attacks especially, the accused witch is given an opportunity to defend herself, but in most cases the verdict has already been decided prior to the attack. The trial then becomes a part of the construction of the guilty witch. In contrast, in the surprise category of witch attacks, the accusers and his/her supporters are so convinced about the identity of the witch that they do not see a need to hold a trial. To them, the sole purpose of the witch hunt is to kill the witch as soon as possible so that they can rid the village of the evil influence.

Another key difference between the two categories is the actual time gap that exists between the point when an accusation is made and the actual hunt. In calculated attacks, this gap can be anywhere from one week to one year; in cases of surprise attacks, the time gap between the accusation and the hunt can range from a couple of hours to a few days. The variation in time gap can be explained by the very nature of the two categories that the participants described. In surprise attacks, the accusers are motivated by what the participants perceive them to have, a real fear in the powers of the witch, and thus there a notion of impulsiveness in the attack. This explains the suddenness of the attack in which the accusers attack allegedly without much planning or preparation. The surprise event takes place in the following sequence:

1. A death or an illness
2. Suspicion of witchcraft
3. Support for the witchcraft evidence
4. Selection of targets
5. The witch hunt

In contrast, calculated attacks have an ulterior motive. The accused woman is a scapegoat in the real scheme of events. Here the sequence is a little different:

1. Conflict between two parties
2. Targets already selected
3. Death or illness in the village, suspicion of witchcraft
4. Accuser group is joined by one of the parties in conflict
5. Name of the witch is proposed and conformed
6. Trial
7. Witch hunt

Calculated attacks are thus more carefully planned, and this can explain why there is some time gap in the chain of events.

Perhaps the most crucial difference between the two kinds of attacks is the complete lack of awareness on the part of the accused woman and her family of an impending witchcraft accusation. Because of the time lapse between the accusation and the hunt in calculated attacks, there is some sort of "preparedness" in the attack that can sometimes be used to prevent the hunt. For instance, in some cases the local police could be notified, the family members or other villagers could use the time to negotiate deals with the accuser group, and in rare cases the accused could have fled the attack (see Basanti's case in the following chapters). This preparedness is not present during the surprise attack type of witch hunt.

Finally, in calculated attacks there is a pattern of events that led to the witch hunt, unlike surprise attacks, which are "sudden" or "surprise" developments. But in both categories of witch hunts, the belief in witches is present among some section of the *adivasi* migrant group. This is a key element that has to be present for witch hunts to occur. However, it is also of interest to note, that the calculated category of witch hunts constitutes nearly 75 percent of the cases in my data set on witchcraft accusations in the Jalpaiguri plantations. This implies that incidents in the plantations are not motivated solely by the fear in witches among the *adivasis*. Rather, most cases of witch hunts are oriented to-wards fulfilling goals beyond the killing of the witch and getting rid of her evil spell, particularly when the hunts involve the pursuit of wealth (the idea of wealth is relative in communities) and power (Sanders 1995, 199). Sanders goes on to argue that witchcraft accusations become complex in societies in which there are differences in political and economic power between social classes (200). At the surface level, the witchcraft accusations in the *adivasi* migrant worker community are taking place within the labor community. There seems to be no involvement of the management or owners (the political and economically powerful social class within this economy) in the witchcraft accusations. However, as the rest of this chapter and the following two chapters will demonstrate, the witchcraft accusations are associated with tensions and social conflict because they generate anxieties.

## Using the Categories to Explain Individuals' Support of Witchcraft Accusations

Although a witchcraft accusation may arise from a preexisting conflict between the accusers and the accused, the involvement and support of the entire village towards the witch hunt should not be overlooked. This is an important point, because if the entire village was not convinced of the guilt of the witch, it would not have supported the hunt and demanded a punishment (Sanders 1995, 199). Second, despite persuasion and enticements in the form of rewards, mobilizing almost an entire village against the witch is not a small feat. It requires extensive planning, as we saw in calculated witch hunt cases, where whisper campaigns against the accused women, i.e., using gossip to incite people to assemble and join a hunt, were deliberate acts of recruitment. Often there are two ways villagers (other than accusers) can take part in the witch hunt. First, villagers can be active participants, whereby they join the initial accuser and become a part of the core group. In the Central Dooars case, Sushil, a friend of the initial accuser, became an active participant when he joined in recruiting supporters against the witches. Active participants decide the forms of punishments for the witch, and they take part in the implementation of the punishment, thus becoming a part of the formal group of accusers. Second, the rest of the members in the community may participate in the hunt by their seemingly passive support. Their seemingly passive participation may involve a variety of acts ranging from nonviolent acts (nonprotests of witch hunts in the community) to violent acts, such as threats to the family of the accused and others in the community. This is a crucial point, because this group does not seem to be directly linked to the accusers. This suggests that this seemingly passive group does not have a self-interest in the accusations. It is this group that was not recruited through enticements but that joined the attack out of perhaps a shared fear of the witch remaining in the community. However, it is this group that often plays a supportive role during the hunt not only by preventing the accused from escaping but also by threatening others who might be reluctant to join the hunt. For instance, going back to the Central Dooars case, the entire village kept vigil outside Padma's house so that her family members could not ask for outside help. One of them held a knife to the throat of a child in the family, threatening to slit him, if they escaped. While the group did not participate in the actual hunt (that involved dragging the women to the house of the accuser and in the killing of the women), it did participate in the witch hunt by keeping vigil over the relatives and supporting the hunt. Typically during the witch hunt in the tea plantations of Jalpaiguri, all villagers in the *adivasi* migrant worker communities participate, thereby making them accomplices in the eyes of the law.

So what makes hardworking ordinary individuals turn into killers overnight? The question that I ask here is not a novel one. It has been asked at numerous times by political scientists and collective behaviorists working on genocides and riots, and this analysis is often dominated by motives and coercions (Fuji 2009; Straus 2006). For instance, in the Rwandan genocides, coercion and threats played important parts in persuading people to join the perpetrators. However, in the witch hunts of Jalpaiguri, the villagers in both categories of hunt joined mostly by persuasion, often with little rewards, and they did not need much coercion. In the interviews, my participants did not mention any threat of coercion that had forced others in the community to join the accusers. Instead, participants talked about how little persuasion was required to motivate the rest of the community to join the accusers. Thus, the participation of the rest of the community in witchcraft accusations is different than the participation of the accusers who had clear motives and objectives: finding a cure for the illness or misfortune or using the witch hunt to avenge personal scores. So there seem to be definite psychological reasons why villagers and people with no apparent motives join a witch hunt. In other words, what is it that prompts individuals to mobilize against a target when the costs of participations are high? What makes villagers and others perceive the target as a threat, i.e., how does the witch hunt start out as a conflict that arises from a personal dispute and then turn into a matter of compelling public concern? Also, at the other extreme, are the costs of not participating higher than the costs of participating during a witch hunt?

Sociologists have often used the concept of moral panics to explain the seemingly irrational violent behavior of societies against individuals or groups who are perceived as threats to moral values and interests. Moral panics have existed throughout history (for example, folk devils), and they continue to exist today. Some contemporary examples of moral panics are those that involve reactions against child abuse (including ritual child abuse, child molestation, and pedophiles) (De Young 2004; Nathan 1991; Critcher 2008; Cohen 2002; Jenkins 1998; Schultz 2008), AIDS victims (Critcher 2008); young, working-class, violent males (Cohen 2002); gay and lesbian populations; "welfare queens;" and single mothers (Cohen 2002). Moral panics involve moral entrepreneurs or barricaders—social experts— who launch moral crusades, help in the diagnosis and solution of threats, and then strategically help in the selection of scapegoats (Cohen 2002). Goode and Ben-Yehuda (1994) best describe moral panics as a concept that is focused on the reaction to disturbances and on the scale of these reactions. So, moral panics are reactions to threat. The scale of the reaction, which typically involves violence, determines the moral panic. "One of the reasons for the concept's success is that it is centrally 'about' a struggle for cultural representations, that is, where the respectable mainstream of society leaves off and the margins or 'outsiders' begin. The moral panic divides the society into 'them' and 'us,' deviants and law-abiding citizens." (33). The "them" is the group that causes threat in the society, and they are "*devianized*" (Ben-Yehuda 1990,100).

Perhaps very crucial to moral panics are the social conditions that give rise to them. Of the many conditions that can facilitate moral panics, two are most important: (1) some form of social disruption leading to an already primed and sensitized public audience and (2) a group of individuals who can be credible targets of moral panics (Garland 2008, 14). The threat in moral panics is often delusional and imaginary. A common, classic example of moral panics for sociologists is the European witch craze, which has often been defined as the most horrific panic in human history (Goode and Ben-Yehuda 1994, 169). During the European witch craze, changes in the social, economic, and moral order; the gradual diminishment in the role of the Church; the rise of state power; and the growth of urban society altered the dominant European outlook and gave rise to skepticism about the existing social order, which was previously clearly defined. Women's roles began to change, thereby creating further changes in the traditional social order. Adding to the stress and confusion, Europe began to experience external catastrophes such as the devastating outbreaks of plague and cholera in the fourteenth century that annihilated populations, climate changes that brought on the little Ice Age, and the appearance of the great comet of 1528 that led to fears about the impending doom. It was a period of confusion and anomie, in which the boundaries between science and magic were blurred and there was a preoccupation with secretive knowledge. As a result of the disruptions, there was a need to redefine the moral boundaries of society. Witchcraft was portrayed as the opposite of true faith. It was an attack on the existing system. It was antireligious. The strain was so great that it had effects not only at the macrosocietal level but at the individual cognitive level. "He was part of a cataclysmic cosmic struggle between the sons of light and the sons of darkness" (Ben-Yehuda 1980, 16). The witch craze won popular support among the masses, because demonology theory was an effective ideology. Ideology provides authoritative concepts that help in understanding situations through images that help in arousing emotions and actions towards goals to minimize strain. The status of women in Europe at that time was going through enormous changes (caused by structural changes in the family, need for women to enter the job market, and demographic changes), and they (witches) became effective blame symbols within this ideology. Women were seen to be in pacts with the Devil against the church, and therefore they became convincing scapegoats during the witch craze. With the rise of secularism in the seventeenth century, the growth of the power of the state over the church that further led to the complete separation of church and state, the need to hunt witches no longer encompassed the moral order of the rational enlightened European mind (Ben-Yehuda 1980, 16–24; Goode and Ben-Yehuda 1994, 193–94).

In the plantations of Jalpaiguri, strain and conflict are always present. Starting with the migration of the *adivasis* from the central states, to the current crisis in the tea industry and ongoing conflicts over wages, strain almost seems to be omnipresent reality in the lives of the workers. For the worker community of tea plantations, the moral order is defined through beliefs in spirits, and all harm within the *adivasi* migrant community is directed towards the handiwork of the witch or other supernatural causes. Faced with poor wages and the associated dismal living and working conditions that accompany a suppressed working class, the community is constantly looking for a seemingly rational explanation to justify their struggles. In a community that has a history of being oppressed and neglected, first by the colonial planters and then by the big corporate houses in independent India, witch hunts are perhaps, as Kai Erickson explained "normal" responses to "abnormal" social conditions (1962). The witches are perfect scapegoats and loci of blame for problems that are beyond the control of the oppressed community. As during the European witch craze, a scapegoat in the form of a witch provides the perfect explanation for the continued ailments in the community. But the question of why women are selected as credible scapegoats and how one can tie witchcraft accusations to the broader conflict between the workers and the management in the plantations still remains to be answered. The two categories of witch hunts show how all women are under the threat of witchcraft accusations in the community. Sometimes they are selected because they or their families have a long-standing conflict with the family of the accused (calculated attacks), but often they are selected randomly, in surprise attacks in which the motives for the accusations are unclear. Echoing Sundar's (2001) observations that the targets do not fit any age, class, or occupational patterns, the categories here show that the selected women do not fit one profile.

Through the categories, I observe that aliments, illnesses, or deaths create a situation of stress and panic in the community, and this panic gives rise to witchcraft accusations against the accused women. Perhaps the most perplexing piece of the puzzle on witchcraft accusations is whether there is any "material" basis for the selection of targets. In other words, despite observations that do not find a pattern with respect to target selections, are there any material bases for connections between the victims of witchcraft (the accuser) and the accused women?

Linking deaths and ailments to dark spiritual beings such as *dain*s is observed in other literature on witchcraft accusations. For instance, among the Mawri of southern Niger, blood-sucking spirits are often blamed for deaths within the community (Masquelier 1997). Masquelier observes how the exchange of objects (food, coins, soap, cloth) can play a critical role in establishing social bonds between individuals or how this exchange can be a medium by which witchcraft is passed from the blood-sucking spirit to the innocent victim. Here, social memory and shared knowledge play important parts in the trajectory or map of social transaction through gift exchange, when no other material basis of witchcraft is observed. The mayyu (witch or witches) makes a pact with the spirits to quench their greedy desire for power and wealth that they do not wish to accumulate through hard work and reciprocal ex-change of goods and gifts. Through witchcraft, the mayyu is able to accumulate riches from the innocent recipient who unknowingly agrees to provide blood in return (Masquelier 1997, 187–88, 196).

So, did the accused women in the plantations of Jalpaiguri have a history of social transactions with the accuser or his family? Were these social transactions material, or did they also involve nonmaterial verbal exchange, such as praise, or good luck charms through which *buri nazar* or evil eye could be transferred? How does shared knowledge of the beliefs in *dain*s, bongas, and other spirits associated with the *adivasi* spiritual world gets transformed into witchcraft accusations? What do these witchcraft accusations say about the status of *adivasi* women within the plantation economy, and their changing roles? Both categories show that the communities experience a moral panic before a witch hunt. For instance, in both the Central Dooars and the Chandmoni tea estate incidents, the ailments and deaths of family members instigated a panic within the community. In both cases, the moral entrepreneurs (which included the core group of accusers, *jangurus*, and members of the *panchayat*) were instrumental in justifying the need to look for supernatural spiritual causes behind the ailments and deaths within the community. Witches were identified as the culprits; they are blamed for all miseries in the plantation-worker communities. Here, the *adivasi* workers, who were constantly under pressure as a result of the nature of the plantation economy, connected the micro-, village-level strain of ailments to witchcraft rather than blaming the deaths on the lack of proper medical aid for the workers. To the community, the ailments became the necessary proof that witchcraft was at work, and joining forces with the accusers became a logical choice—a choice that was necessary not just to get rid of the witchcraft temporarily but to seek justice. One *adivasi* participant explained:

> There is so much pressure and struggle in our daily lives . . . one has to do something . . . kill something . . . so that we feel that momentarily we have some power over our lives. It perhaps gives the community some respite. Momentarily of course, till the harassment by the police and outsiders start. Hospitals, medicines, doctors are something we do not have here. So at work we have the troubles over wages and treatment. And at home it is the old story of ailments and deaths.

The *dain* becomes the symbol of all oppression and misery, and thus the witchcraft is no longer a personal matter. It is now a concern of the community. So how do witchcraft accusations within the *adivasi* migrant worker community become a mirror of the community's struggles with the management? How do these microstrains within the community become a reflection of the macrostrains that the workers experience as a part of the wage plantation economy? In the next two sections I will look into the two groups, the accusers and the accused, to find links between the micro- and macrostrains.

## The Accusers

In this section, I take a look at the accusers closely. The numbers from the data set on witchcraft accusations in Jalpaiguri suggests that almost 92 percent of the accusations in Jalpaiguri come from males, while women constitute 8 percent of the accusers. It is interesting to note that though 92 percent of the direct accusations of witchcraft came from men, women could have been indirectly involved in the accusation. By indirect involvement I imply, that because social exchange in traditional communities is gender segregated (for instance, women tend to exchange gifts between themselves, and social interactions such as ties of friendship, social bonds, or gossip are also gender specific), women are most likely to be involved in conflicts with other women in the community, as opposed to with men, and the women are the ones who start the initial witchcraft accusations. For instance, conflicts over household goods, such as sharing of water pitchers and encroachment of kitchen gardens, are frequent; and women may accuse each other of manipulations. Such conflicts frequently give rise to name-calling (*daini*) between the women, and when there are suspicions of witchcraft by one woman or her family, accusations are typically made against the other woman. Generally, men are the heads of families, and it is men who negotiate with the *janguru* and present the formal complaint of witchcraft accusation to the village headman. This could be the reason that the numbers in the data set point to such high evidence of accusers being male.

Furthermore, on the point on social interactions being gendered in the *adivasi* community, of the few cases in the data set that did point to males being accused, the accusers were also men. Typically in these cases, the accuser is also quick in dispensing justice to the accused. However, I do note that accusations against men are not common in Jalpaiguri, and most of the cases where the accusers were men were located in the police archives. I did not come across any male victims of witchcraft accusations at the time of my study. For instance, in a case recorded almost a decade ago, Lalit Oraon accused his friend Sudhir Oraon of witchcraft. Lalit was going through personal troubles with his job at the plantation factory and had recently lost his job. He blamed Sudhir for his misfortunes, because he felt Sudhir was jealous of his permanent worker status in the plantation, a status that Sudhir failed to negotiate despite working for many years at the estate. One evening, when the two men were drinking, Lalit accused Sudhir of using witchcraft against him that caused him to lose his job, and the two friends started quarrelling. Suddenly Lalit lost his temper and slit Sudhir's throat. Sudhir died instantly, and Lalit was later arrested for homicide.

In both categories of hunt, the accusers played a determining role in the witch hunt. They were the ones who played a crucial role not only in selecting the target but also in providing validity to the existence of witchcraft. The number of core group accusers in a single case of witch hunts could be anywhere from one to groups of 20 or more. In these cases, in which there was more than one individual accuser, the initial accuser was typically the individual who suspected witchcraft against himself and his family members (for instance, Nepul and Suresh in the cases at Central Dooars and Chandmoni). After the initial accusations were made, the accuser was joined by relatives and friends in the accusations against the witch. Nepul was supported by his son Benglu and later by his friend Sushil. These three men were joined by three other men, thereby forming a group of six accusers against the two accused women in Central Dooars. Typically in the tea plantations of Jalpaiguri, about 75 percent of the cases in the data set had anywhere between one and ten accusers in the core group.

The categories and narratives in this study also show that, among the *adivasi* migrant worker groups, the witchcraft accusations came from individuals who were related or known to the accused in some way: they had family ties or were workplace or village acquaintances. In other words, the accusations against the accused did not come from strangers. Nearly 24 percent of the accusations in the data set came from family members of the accused who were related through blood or marriage, 67 percent of them came from neighbors and other acquaintances in the village, and 8 percent of the accusations came from fellow workers/colleagues.

TABLE 4.1: Relationship of the accusers to the accused

| | |
|---|---|
| Family members or relatives of the accused | 24.03% |
| Neighbors, friends, and villagers | 67.6% |
| Fellow workers | 8.10% |

The above statistics are similar to Karlsen's (1998, 46) observation that most witchcraft accusations in colonial New England originated in conflicts among people who knew one another: "No one could be certain that an angry encounter with a neighbor would not elicit an accusation" (48). The observation that ties of friendship could also elicit hate is similar to what has been seen in witchcraft in postcolonial Africa, where, as Ashforth (2005) describes witchcraft, it is a human action that is driven by hate, jealously, and envy. However, as observed through the categories of witch hunts, among the migrant worker communities in Jalpaiguri, not everyone was equally vulnerable to accusations of witchcraft, even though everyone (particularly women more so than men) in the village was under the threat. The accusations of witchcraft were directed at particular individuals based on some widely shared assumptions about what the shared image of the witch was like. This included physical features as well as personality traits. It is at this stage, the stage of selection of targets, that the moral entrepreneurs played an important role.

The term "moral entrepreneur" was coined by Becker in *Outsiders* (1963). According to Becker, moral entrepreneurs broadly fall into two categories: rule creators and rule enforcers. Rule creators can be seen as moral crusaders or individuals who are concerned chiefly with the successful persuasion of others towards morals, but they are not concerned with the means by which this persuasion is achieved. Successful moral crusades are typically those in the upper social strata of society. There is political competition in which these moral crusaders originate, and they organize crusades aimed at generating reform, based on what they think is moral and what they think is deviant. To operate, moral crusaders must have power and public support. They must generate public awareness of the issue and be able to propose a clear and acceptable solution to the problem (Becker 1963). The success of the moral entrepreneurs depends on, among other factors, their ability to mobilize power against the perceived threat and create public awareness and their ability to suggest a clear and acceptable solution for the issue or the problem (Ben-Yehuda 1986, 496). Typically in the plantation, the *janguru* plays the role of the moral entrepreneur in the community. As rule enforcers and rule creators, the *janguru* plays an important role in the daily spiritual guidance of the workers and represents a benevolent power that is contradictory to the malevolent power of the witch. For example, in the Chandmoni incident, the *janguru* was instrumental not only in identifying witchcraft behind Anil's death and the other epidemics in the village, thereby creating the moral panic, but also in overseeing the punishment of the witches. Similarly, in cases in which the *janguru* is not involved, the role of the moral entrepreneurs is taken over by the core group of accusers (Central Dooars case), and sometimes the accusers and the *janguru* work together against the witch, who is the symbol of deviance, in the community.

## The Accused Witches

In both surprise and calculated categories of hunts, *adivasi* women are the overwhelming targets of witchcraft accusations and witch hunts. For instance in the data set constructed for this study, a preliminary descriptive number count revealed that 84 percent of the accusations were against women. Accusations against men comprised approximately 15 percent of the cases. The numbers in the Jalpaiguri witchcraft accusations are similar to the witchcraft accusations in other regions and noted in the literature. For instance, Karlsen (1998) comments that in the New England witchcraft accusations, 78 percent of the accused were females. The accused men were "suspect by association: they were husbands, sons, other kin, or public supporters of female witches" (Karlsen 1998, 47). Among the *adivasi* migrant workers in Jalpaiguri, the accused men fell largely into the category of family members of the accused women. I was unable to get direct access to cases where men were victims of hunts. The cases that made it to the data set came from police records and newspaper archives. It was difficult to trace the male victims for most of the police cases, because the locations and addresses were missing in the data set. But the cases that were retrieved from the archives did mention that sometimes the entire family of the accused woman was attacked as retaliation against the witch. A small number of accusations against men could also come from independent accusations, typically from male accusers, as we saw in the case in which the accusations were between two friends. A few cases were also recorded in the police archives against *janguru*s who were accused by their fellow males of conducting misfortune on others. But these cases of accusations against *adivasi* men in the plantations are exceptions rather than the rule. The overall reported cases in the data set do point out that women are more likely to be suspects compared with men in cases of witchcraft suspicion, and the repercussions of an accusation were likely to be far graver and longer lasting for a woman than for a man, despite having strikingly similar personal circumstances and evidence between the two genders (52). Thus, for similar cases of witchcraft suspicions that involved both men and women, the punishments for the women who were accused would be more serious in nature than the punishments, if at all, for the men who were accused.

Nearly 78 percent of the accused women fall above the age category of 40 years and above, and the bulk fall between 40 and 60 years. This is an interesting statistic, which corresponds with the findings in New England where women under 40 were unlikely to be accused of being witches in the Puritan society (65). Regarding the religious background of the accused, 93 percent of the accused were *adivasis*. Among the *adivasi* accused category, the Munda and Oraon groups, the two most common groups of *adivasis* in the plantation areas, comprise 50 percent of the cases. Christian *adivasis* comprise nearly 5 percent of the data on accused individuals. Most of the Christians are under the "converted Christian" category and the "tribal Christian" group.

Among the accused women category, 62 percent of the accused were married, while nearly 30 percent were widows. About 1 percent of the accused were widowers, while nearly 6 percent were single men or women. The predominance of the married women in the accused witches' category probably had a lot to do with their relationship with older female family members (71). As seen in the previous cases of witch accusations in New England, the relationship the accused women had with their families, particularly with their female in-laws, was instrumental in providing support for accusations against the accused women. We will observe this in more detail when I discuss Basanti's case in chapter five.

## Conflict Between the Workers and Management and Some Concluding Thoughts

So how does one link the witchcraft accusations taking place among *adivasi* migrant workers in the tea plantations to the broader conflict between laborers and management? How do seemingly microlevel strains within the workers community connect to the macrostrains experienced in a wage economy? While the connections between the two do not seem to be obvious, closer examination of the events reveals that the witchcraft accusations serve two purposes for the community. At a local level, witchcraft helps in giving the *adivasi* workers a sense of control in their lives. Particularly relevant to this argument is the community's mobilization before the witch hunt, even though the witch hunts could be motivated by personal interests of the accusers group or sudden attacks that are provoked by unexplained illness or deaths. As one of the participants explained in a previous subsection in this chapter, the community develops a desire to do something about the situation or to take control over the forces (witchcraft) behind their miseries. Here, their shared knowledge of the witch and her powers comes into play. At the macrolevel, these witch hunts represent the broader conflict between the *adivasi* migrant workers and the plantation management. This is a more complex argument to be explained, and I will devote this section, and the next two chapters to explaining how witchcraft accusations are indeed a manifestation of the conflicts between the workers and the managements.

The link between witchcraft accusations as situated within local patterns of change and wider transformations that is embedded within the larger context has been explored before. For instance, Niehaus (2001) comments that central to the dynamic character of witchcraft accusations are the social and cultural transformations that accompanies it (Niehaus 2001, 7). Similarly, Geschiere (1997) demonstrates that witchcraft in Africa has both accumulative and leveling aspects. On one hand, witchcraft provides indispensable support for the dominant groups to accumulate greater wealth and influences, or to defeat political opponents. For example, people in power could use witchcraft to watch over the community and drive off evil doers. Among the Beng of the Ivory Coast, witchcraft was used by the kings and diviners to keep their enemies away. The leveling power of witchcraft is observed in its covert use by individuals who are envious, deprived, and resentful. In those cases, witchcraft becomes a weapon of the weak that can be used to level inequalities. For example, among the Zambiam Chewa older women were accused of witchcraft that prevented fertility and progress (Niehaus 2001, 9–10). Among the *adivasi* migrant workers, one does observe witchcraft as a way that the subordinate and oppressed community, a community whose very existence is a history of continuous marginalization leading up to today (Bhowmik 2011), comes to represent a weapon of the weak. Here, the weapon of witchcraft is not directed against management, a logical target given the conditions of the workers, but against fellow *adivasi* migrant workers. So, in a sense it becomes a weapon of the weak that is targeted against the weak, and that does not seem to make much sense in furthering the argument that these witch hunts are essentially representative of the bigger conflict between the two classes. So how does one make the connections? It is here that I turn to others in the literature to create a background for my argument.

Peter Geschiere (1997) suggests that there is an ongoing relationship between witchcraft and the people who are involved wherein witchcraft applies not only to local politics within the village but also extends itself to "modern" relations of the state and national politics. Thus the comment by Peter's assistant that "where there is electric light, witchcraft will disappear" is filled with misconstrued optimism based on the western conception that belief in witchcraft or sorcery is traditional and will automatically disappear with modernization (Geschiere 1997, 2). However, Geschiere argues that in contemporary Africa, discourses on sorcery or witchcraft are intertwined, often in surprising ways, with modern changes and with democracy. For instance, modern techniques and commodities (flying a plane, pilots) are central in rumors on the occult. In Africa they are the subject "of constant reformulations and re-creations, which often express a determined effort for signifying politicoeconomic changes, or even gaining control over them. In many respects, then, one can speak of the modernity of witchcraft, where witchcraft continues to exist in modern contexts with often surprising force" (1–3, 8).

The stress and anxiety experienced by the *adivasi* migrant workers in the wage economy made witchcraft accusations perhaps integral to their experience with modernity and its climate of exploitation. In this way the migration from peasant-based agricultural worker status to that of wage earner in a plantation economy, a product of "modern" western capitalism, made witchcraft accusations essential to cope with the daily lives in the plantation. This link between economic anxiety experienced by migrants and witchcraft appears in the literature as well. For example, Parish (2005) mentions the anxiety and apprehension of West Indian migrants that is caused by declining economies both in their native Ghana and in their adopted home in Northington, England. The uncertainty of leaving behind families in Ghana and migrating to new lands, along with the separation of families and children, made the migrants' experience a tenuous one, and as a result, they questioned every aspect of their financial affairs (Parish 2005, 114). Anxiety and desperation to escape the plight of economic decline created the diasporic witch, who travelled with the migrants and became more knowledgeable than the homeland witch (118). Rather than being sidelined by technology and capitalism in the new land, witchcraft became an integral component of modernity and its climate of exploitation among the diaspora (110–18).

Continuing the discussion of witchcraft accusations as a dynamic phenomenon that adapts to the changing contexts, Redding (2006) describes how in South Africa taxation, state legitimacy, and witchcraft accusations were linked throughout the history. In the early 1900s, those who did not align with the rebels could be named as witches and burned out of their huts, and many Africans who paid taxes feared being named as a traitor or a witch by the rebels. With the dismantling of the apartheid state in 1990s, issues of witchcraft and morality emerged as comrades. New changes and a new order exacerbated old conflicts and created new ones. In the twenty-first century, taxation has played a minimal role in witchcraft accusations (204–206). Redding (2006), Parish (2005), Geschiere (1997), and Niehaus (2001) all point out how witchcraft accusations situated in traditional communities are connected to bigger conflicts and how such accusations continue to exist with ongoing tensions. Witchcraft beliefs shifted between moral boundaries and have the capacity to act in diverse ways in a contradictory world (Comaroff and Comaroff 1993, xxi). This chapter brought forward the key actors in witchcraft accusations and presented a profile of the accusers and the accused. In the following two chapters, I situate witch hunts within the context of gender and class politics, wage struggles, and epidemics in an attempt to delve deeper in the plantation class struggles that are instrumental in continuing the witch hunts and giving rise to future witchcraft accusations among the *adivasi* migrant workers.

# Chapter 5

# Women, Moral Boundaries, and Gossip in the Plantation

## The Story of Basanti

I first met Basanti in the summer of 2005. Basanti, who at that time was 27 years old, was living with her two children (a seven-year-old daughter and an infant son) and her husband at her mother's house in Mourighat (another tea estate village), about 30 miles from Jalpaiguri city. When I reached Mourighat for my first meeting with Basanti, it was nearly noon. It was not hard to locate Basanti's house, because the villagers were familiar with "the house of the *dain*."

My first impression of Basanti was that of a woman with beautiful sad eyes and a smile that bespoke of her sufferings and sorrow. I was seated in a room that was an unfinished brick structure with exposed the red bricks joined with grey cement. The room's only furniture was a *chowki*, a wooden plank raised on a few bricks and some wood to form "legs" of the bed. On the *chowki*, was a child of about nine months who had an eye infection. My visit raised a lot of curiosity among the family's other children (Basanti's older daughter and her cousins), who stood at the entrance to the room and peeked in. Basanti's husband Alfred and her mother Smita joined me in the room as Basanti started to narrate her story.

Basanti's troubles started three years prior when she first met Alfred (who was known as Joga at the time). At that time, Basanti was a widow (her first husband died of an undiagnosed illness) with a child (her daughter) by her first husband. Joga and Basanti fell in love and decided to get married, much to the opposition of his mother and sister, who were reluctant to let Joga take on the responsibility of a child from his wife's previous marriage. Joga was a worker at the tea plantation, and after the wedding, the couple moved to his home, which he shared with his mother and sister.

From the outset, Joga's widowed mother and sister disliked Basanti. Arguments between the three women in the household became a daily affair and often resulted in name-calling. One of the common slurs used against Basanti by her in-laws was *daini*, and Basanti was also accused by her in-laws of "eating her first husband," causing his death. The three women disliked each other, and very soon Basanti was left with no friends among the neighbors in the village. Basanti had moved to the village after her marriage, she was a newcomer in the area, and her in-laws conspired to socially isolate her. In an attempt to bring some peace to the household, Joga decided to move his wife and stepdaughter to another house in the same village. With the help of his friend Lekha, who was also a worker in the tea plantation, Joga built a house on a plot that they co-owned. Lekha, along with his family, also built a small hut in the same plot, and the two families became neighbors. The families lived amicably for some time, until Lekha started making claims over the plot of land that was jointly owned.

The two former friends were now in constant conflict, and very soon the wives became engaged in daily brawls over water and vegetables from the kitchen gardens. Soon after Lekha's three-year-old daughter fell ill. Lekha's wife started complaining to the villagers that Basanti was the cause of her daughter's illness, alleging that Basanti knew witchcraft. Basanti's mother-in-law joined in the accusations with Lekha's wife, and Basanti's reputation as being a witch grew in the village. Thereafter, wherever she went, Basanti had to bear insults and taunts directed against her, and her husband faced harassment at work from the fellow *adivasi* workers. A village trial was held to put an end to Basanti's mischief and to prevent the witchcraft from spreading on to the rest of the villagers.

At the village trial, Basanti was asked by the *panchayat* to release her witch's spell on the child, and she was threatened with punishment upon refusal. During the meeting, Basanti tried to reason with the people regarding the absurdity of the accusations against her. She argued that Lekha's child had been ill from birth, because she had been born with jaundice. However, no one supported Basanti. The strongest supporter of the accusations against Basanti was her mother-in-law, who gave dramatic testimony in front of the *panchayat* as to how Basanti had plotted and killed her first husband and how she was planning to kill her second husband too. She provided narrations of how, at night, Basanti changed shape into a horned animal and would go on the prowl for her victims. Basanti was thus portrayed as a blood-thirsty and evil woman who had questionable morals. As the evening drew on, the villagers became more convinced about Basanti's being guilty of witchcraft and threatened her into a full confession of her crimes. Fearing for her life and for the life of her unborn child, five-months-pregnant Basanti gave a full confession of her guilt and told the villagers that she would take her spell off her neighbor's child. She also gave them 1,500 rupees as payment of a fine.

However, Lekha's daughter's condition worsened after the trial, and a few days later the child died. At around 5 p.m. that evening, a group of 15 men, led by Lekha and armed with sticks and kukri, started coming towards Basanti's house. Basanti was at home with her daughter, and when she saw the men approaching her house, she quickly went inside and locked the door. Very soon after that, the men started banging on the door and chanting "kill the *dain.*" The weak door gave way, and the men entered the room and grabbed her. The smell of *haria* was very strong in the room. The men had red eyes—the kind of eyes that saw no reason and were filled with cruelty. Basanti feared for her life as she saw a kukri pressed at her neck. Suddenly, Joga arrived home with a few of his friends and managed to drive the group away.

That night Basanti fled with her family 20 miles to her mother's home in Mourighat. Basanti's mother, Smita, lived with her son, his family, and her youngest daughter. Smita sheltered Basanti in her house, much to the displeasure of her son, who did not want to take on the responsibility of another sister and her family. After spending a few days in the shelter of his mother-in-law, Joga had to return to his village or else he would lose his job at the plantation. After Joga returned, Lekha and his friends found out about Basanti's hideout. The men hunted down her mother's house and threatened to kill Basanti. However, the local *panchayat* of Mourighat and its members came to Basanti's aid and managed to temporarily drive the men away.

Joga, who continued to live in his village, converted to Christianity to escape the taunts he and his wife faced. Christian *adivasis* in the region have the reputation of being "progressive minded," that is, the impression is that they are more "civilized" (meaning modern) than other *adivasis*, and thus accusations of witchcraft are less common among them.[1] Joga changed his name to "Alfred," much to the chagrin of Smita. When I met Basanti for the first time in 2005, she had already given birth to her son. Her husband visited her every weekend. The threats from his village continued, thus making it impossible for Basanti to go back. Lekha continued to fight over the plot with Alfred.

A year later, in the summer of 2006, I went back to visit Basanti in Mourighat. Basanti's husband, Alfred had committed suicide by consuming pesticide a few months prior to that. Basanti told me that Alfred became increasingly depressed about living away from his family. He faced constant pressure against his wife back in his home village, and he could not take the insults against Basanti anymore. Finances were very tight in Basanti's mother's household, because her son did not support his sisters and mother. The youngest sister had taken a job in another plantation to support her sister and mother. Basanti's mother-in-law was trying to persuade Basanti to give up her claim to Alfred's job at the plantation so that her daughter could get the job.[2] In return, Alfred's mother told Basanti that she would drop the witchcraft accusations against her.

Mourighat had one of the highest numbers of witch hunts and witchcraft accusations in the district of Jalpaiguri, and local activists were working hard to promote anti-witch-hunt campaigns in the villages. I helped Basanti and her children relocate to a shelter run by a local NGO who conducted anti-witch-hunt campaigns. But, Basanti returned to Mourighat a week later because she missed home.

By the end of summer 2006, when I left the field for that year, Basanti's troubles were far from over. Her mother was looking for a job as a *dai* (midwife) because it would give her and her family some respect and credibility. The witchcraft accusations against Basanti had not stopped, and this made it difficult for her to return to her husband's village. Basanti refused to let her sister-in-law take her husband's job, and she continued to fight with Alfred over the land.

## Some Comments on Basanti's Case

Basanti's case fits almost perfectly under the second category of witch hunts: calculated attacks. Here, the accusers used the prior conflicts to manipulate accusations against Basanti. Basanti's reputation as having knowledge of witchcraft started much earlier than Lekha and his wife's accusations against her. It started when she came to live with her in-laws, who used her previous widowed status as evidence of her evil nature. By using their own friendship networks to isolate Basanti, the in-laws had already successfully alienated her from the rest of the women in the village. Thus, when the accusations against Basanti were brought by Lekha and his wife, it was easy to gather support against her, and the villagers very willingly joined in the witch hunt. The death of Lekha's child after the trial further justified the witch hunt against Basanti, and the villagers continued to harass her.

# *Daini*: The Powers of the Dark Lady With Horns

The witch can possess anyone in the village. A careless remark about the weather, the ramblings of an old woman, a woman returning to the hut in the dark—all can be seen as signs of a witch's possession of another person. Then these signs get attached to the woman with whom they have been associated, and the woman herself comes to be seen as the witch; she is no longer the mother, the sister, or the daughter she had once been. Strange misfortunes occur where the witch lives: death of children, stomach ailments, and bareness. Cows become dry, and roosters and pigs die (Chatterjee 2001, 272–74; Devi 1990).

Perhaps there is an explanation for why *adivasi* women's bodies are thought to be more susceptible to the influence of a witch. As mentioned in the earlier two chapters, *adivasi* women occupy the lowest status at home, in the community, and within the plantation working class. Their work is undervalued and they are paid lower wages than the male *adivasi* workers. They are vulnerable to sexual advances of the managers, their morality is always under question, and their bodies are exotic and forbidden at the same time. They are objects of fetish for the planters and the managers, and they are often coerced into sexual relationships that are secretive and forbidden. It is common knowledge in a plantation that whenever such relationships take place, the *adivasi* men are powerless if a manager "fancies" one of their female relatives. The attitude of the *adivasi* men and women, and that of the others in the plantation villages, is one of repressed anger and acceptance, lest they lose their job. Often their anger is directed at the women, who are viewed as promiscuous and responsible for provoking the planters and other men. The women are objects of ire by the men because of their exotic, lustful, and savage bodies, which are responsible for the spell they cast on the planters and managers. These women are both desired and forbidden in a social structure that is based on patriarchal rules. For the planters, they are desired, as someone who is both exotic and repulsive: a forbidden fruit. For the *adivasi* men, these women are promiscuous, lack morals, and seem to be beyond the control of the men. The *adivasi* women are weak individuals; they are sinners who attract evil (witch) (Chatterjee 2001, 6–8, 26–27, 163–66, 272–73; Devi 1990).

Narratives from the participants (both men and women) in my study describe how, after possessing the weak woman, the evil eye of the witch that is now inside the woman, operates through *ban mara* (shooting of arrow). The possessed woman and the witch are now the same person. It is through the use of *ban*, where the arrows are filled with evil venom, that the witch is able to cause illness in her victims. Radha, an *adivasi* woman in her thirties, who was candid regarding her beliefs in witchcraft during interviews, remarked, "Do you know *ban mara*?" When I nodded my head in negative, she seemed surprised at my reaction and explained, "You do not know? Witches can shoot arrows . . . *ban* is a terrible thing. With *ban*, they can harm anyone. They can even harm you. The wind carries the *ban* to their victims' houses."

All the cases in this book point towards how the victims of the possessed woman (who has now become the witch) could be anyone: men, women, children, and animals. Ailments caused by witchcraft may vary from very specific illnesses to general ill luck, such as drying up of breast milk, infertility, and death of livestock. For example, in one of the cases from the police archives, a report about an assault against an accused woman described how the woman in a plantation village was responsible for causing cancer in the villager. The victim of witchcraft was a fellow villager (the accuser) with whom the accused witch had quarreled. It was also reported in the statement of the accuser that the witch had also caused her own daughter-in-law to be barren and that she was responsible for numerous illness (ranging from common colds to serious ailments) in the village.

The narratives of this study did point out that among the *adivasi* migrant workers, the nature of maleficium, though harmful in variable kind and degree, could be passed through the wind or a stare, or it could be hidden in food or personal items belonging to the victim. The witch, thus, symbolizes evil and can harm anyone who is around her. However, even though the witch's power could bring harm to anyone, her victims tend to be close neighbors, relatives, and people who knew her well enough to anger her.

Shamita (a Nepali participant in the study) describes the *adivasis* as being especially fearful that small children will fall prey to witches. Because child health and mortality are common concerns in the region, child health-related accusations are fairly common. The illness and the death of Lekha's daughter was credible evidence for witchcraft accusations against Basanti. Particularly for child death-related incidents, like similar incidents of death and illness where witchcraft is suspected, it is fairly difficult for the accused woman to get rid of the reputation as being a witch. Sometimes there are cases where an accused woman is able to overcome the accusations against her. However, these cases are exceptions. There are rare cases where the woman is able to succeed particularly because of outside intervention. Referring to Ramani, an accused woman whom Shamita rescued from a witch hunt, Shamita narrates:

> She [Ramani] stayed in my house for four years after that incident. In defiance of the entire community, I gave her shelter. She looked after my children. My children were all small. My daughter was brought up by her. She fed her *bhath* [rice], bathed her. Nothing happened to my daughter and to my family.

Shamita's success in being able to give Ramani a relatively trouble-free existence was perhaps possible because Shamita did not belong to the *adivasi* community. She is a Nepali woman and is actively engaged with the NGO that is supportive of anti-witch-hunt campaigns. She continues: "After four years, when the community began to see that nothing happened to my children or my family, they slowly started accepting Ramani back." By letting Ramani closely interact with her children through their food and clothing, Shamita strategized that this might convince the community of Ramani's innocence. As mentioned before, witchcraft is often passed through gifts and is thought to be hidden in food and clothing. For example, the exchange of food can be a symbol of social closeness, but it can also be a medium through which poison can be transmitted to unknowing victims (Desai 2008, 103–105). When Shamita's children grew up to be healthy, Ramani was able to somewhat get rid of the witch label that had been attached to her.

The passing of witchcraft through food and other objects plays a critical role in the reassertion of a link between witchcraft and its victim. The recipient becomes vulnerable to the witchcraft, and the gift signifies that the victim is now a source of sustenance for the witch. Witchcraft thus involves

> remembering the specific transaction or event during which the victim took something from the spirit . . . and which triggered the . . . attack . . . . Through the process of remembering that 'something took place' between the alleged maybe and . . . victim—something that becomes significant only because it led to an innocent person's death—villagers not only ascertain that there was a spirit attack and that they have tangible proof of crime that was committed. By focusing on the transacted object as the only concrete evidence that contact oc-

curred between the spirit's master and the dead person, they were also able to fix the event in the collective memory (Masquelier 1997, 189–90).

Thus we see that objects become powerful mediums for bringing together fragmented memories that are connected to the victim's last few moments in life. These objects become powerful evidence that witchcraft has taken place. Collective memories and shared knowledge become crucial during witchcraft accusations, as we will see in the following case.

Chaili, a widowed woman in her sixties, was accused of witchcraft when her neighbor's child fell ill after she bought him some sweets. Chaili was childless and lived alone. She was very fond of other children in the village, and she often gave gifts of candy and sweets. When the child fell ill, his father believed that the witch had poisoned the sweets. It was the "only" thing that the child ate before he fell ill. Being barren made Chaili envious of other women and their children in the village. Here, both an intent (jealously) and evidence (sweets) of witchcraft was established against Chaili.

## The Accused Women and Power

What social and economic powers did the accused women (Basanti, Savitri, Padma, Atashi, Binshu, Dhanni, Sanchari, and Manshi) have that led to the accusations against them? Were they women with property? Or were they women who violated socially sanctioned rules? The answer to these questions requires a closer look at these women and at others who were accused in the plantations.

One ongoing theme in the stories and lives of the accused women was that they were all ordinary women with ordinary troubles related to money and family. Their troubles were nothing out of the ordinary compared with those of their supposed victims. Their lives were similar to others in the *adivasi* migrant labor community, meaning that their social and economic positions were similar to the rest of the *adivasi* workers in the tea plantations. The accused women had family members who fell ill, died, and lost income. Basanti's son had ailments, and Alfred committed suicide. Basanti's life was no different from the lives of other women in the plantations. Basanti's social status was no different than that of the other *adivasi* women in the plantations. Perhaps her own personal share of misfortune was more tragic; she lost both of her husbands at a young age and she was a single mother with no income. Joga's entry into her life brought some stability and a change in her luck. Family life was blissful, and they had a son. Basanti's physical appearance was like any other young woman on the slender side. In summary, Basanti and her life were normal and ordinary. So, what was unusual about Basanti that made her transform within only a few months from being an ordinary wife and mother into being a credible witch, in the eyes of the community?

Scholars on witch hunts in various geographical settings have come up with a number of suggestions about which individual characteristic make women vulnerable to witchcraft accusations. These characteristics of witches comprise a range and are sometimes contradictory. They include the following:

- Having weak physical and psychological health (Bever 2002; Kivelson 2003)
- Being socially powerless (Hoak 1983)
- Having social power: elites who do not conform to tradition (Kohnert 1996)
- Having the ability to cause physical harm against people with whom they are in conflict (Latner 2008)
- Fitting the stereotypes associated with the image of witches (Niehaus 1993)

For example Latner (2008) describes them as "logical targets of the accusers" who possessed "characteristics that for seventeenth-century beliefs about witches" (Latner 2008, 149). They were poor, middle-aged or elderly women who were either single or widowed and were involved in neighborhood disputes. They were also often either related to or friends with other accused witches. The women became accused as result of conflicts between close family members and neighbors, particularly when their families were of different social standings (Delius 2001; DeWindt and Reiber 1995; Mixon and Trevina 2003).

In early modern England, witches were typically women who were bad mothers. A bad mother is one who used her powers of nurturing to cause malevolence toward her neighbors. Her children were demonic imps who caused harm to good mothers and their children. Arguing why witches were women, Willis contends that witches are typically women, because women are mothers. Witchcraft accusations have brought out fantasies of the malevolent mother, a mother who is a traitor, who instead of protection causes harm (Willis 1995, ix–8). In an attempt to understand what was characteristic of the accused woman that could convince an entire community of her witchcraft, Willis analyzes each "instigating" characteristic of a potential witch proposed by scholars on the topic. To her, the generalizations proposed by scholars, such as a threat to the patriarchal order, unpleasant personality, and sexual promiscuity were weaker theories that do not apply to the witches in modern Europe. Instead, Willis urges us to take on a closer look at the gender relations and the quarrels that start the accusations between the witch and her accusers (44). Village-level conflict that led to witchcraft accusations often grew out of quarrels about who had household control of raising children and feeding the family, jobs that were typically assigned as women's work. Willis argues that instead of following the widely held feminist view that women who were accused violated patriarchal standards, perhaps accused women were as likely to be conforming to the norms as the accusers (13). Willis goes on to explain that "curses," the most crucial part in all witchcraft accusations, are a part of the nurturing behavior of women and not a violation of feminine conduct. Curses are often directed against the other party to protect the loved ones. Thus, both the accused woman and the accuser woman are parts of a complex struggle of power in a patriarchal world.

Name calling, slurs, and curses are very common among women's household conflicts among the tea plantation *adivasi* migrant worker community. The slur *Daini* is the most commonly used between women both within and outside the family. For instance, during interviews, women participants would often describe other women whom they disliked as "*daini, dain, churail.*" Such name-calling also extended between the non-*adivasi* participants. Such references would come up particularly while describing characteristics of jealously that might stir up evil eye against anyone the *dain* felt envious towards. Typically in patriarchal structures women are responsible for the well being of their families. Death, loss of jobs, and misfortunes are often blamed on the young daughter-in-law. Young brides are sent home if her new family encounters misfortune. In Basanti's case, she became a symbol of both bad luck and good fortune. The death of a young husband is blamed on the young woman, and an accusation of the bride "eating her husband" is a common accusation from family members and others.[3] For example, among the Ho and Munda groups, who share similar myths and legends about witches, there is a belief that brides who are witches in disguise "eat their husbands." (Bosu Mullick 2000, 347–48).

Basanti's good fortune came with her second marriage to Joga, who had a steady job in the plantation and was doing reasonably well. Basanti's entry into the new household with her daughter from her first husband signaled the end of the control of household by her mother-in-law and sister-in-law. For them, Basanti was a threat: a young woman, getting a share in the household resources, and control over Joga's income. The couple's devotion to each other, steady income, and the potential birth of their child, became a threat to the two single women of the family, where Basanti's marital status, economic stability, and her fertility were a warning to them against their potential loss of control.

In searching for answers on specific characteristics of potential witches, I asked the participants who had played the role of accusers in incidents of witch hunts to describe the characteristics of accused women that made them certain of the accused dark powers. Pukahni, an 18-year-old female plantation worker whose father was one of accusers in a witch hunt incident, told me, "Yes there are [witches]. I have seen them. I went out in the night to relieve myself. As I came back to our house, I saw Liti [the accused witch] standing behind our fence. Liti was naked. She had horns and her mouth was filled with blood. I was very scared. I ran inside and saw my mother vomiting blood." Pukhani's mother had tuberculosis, and after this incident, the family accused Liti, a poor *adivasi* woman, of witchcraft against Pukhani's mother. Liti's identity was confirmed by the village *janguru*.

A shadow in the dark, fantasies of the features of dark woman were present in Pukhani's narratives. To her, the continuation of her mother's tuberculosis, prior to the encounter with Liti was not relevant. Liti's naked body image with a bloody mouth, symbolizing both an insatiable thirst for sex and blood, gave Pukhani the motive behind her mother's illness. Healthy women do not fall ill unless witchcraft is involved: witchcraft, which is transferred through a woman, who instead of nurturing, destroys.

Sumi, a woman in her thirties, told me about her neighbor, whom she suspected to be a witch. According to Sumi, the woman [her neighbor] was ill-tempered and often quarreled with her. Particularly significant for Sumi were the curses that the woman hurled against her.

> Once she cursed me that my child will die and we will die childless. After a few days, I found a small packet of *sindoor* and rice in my yard. I threw it away. My child became very ill after that. I went to the *janguru*, who gave my child medicines and conducted rituals to get rid of the *kala nazar* [evil eye]. My child became all right after some days, but I never let him play with her children or eat food given by her. I know she is a *daini*. I am scared of her.

Sumi's narrative reflects the role of curses in everyday women's lives in the plantation narrative. Curses are common exchanges during quarrels, particularly those between women. Both Sumi and her neighbor exchanged curses against each other family's well-being, and both women were mothers. Sumi, too, had called her neighbor names and cursed her family. It so happened that in this case, the *sindoor*, and pieces of rice found in Sumi's yard, perhaps parts of household garbage, got transposed into a spell. Open garbage is common in the plantation labor lines, but in this case the illness of the child gave Sumi reason to suspect her neighbor. Perhaps it was Sumi's own fear of her own spells working that made her cry wolf first.

I also asked relatives of accused women and the accused women themselves, whether they knew why they were singled out as witches. Almost all the participants expressed surprise at the accusations, and they came up with a variety of factors behind the blame. For some, witches, even though existing, did not exist within their own households. For example, Lattu, a young boy whose grandmother was murdered in a hunt, described her as a gentle, mild-natured woman who to his knowledge had never uttered curse in her lifetime.

> No . . . my grandmother was not a witch. She loved me a lot. She used to sing for me and put me to sleep. She is not a *dain*. I never heard her chanting mantras or hurling *gala-gali* [curses] at anyone. Yes there are witches . . . but not my grandmother. She was ill. I did not know that they would take her. They [the accusers] carried her away.

Similarly Shipli, a 45-year-old female *adivasi* tea plantation worker, whose mother was accused of witchcraft, described her mother as a good woman.

> My mother was a good woman. She did not have any knowledge about witchcraft. They blamed my mother. They are lying. Maybe the *janguru* came and did some rituals [at the house of the sick child] . . . I do not know.

I asked her whether the child who was ill became well after her mother was murdered. Shipli nodded her head and said yes.

Some of the participants pointed to physical characteristics such as age (old women), hunchback, skin color, and hair as features that were used to single out accused women. For instance, Lata, a 29-year-old *adivasi* woman, expressing surprise at the accusations against her mother reasoned: "Who knows why they accused mother of witchcraft. Maybe . . . because she had a hunchback?" Bila, a 33-year-old *adivasi* woman, struggled to come up with an explanation for the accusations against her mother: "I do not understand why this happened. Does having white hair make one a witch? She was a good woman."

Some interesting descriptions of the popular image of the *dain* were shared through the above interviews. Relatives of the accused women consistently insisted at various points during interviews that the accused women were good women, who did not curse. Curses are such a daily part of the vocabulary that they are not taken seriously, but they are treated with suspicion if someone falls ill. This relates to ideas about the power of a collective memory about witchcraft being transmitted through gift-giving. Thus curses are dismissed and taken seriously at the same time. For others, the accused women were mothers and grandmothers whose physical features rather than their tendency to curse perhaps led to their accusations. For the accusers, the *dain* was a blood-thirsty woman whose naked body was evidence of her promiscuous nature. For others, it was her jealous nature that caused illness in others.

Closely related to the power of the curses, the evil eye of *dain* was feared by villagers for its ability to cause harm to the victims. My translator took me to meet Ramani, the 60-year-old woman who was ostracized by the entire village on suspicion of witchcraft and later rescued by a Nepali woman. Narrating the incident, Ramani reasoned that her dark skin tone caused trouble.

> I was kicked out of the village. They told me that I had buri nazar [evil eye]. My dark skin tone was a problem too. I came to Shamita's house for help. Shamita calls me kaki [Auntie]. Ask her if I had never any *kharap bath*? [4] They said my *nazar* [eye/look] was *kharap* [evil]. *Bohut juta bath hai* [This is a terrible lie].

Similar to Ramani's experience, for some accused women it was the reputation or suspicion of having an evil eye that led to witchcraft accusations against them. Lajju was a 33-year-old *adivasi* plantation worker who lived with her husband and children. The villagers were always suspicious of her behavior, and Lajju was often involved in fights as a result of accusations of witchcraft against her. One participant described her: "She was not known to keep quiet if someone accused her of witchcraft. She would argue back with curses against the entire family. . . ." Lajju was described by the villagers as a bad-natured woman who was constantly fighting with everyone, including her husband. Lajju's neighbor's child and her [Lajju] husband began to fall ill very frequently, and the local *janguru* was unable to find a cure. The *janguru* told the rest of the villagers that Lajju's evil powers made his medicines useless. The entire village, along with Lajju's family, which included her husband, was involved in a witch hunt that resulted in Lajju's murder. Cases like Lajju's are numerous in the police files from the Jalpaiguri plantations. These case reports record "suspicion of witchcraft" as the cause behind the witch hunts. Mere suspicions of the evil eye turn husbands against wives, siblings against siblings, and neighbors against neighbors. For example, in another case recorded in the police archives describes the statement of an accuser, the husband of the accused dead woman. The husband was suspicious that his wife used witchcraft against him that resulted in his stomach ailments for the past 10 years. According to the husband, his wife had a nasty temper and the couple was frequently involved in domestic squabbles. He never felt safe around her, and later on he refused to eat food prepared by her. Here, regular domestic strife between couples is interpreted as evidence that witchcraft caused stomach illness in the husband.

For others, the evil eye is useful to the *dain* to satisfy her insatiable sexual desire. Rimi, a 45-year-old *adivasi* woman whose husband deserted her for another woman [Subra], accused Subra of using witchcraft on her husband to cause him to leave his wife. After a few months, when Rimi's son fell ill, the couple (who had since reconciled) began to suspect Subra of using witchcraft on the child because she was jealous. In another case, an *adivasi* man suspected an *adivasi* woman of using witchcraft against him because he had made sexual advances towards her on a previous occasion. According to his police confession (he killed the woman), the woman, who spurned his advances, was a witch who made him fall ill as an act of revenge. Willis's (1995) argument that in witchcraft accusations both parties of accusers, which consist of men and women, and accused women are involved in a complex network of gender power relations and bargaining, seems particularly relevant in the plantation community. For the woman whose husband had left her for another woman, the accusation against her husband's lover is an act of revenge and a personal act of triumph. For the spurned man, the act of branding his lover as a witch, and for the ailing husband of a dominant wife, witchcraft accusations, were acts to preserve hegemonic masculinity.

In answer to the original question of this subsection, what characteristics made an ordinary *adivasi* migrant woman worker transform into a credible witch, it is hard to point to any single characteristic, cause, or factor that is decisive in the identification of the witch. The witch can be selected on the basis of a single factor or a combination of factors, and each case is different and unique: domestic quarrels, reputation, physical traits, gender and proximity to the ill individual are some of the factors. However, a woman could have all of these characteristics and never experience a witchcraft accusation. Similarly a woman can have none of these characteristics and still be branded as a witch.

Through the in-depth interviews with both the accusers and the accused parties one might wonder whether it is possible to construct a consistent image of the *dain* in the plantation community. In the interviews, a wide assortment of characteristics was used to describe the witch. In some interviews, the witch was described as being naked with horns, sucking blood from her victims, possessing some physical "peculiarity" like hunchback, or having dark skin tone and white hair. The accusers described the *dain* as having behaviors that were considered to be problematic for "good women": she was naked, blood thirsty, quarrelsome, jealous, or of loose morals. For the accused women and their relatives, normal physical characteristics of individuals were used to describe the *dain*: physical deformities, graying hair, and dark skin tones. Of course, these descriptions differed from participant to participant. This made it very difficult to come up with a definite description of the physical features of the *dain*, and so, a unified description of what a witch looks in the plantation was never possible from the quotes. There was only one quote that suggested that witches had horns and usually operated naked, but when asked to give physical description of the witch, most of my interviewees seemed confused.

The accused women were between the ages of 40 and 70, and their marital status was either married or widowed. This is an interesting finding, especially if one compares these findings with the findings from the New England witch hunts, in which single, married, and widowed women were found in significant numbers among the accused (Karlsen 1998). Married women dominated the accusations in New England, though Karlsen argues that had more to do with their relationship with older women in the family. Karlsen goes on to argue that the marital status of women was crucial in determining their relationship to their family and to the community. One can see the relevance of this argument when one looks at the cases among the *adivasi* workers in the tea plantations in which the accusations start mostly from conflicts among women. As seen in Basanti's case, her reputation as a witch grew during her initial conflict with her mother-in-law, who accused her of being responsible for the death of her first husband. This accusation played a crucial role in strengthening the accusers (Lekha) complaint that Basanti knew witchcraft. It was her troubled relationship within a community that ostracized her and where she had no supporters or friends, that worked against her when the accusation from Lekha surfaced.

However, Karlsen's argument that even the most unlikely women among the accused typically exhibited some of the characteristics of the witch (Karlsen 1998, 47) does not seem to hold true in the Indian plantations. In the context of the tea plantations, the fear of the bad mother causing harm to others through her evil eye and through gifts and the resulting manipulation of gender politics between women (Basanti's case) provide clues to the transformation of ordinary women to witches. In the following section, I will discuss how household quarrels get manipulated through rumors into witch hunts, and I will discuss what these conspiracies tell us about the broader conflict between the workers and the managers in the plantations.

## Rumor, Moral Boundaries, and Conspiracy

For Balwant, a male *adivasi* social activist in his forties, most witch accusations stem from fights between women through what he calls *ghorelu jogra* or everyday household quarrels or conflicts between relatives or neighbors that are nonserious in nature to start with. Because the houses in the labor lines are in close proximity, occupants are frequently involved in each others' lives, and these daily interactions also attract conflicts. The idea of *ghorelu jogra* could range from arguments over distribution of common recourses, personality clashes, or jealous fights. To him, these petty conflicts, usually between women, get transposed into a conspiracy of calculated attacks of witch hunts against the accused women, in which men play a prominent role in instigating the hunt.

> If you look carefully you will see that women play a very small role in the conspiracy. Their [the women] numbers in the conspiracy is very small. It is the men who call the shots. Once the men start the conspiracy then their women folk begin to play a more active part in the conspiracy. They believe their men blindly and without understanding the events support the men.

Balwant's comment illustrates the complicated nature of the gendered politics in witchcraft accusations. What starts as a petty conflict between two women gets instigated into a full-fledged witchcraft accusation against the accused woman, in which the men in the other woman's family play an important role. It is the men who consult the *janguru*, help in identification of the *dain*, prepare the necessary support for the witch hunt, and play a crucial role in the trial. During the initial stage of the accusations, the women on the accuser's side play a smaller role. After the *dain* gets identified, the women play a bigger role in the whisper campaign and in lending support during the hunt. Balwant's argument that most witchcraft accusations stem from household quarrels between women is similar to the arguments by some feminist scholars on witch hunts. What is crucial here is how these seemingly nonserious household quarrels get transposed into witch hunts. Basanti explains how the first accusation against her was started by Lekha's family:

> My friend's daughter was ill for some time. That baby had jaundice. You can tell from her belly and skin color. I used to tell her show a doctor. Her [the baby's] stomach became really big. I really meant good for the child. But Dipti would not listen. She would bring medicines from who knows where [the *janguru*] and give it to the child. Would these medicines cure her? Tell me? I used to repeatedly tell her to show to a good doctor. That's why she [Dipti] used to get angry and tell me, "What does it matter to you to say these things? Are you giving taka [money]? Is your father giving the money?" She used to talk like that. Towards the end they took the baby to the government hospital. But it was too late. The baby died . . . After the baby died, Lekha, Dipti and her brother came over to my house with a *chhuri* [crude knife] and threatened me: "You have eaten our child." Prior to this incident, I never had any accusation of

> witchcraft against me. Lekha's daughter died. After her death my husband was physically assaulted by Lekha and his friends. Later they came to my house with a kukri [knife]. I ran away.

I asked her whether she and her family had any conflict with Lekha and his family. Basanti said: "No fight. . . . This was the first fight," [implying the physical assault and threat]. I asked, "How did he come to the conclusion that you were the witch who had caused the mischief?" She replied, "From his head (*mathar thekey*). . . . Everyone said that I was a *dain* . . . he too started believing it." I asked, "But why you? Was there a *janguru* involved? Did you have any animosity with anyone?" Basanti said:

> Well you can say that there were some bad feelings between me and his wife. I came to this place after my wedding [referring to the village]. She [the neighbor's wife] did not like me and we often quarreled over pigs and water. And then, when she [child] died, I was the witch. This was natural according to everyone.

I must mention here that in prior interviews with me, Basanti had not mentioned her own personal conflicts with Dipti. This came as a surprise to me, because Basanti often spoke about how the two families had been good friends prior to Lekha's accusations. In my follow-up interviews, Basanti reflected that, even though she and Dipti often fought, things became normal after every fight, and her conflicts with Dipti were nonserious in nature. Basanti's reflection brings forward how conflicts between women in the labor lines are a part of their daily experience, and these are not given much attention, except when an innocent person (here, the child) becomes fatally ill. The process of remembering the specific event, here the conflict between Basanti and Dipti, brought forward witchcraft accusations against Basanti (Masquelier 1997). Basanti's quarrels with Dipti and Joga's conflict with Lekha played a crucial role in the witch hunt. Basanti's accusation is an example of a case in which personal conflicts evolve into witchcraft accusations. Basanti's quarrels with her in-laws, the death of her first husband, the conflict with Dipti, and the sick child were all pawns in the bigger conflict between Joga and Lekha over property. When the witchcraft accusations against Basanti started, the preexisting conflict between the men got pushed into the background.

Balwant's argument that women play a small role in the bigger conspiracy of men is possibly best explained by Sukhni, a 40-year-old female plantation worker whose husband was in prison serving out a murder sentence for killing an accused witch. Her narrative echoes the sentiment of other women conspirators in the study: "Today if my husband says that this is right [accusation against another woman], why will I not support it? She is a witch and my husband is speaking the truth." Upon asking Sukhni how she knew that the accused woman was a witch, she replied it was because her husband had told her so.

Most of the women from the accusers group join the conspiracy as a form of "bargain" with the men. Their participation in household quarrels, often an everyday event, is not a part of the conspiracy. Rather the conspiracy is to make the women believe that the other woman is a witch. Among the *adivasi* migrant worker communities, as is the case with most patriarchal societies, a woman's economic security and social position is controlled by men. Even though *adivasi* women are employed in the plantation, they are paid lower wages than men, and their incomes are controlled by their male family members. Referring to the resistance to abortion and condom use by women in some African societies, Nathanson and Schoen (1993) argues:

> To the degree that women are economically dependent on men . . . women's power in the heterosexual market place will be a function of the value attached to their sexual and reproductive resources, and they will have a strong vested interest in seeing that the value is maintained (287).

This patriarchal bargaining framework has been used to explain, for example, why women accommodate gendered practices of religious traditionalism, veiling, and constraints on sexual behavior (Chong 2006; Kandiyoti 1988; Nathanson and Schoen 1993), and it has proven to be very useful in documenting the reasons for women's choices to accommodate patriarchal norms (Chaudhuri, Morash, and Yingling forthcoming). Kandiyoti (1988) argues that women cope within patriarchal constraints with strategies that involve making bargains towards the goal of maximizing financial security and life options within constraints of the patriarchal bargain. Patriarchal bargain has been defined as a difficult compromise between acting with unrestrained agency and accommodating the constraints on agency that are due to "rules and scripts regulating gender relations" (Kandiyoti 1988, 286). Women employ varying strategies to cope with patriarchal arrangements in families and communities as they "contest, negotiate, participate in and reproduce patriarchal relations" (Shankar and Northcott 2009, 425; Gerami and Lehnerer: 2001). Similar to Willis's (1995) arguments for the English witch hunts, the *adivasi* migrant women in a traditional setting within the family bargain their domestic service, which includes listening and supporting her husband without question, in return for economic and social support from him.

Rumor plays an important role during the whisper campaign against the accused woman. In Basanti's case and in similar cases, rumors of the evil powers of the *dain* were spread throughout the community in a whisper trail. This crucial phase is essential in alienating the accused women within the community and in motivating a community to react against her, and ultimately in the successful implementation of the conspiracy during the witch hunt. Writing about how rumor and gossip are important catalysts during witchcraft accusations and sorcery, Stewart and Strathern (2003) argue that through rumors the actors (meaning the accusers) become powerful against their enemy (the witch) by means of conflict, violence, and scapegoating. Theoretically, witchcraft here is viewed as processual, i.e., as a social action that is enacted through sequences of action. Rumors emerge during the developmental stages of stress in a community, particularly during the formative phases of witch hunts, and they create a network of communications that leads to merging of mutual fears and crystallization of accusations. It is through rumor that the accusers demonstrate their aggressiveness against the all powerful witch (Stewart and Strathern 2003, ix–xiv). Stewart and Strathern further argue that in communities where beliefs in witches and sorcerers are predominant, claims and counterclaims of their activities "flourish in the shadows, fed by gossip and rumor, and emerge into public debate or accusations, only in times of specific tension, most often following the actual sickness or death of someon" (7). Rumor spreads rapidly and produces its own truth through repetition. It can absorb and accommodate many meanings, and it is a particularly potent vehicle for political purposes. For example, rumors of pollution triggered the revolt of 1857 (also known as the *sepoy mutiny*) that shook the British army in India (102–103).

Among the *adivasi* migrant workers in the plantations, the whisper campaigns are used to make the witch feel alienation from all networks and thus powerless. This is achieved mainly through the accuser's networks of friendship. In Basanti's case, her mother-in-law used rumors to alienate her from the village. The stage was already set against Basanti when Lekha accused her of witchcraft. Further, Joga was pressured at work by the rest of the *adivasi* workers to leave his wife. Basanti's daughter complained that other children in the village refused to play with her. Rumors and whispers against Basanti reached a peak when Lekha's child became ill, leading to her trial.

Bhagawan, a 60-year-old male *adivasi* retired plantation worker, explains how the process of rumor and gossip works in the plantation:

> This is how it works over here. I [Vishnu] have a wife and my neighbor has a wife. This is suspicion . . . all in the mind, that my neighbor's wife is evil. . . . Vishnu's wife was pregnant. There were a lot of complications during delivery. Her ailments remained undiagnosed . . . in Sadri we call it *pichla-rog* . . . during child birth women become weak. And if they do not eat properly the weakness becomes acute. So because of these reasons, after the delivery Vishnu's wife died. After she died, it meant [to Vishnu and family] that there must be some *meye-cheley* [woman] around me that had done mischief with the help of *dain-viddhya* [witchcraft]. Because of this my *shustho* [healthy] wife, *amar bhalo bou* [my good wife] died while giving birth to our child.
>
> . . .
>
> Then what happened was Vishnu went to the *janguru* with rice, *dal*, flowers and *haria*. The *janguru* has his personal motives behind this. He saw that this was a good way to get some profit out of this consultation. The *janguru* chanted some mantras, conducted some rituals and "planted" suspicion in Vishnu's mind about his neighbor's wife. If the *janguru* did not do this, then how will he make ends meet? He got five hundred rupees [approximately ten dollars], black

> hens, two goats out of this. He brainwashed Vishnu and told him that there is some dark skinned woman who lives near your house who has done jadu mantra [witchcraft] against your wife. Vishnu came back home and sees his neighbor's wife who is dark skinned.
>
> . . .
>
> Thus it began . . . two three *matabor* (headmen) got involved . . . they feasted together . . . drank a lot of *haria*. Then they all started saying, "Yes you [Vishnu] are right. This is the work of that *shaalir beti* [curse word]." Then the torture against the accused woman began. The entire village started avoiding her. They held a trial against her and in the trial, where the *janguru* was present, it was decided that they would "drive" the witch out of the accused woman. They started hitting the poor woman with sticks and stripped her. The beating continued for five hours. *Daini o morlo, meyetao morlo* [The witch and the woman were killed in the end].

Bhagawan's narrative highlights the role of ordinary villagers. They participated in the whisper campaign and supported the violent attack against the accused woman. Rumors are not trivial components of the social process but central and fundamental processes. As we read in the above quote, their source of power lies in the networks of informal communication. Stewart and Strathern (2004) demonstrate through examples of witchcraft accusations how these informal channels can be subvert power or give rise to new sources of power and thus produce serious social upheavals (Stewart and Strathern 2003, 203). Among the *adivasi* migrant plantation workers, the goal of gossip and rumor is to get rid of the witch who is responsible for misfortunes and to threaten the moral boundaries of the community. Rumors are an important tool for social control for the maintenance of moral boundaries. Balwant the *adivasi* social activist explains:

> You will see that in areas where there is little education . . . and no resources for education . . . some *matabbar* people take advantage of the situation. To teach someone a lesson, to exert their influence over someone, they might start to malign the reputation of the individual, accusing her of practicing witchcraft. These people they take advantage of the superstition of the tribals. Who are these people who get accused? They could be relatives of individuals over whom the *matabbar* wants to exert his influence . . . it could be a woman who has some money, property. They target the women of such family. Then if someone in the neighborhood runs a fever, has malaria or dysentery [both common ailments in the plantations], then these people [he accusers] come together and start making trouble. They start spreading rumors about the accused woman . . . the illness was started by the woman. Naturally the illiterate people in the village do not understand the politics. They do not understand the illness too. All they understand is *daini protha* [witch] and *jaddu vidya*. They then join the harassment against the accused woman.

Chanda, another social activist explains why it is easier to blame women in order to exert moral boundaries: "It is easier to blame the women. . . . They are the root of all trouble." She goes on to explain: "In a society the women are always the victims. If there is any trouble the first name you will hear is that of a woman." Chanda's views seems to be similar to the arguments of scholars on witchcraft in New England, where the idea that witches were women was held by local authorities, magistrates, and juries, that is, men who had the power to decide the fate of the accusers) (Karlsen 1998, 48). Balwant's quotes, the narratives from the Central Dooars and Chandmoni estate cases, it is men, typically in positions of power that decide on the target.

Witch accusations are rarely made against total strangers. It is common for witch accusations to be made against neighbors and relatives. As our discussions of both types of attacks have shown, in both surprise and calculated attacks, no strangers were accused. The targets of witch hunts are usually selected from groups and people who have been involved in prior conflicts. The individuals selected have to be credible as targets and also vulnerable, with little power or means of retaliation. *Adivasi* women, by virtue of their lower social status, because of their gender, and because of their proximity to sources of conflict (typically with other women in the family or neighborhood), make perfect witches.

However, sometimes the accusations stem from a surprise fight in which a "credible target" is absent. Ramdev, a 40-year-old male plantation worker, narrated a recent incident: "That day was a market day. All the boys drink [*haria*] that day. A fight broke out between two groups. Cursing, verbal abuses started along with accusations of witchcraft. Each group started calling each other *dains* and started to attack each other." I asked whether the two groups had any conflict before that. Ramdev said: "There was some conflict over property . . . the usual . . . but nothing that warned us of the attack." For the *adivasis* in the plantations, calling someone a *dain* or a *daini* is the strongest of curses.

## *Haria*, Women, and Workers Feelings of Conflict Against Plantation Owners

In almost all the descriptions of the accusers, participants spoke of the intoxication and exchange of *haria* that takes place before the hunt. Alcohol is used as an enticement in attracting supporters against the witch. *Haria*, a rice brew, has ritual significance for the *adivasis* in the plantations and is offered to guests (including me) as a welcoming drink. I was always greeted with a glass of *haria* during my visits to the labor lines in late afternoons, and my resistance to drink it was considered sacrilege by my participants. Piya Chatterjee (2001) writes about the importance of the drink among the *adivasis* during rituals as a part of the animal sacrifice. She refers to a comment by an *adivasi* woman, who talks about the connection of *haria* with *adivasi* life: "If the *devta* [God] has asked you to have *handia* for the *puja*, to offer to the *devta*, then how do you say no to it? As long as *handia* is in our rituals, nothing will stop us from drinking it . . ."

(Chatterjee 2001, 284–85). *Haria* thus represents a sacred drink that is also believed to have medicinal powers for the *adivasi*, especially to cure gastroenteritis, and it is often drunk to satisfy hunger pangs among the *adivasi* migrant workers (284). Participants in my study spoke of how *haria* gave them the power to kill the *dain*. Sushil (an accused in the Central Dooars) reflected on how the stress of daily life on the plantation, the frustrations of not being able to improve their lives, and the drinking of *haria* are connected.

> Sushil: [W]hat can we do? We work all day, eat a little . . . that too *tao bhalo mondo noi . . . je tuku nah holley noi* [eat barely to sustain ourselves] . . . when we get our wages, infrequently, we want to enjoy for that day. Do we think of consequences then? Saving the wages is a distant thought . . . our only thought is to enjoy for sometime so that we forget the troubles of the week . . . forget our daily troubles at home. . . . *Haria* makes us feel good. We start to think differently . . . there is a lot of anger inside us. Our plantation was closed for three months . . . no one cared whether we ate or not . . . people were falling ill . . . drinking *haria* gives us a lot of strength. Our mind works differently . . . our anger takes on a different meaning. We start to think of killing the *shaali*.
>
> SC: Who is the *shaali*?
>
> Sushil: The *daini shaali* . . . she is the one who is responsible for all our troubles and misery. *Haria* gives us the strength to deal with her. It gives us inner strength.
>
> SC: Do you not think of going somewhere else?
>
> Sushil: Where do we go? Where do we go leaving this tea garden? . . . What can we do? . . . We do not know how to read or write.

Sushil's comments on the lack of opportunities for the *adivasi* migrant laborers outside the tea plantations are further echoed in the response of another participant who spoke about the state of education in the plantation: "[T]he schools do not teach . . . all we know is how to be workers in the plantation." The long history of the politics of liquor in the tea plantations is reflected in Sushil's comments on how *haria* helps him and others forget the misery. His comments reveal how helpless the workers feel against a management that closed the plantation and did not pay its workers. Scholars working in this region have commented on how violence against women among the *adivasi* tea workers is related to alcohol (particularly to *haria*) abuse and is triggered by conflicts over wages and conditions of work and pay in the plantations (Bhowmik 2011; Chatterjee 2001). The politics of *haria* has its roots in the colonial times, when the British Government controlled government taxes on liquor (*daru*, the legal distilled raw alcohol). The *adivasis* consider *daru* to have devastating effects on health, in contrast to *haria* a ritual brew approved by devta. *Haria* has always been sold illegally in the plantation, and while the planters of the past and present complain about drunken workers, the planters "also used alcohol as a strategy of labor control and discipline. The iconic *matal*, or drunkard, typified male working-class otherness, though the political economy of his drink was itself implicated with wage-labor regime" (Chatterjee 2001, 284).

The frustrations of daily life for the *adivasi* workers, the significance of *haria* in their lives, the ill-legitimization of *haria*, and the hegemonic culture of patronage and servitude in the plantations are all reflected in the legacy of violence against the *adivasi* women in the plantations. Chatterjee (2001) argues that the other-ing of the working class masculinity, by calling them *jungli*, creates an experience of alienation among the male *adivasi* workers that is about emasculation and the erosion of masculine authority and honor. The employment of *adivasi* women as wage laborers has a further effect on the displacement of masculinity among the *adivasi* men, who turn their alienation into violence against the women (Chatterjee 2001, 283–84). This violence against women, both inside the household and in the form of social violence (rape, witchcraft accusations, and hunts), give the men in the community a sense of control over the alienation they experience as wage workers in the tea plantations. In this sense, the witchcraft accusations are manifestations of conflict between the *adivasi* migrant workers and the management.

But does violence over women restore masculinity and bring order back to the *adivasi* men? Violence is often a means to disrupt order (riots, genocides), and it is often the beginning of anomie. However, in the context of witch hunts, the violence against the accused woman is symbolic: it gets rid of the plague that is responsible for the misery. Violence can be both disruptive (from the point of the planters, police, and the non-*adivasi* community) and restitutive (justice for the wronged, in this case the *adivasi* community). Through the use of rumor and the strength of *haria*, the *adivasi* workers sees the *dain* as an image of his misery—an image that can be shamed and destroyed, thereby restoring to the *adivasi* man his honor. In the following section of this chapter, I present the punishments for the *dain*.

# Punishments

## Clippings from Local Newspapers in West Bengal

### *Clipping 1:*

> Lakshmi Murmu, a 22-year-old widow, was locked up in a room by fellow villagers. The villagers tried to set the room on fire because they believed that she was a witch. Police said she had been staying with her parents at Bohar Mandirtala village near Memari, about 90 km from Calcutta, ever since her husband died four years ago. On Thursday, a *janguru* told Lakshmi's uncle

Lippo that his daughter Pushpa, 17, was suffering from mental derangement because of her cousin's (Lakshmi) influence. "She is a witch, she should be driven out," the *janguru* pronounced. The day after the verdict, Lippo, accompanied by seven-eight others locked her up, beat her and tried to set the room on fire. Lakshmi, however managed to flee the room and finally reach her sister Sefali's house in Bhatar, 50 km away. ("Witch Widow Punished," *The Telegraph* (Kolkata), December 7, 2005.)

## *Clipping 2:*

A day after watching a family of five being beheaded in accordance with a kangaroo court's decision, workers of Dil-dal tea estate organized their funeral and celebrated what they believed was the end of witchcraft in the area. The bodies of Amir Munda, 60, and four of his children were burned on a single pyre on the banks of the river. There was hardly any sign of remorse on the faces of the 150-odd people who witnessed the last rites of the family around 3.30 pm. Some of the slain Mundas' relatives were present at the funeral, but remained tight-lipped over the public beheading. Their stoicism was not surprising, given the surcharged atmosphere. The prime accused told interrogators they were convinced that killing Amir and his children was the "right step" to ensure the safety of their community. Sources said the killers actually rued the fact that they were forced to spare Amir's pregnant wife Terosi, his daughter-in-law Mukta and his three grandchildren—Bhola, Bhoni and Pappu. The surviving members of the family are believed to be in hiding. ("Family Killed for Witchcraft," *The Statesman* (Kolkata), March 19, 2006.)

## *Clipping 3:*

A woman was arrested for branding another a witch. The arrest followed after Chandmoni Lohar of Bhatpara tea estate of the Kalchini block, 48 km from here, filed a case at the additional chief judicial magistrate's court on April 11. A couple of weeks ago, she had lodged an FIR with Kalchini police against five persons. Being branded a witch, Chandmoni was beaten up by a few villagers, who suspected that she was behind a matchmaking, which they disapproved of. When Sanjoy Singh of the estate married Sumitra Lohar, the latter's family thought it was Chandmoni's doing and decided to teach her a lesson. Sumitra's brother Shibu, his wife Kamala and three of his relatives went to her home and beat her up, kicking her and hitting her with brickbats, a villager said. The police rescued and later admitted her to the Latabari health centre, the villager added.

Chandmoni is yet to get over the trauma. I am staying at a relative's place and scared to go home, since Shibu and others are still threatening me, she said. Her daughter expressed unhappiness over alleged police inaction. Bhashkar Mukherjee, sub divisional police officer, Alipurduar, however, said: "We started a case before the second was filed in court. We have also arrested one of the accused persons. The rest are still absconding." ("Arrest over Witch Hunt," *The Telegraph* (Kolkata), April 13, 2006.)

The above quotes from local newspapers suggest a variety of punishments for the witch. Sometime the punishment is administered by the family of the accused (Clippings 1 and 3), and often it is administered by an entire village (Clipping 2). The belief in the witch is so strong that sometimes the family members of the accused woman become mere spectators to the events. As Clipping 2 and previous quotes in sections before this suggest, the relatives are threatened with death by the villagers, who think that they are doing the "right thing."

Beheadings and beatings that lead to murder are two of the common punishments for the witch. Sometimes the punishments involve rape, but this typically occurs in cases where the accusation is preceded by other motives on the part of the accuser. In other words, rape is not a common punishment in the surprise attack category of witch hunts, although rape can be a form of punishment in the calculated attack category. For example, in a case reported in the police archives, the accusers murdered the entire family of the accused woman, including her husband and children. One of her daughters was not present in the house at the time of the murder. The accusers (all of them men) waited for her and took turns in raping her after she came back. The accusers had a long-standing conflict with the accused witch and her family. Rape was thus used as a form of revenge against the other party instead of as a form of punishment against the witch.

Dulari, whose story is discussed in detail in chapter 6, narrates how her accusers raped her.

> Then the fights started [between her husband and his friend]. It continued for a month. They [her husband's friend and his wife] used to threaten us . . . told me all the time, "I will cut you, drink your blood, eat your flesh, burn your house." They did not talk to us anymore, used to hurl abuses at us. Then one day I was alone in my house. He threatened me [sexually]. I told him that I will go and complain to his wife. He then attacked me brutally inside my house. His wife stood outside and watched it all. And he . . . what do I say.

Dulari was extremely upset during this conversation and had difficulty recollecting the incident. The rape had shamed her so much that she could not call the incident "rape." She was traumatized by the entire incident and was in shock. To Dulari, the consent of the wife in her husband's act of raping her was a sign of betrayal.

Basanti relates her sexual assault: "Lekha and his friends came over to my house with a kukri. I locked the door to my room and waited in fear. Lekha broke the doors and windows at my house." She continues: "I pleaded with him to spare me. But he did not listen. He said I was a *daini* who had eaten his child." Lekha entered her room and tried to rape Basanti, who was pregnant with her son at the time. She talks about the reaction of the villagers during her attempted rape.

> There were a lot of people who had gathered outside my house. No one said a thing. Everyone was scared. Nobody told me anything even after the incident [attempted rape]. I did not have any justice. I am very sad. But what can I do? I will be looked upon as "bad" by everyone after this incident. They will say that I have been punished because I am a *daini*.

Other gendered punishments against accused women involve stripping or tonsuring the head of the accused woman. In a case from the police archives, the accused witch was "shamed" in front of the village. "Her head was tonsured; her face was covered in soot. She was then paraded naked all over the village." In this case, as is typical in the cases of rape, the dignity of the women victims (accused witches) was taken away by the village as a form of punishment. The woman is made to feel powerless through these punishments. Sometimes the accused woman is publicly shamed through rituals. In an incident in a tea plantation not far from the city of Jalpaiguri, a suspected witch was forced by the entire village to confess to witchcraft. After her confession, the villagers made the women conduct death rituals for her living parents. The death rituals signaled the triumph of the villagers over the witch emotionally, in a society where death is the most feared outcome for individuals.

Social isolation and fines are forms of punishments against accused women that seem relatively lenient compared with the horrific nature of the violence in the previous examples. Here, the punishment for the witch is decided either by the accusers' family (surprise attack) or by villagers through the village council (calculated attack). In cases of village meetings or trials, the accused witch might be given a chance to defend herself. In most cases, she ends up confessing because of threats on her life, and her punishment could be anything from severe beatings leading to murder to fines and other monetary compensation for the family of the accusers. In some incidents, the witch pays for the rituals that the *janguru* conducts to "tame" the witch. For instance Mita, a 27-year-old female *adivasi*, "had to pay two thousand rupees (approximately $40) for the feasting. I borrowed money to pay for it . . . *haria*, meat, and rice."

For the police, such punishments (fines) against the accused women are considered to be relatively "harmless" and are treated with a dismissive attitude against the *adivasis* that often accompanies investigations on witchcraft accusations. This attitude is based on the wild image of the *adivasis*; they are expected to act in these ways. For instance, in one of the reports from the Jalpaiguri Police Archives, the report dismissed the witch hunt: "There was no witch hunt, but the identified witch had to pay a fine to the accuser. . . . Later she fled the village and never returned."

In other words, the justification for punishing the witch arises primarily out of a deep-rooted fear and hatred for the witch. The accused woman's body becomes the icon of misery in plantation life, in which emasculated *adivasi* men seek their revenge by shaming and humiliating the woman, thereby asserting control over their own lives. In the next subsection, I discuss in detail the witch hunt, which is the most fascinating of all punishments against the *dain*.

## The Witch Hunt

As previously discussed, not all punishments for the accused woman take the form of a witch hunt. A witch hunt takes place when two or more people are involved in a process of identifying and punishing the witch that involves mobilizing an entire community against the accused woman. The crucial part of the hunt is the phase where the accused woman is hunted by a group of people; that group could be any size—from from two people to a whole crowd. The main actors in the hunt are the accused, the accuser/accusers, the victim of the witch's evil eye, and the *janguru*. A witch hunt involves the following steps:

The first stage involves "the instigation for the witchcraft accusation and identification of the witch." As discussed in previous sections, the instigation for witch hunt can be anything from revenge over personal conflicts, illnesses, or diseases. The witch is identified in most cases with the help of the *janguru*. During this stage, the accused witch may or may not be aware of the accusations against her. If it is a surprise category of attack, then the accused is unaware of the accusations. The accuser, on the other hand, is aware of the witch's craft and her mischief, which most commonly is manifest in the form of illness.

At the second stage, a "whisper campaign" takes shape. This is a crucial phase because during this stage the accuser starts campaigning and gathering support in the village against the witch. There is a possibility of this stage being discrete, as evident in cases of "surprise attacks" in which the accused witches and their relatives are unaware of the oncoming attack. If the accused witch and her family are aware of the attacks, then she (and her family) may start facing social ostracism from the villagers. If the accused witch is fortunate, she may ask for help from the police during this time through written complaints.

The third stage involves a trial. Prior to the witch hunt, there may or may not be a trial. Trials are never held during surprise attacks on witches. If a trial is held prior to the hunt, then it can be of two types: formal and informal. In formal trials, the entire village becomes involved. The trial takes the form of a village meeting, with the *panchayat* and the *janguru* presiding. Both parties (accusers and accused) take part in the meeting, and the accused has some chance of a defense. In the informal trial, held either at the courtyard of a villager (usually in some relation to the accuser) or at the *janguru*'s house, the accused has little chance of a defense. It is during the trial that the punishment of the witch is decided, if she is proven guilty.

The trial is typically followed by a witch hunt. During the witch hunt, typically two or more individuals attack the accused and administer the punishment to the witch. Witch hunts involve some form of violence in the form of physical abuse on the accused witch. The abuse can involve mob beating, stripping, tonsuring, rape, and murder. For example, in the case in Central Dooars, when one of the women tried to escape, the mob hunted her down. They then dragged the

A shot of the tea bushes.

Women workers going home in the evening after a long day at the tea plantation.

A bamboo bridge on the road to Beech Tea Estate.

Crossing dry river beds; the area is flooded during monsoon season.

A *janguru* and his wife in the courtyard of their house. Both of them also worked at the plantation as labor.

An example of what a house looks like in the labor lines.

Local school destroyed in a recent storm in Chandmoni.

The same school, now used to store firewood.

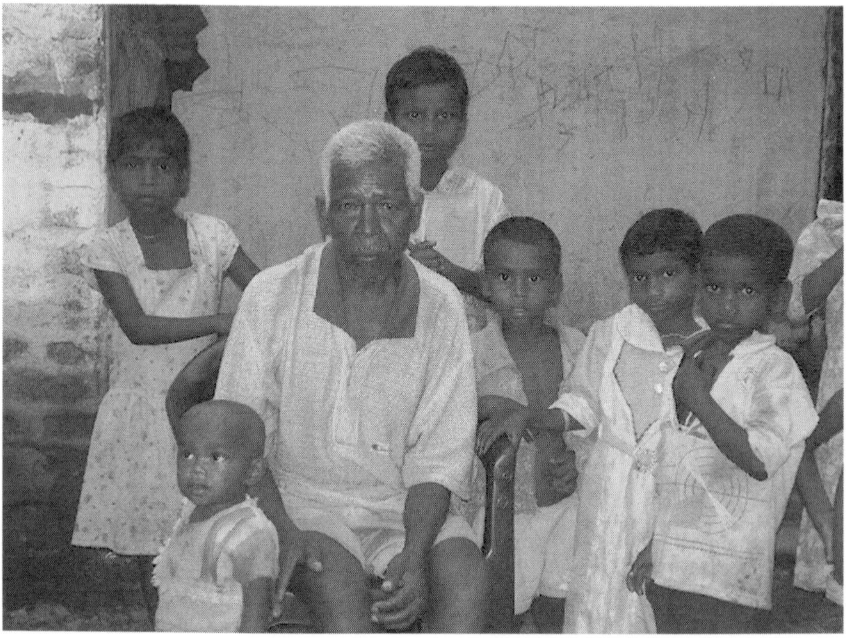

Husband of one of the victims in the Chandmoni witch hunt incident.

Savitri's son and daughter in law, in front of their home in Hatimtala, Central Dooars.

Photograph of Ramani, an accused witch who wants her story told.

A microcredit meeting on a Sunday afternoon at a school playground.

two women into the house of the accusers and beat them. After beating them, they pushed the two women down a high drain and hurled big stones at them until they died.

The following table outlines the steps in a witch hunt, as presented in the four case studies discussed in this book.

TABLE 5.1: Steps in a witch hunt

| Steps in a Witch Hunt | Calculated Hunts | | Random Hunts | |
|---|---|---|---|---|
| | Basanti's case | Dulari's case | Chandmoni case | Central Dooars |
| Instigation | Yes | Yes | Yes | Yes |
| Whisper | Yes | Yes | No | No |
| Trial | Yes | Yes | Yes | No |
| Witch hunt | Yes | Yes | Yes | Yes |

The steps discussed in the witch hunt are ideal types, and not all incidents of witch hunts involve all the steps. The steps are also not chronological and may be combined with one another. These steps are typical in both categories of witch hunts. In surprise attacks, steps one and two, which involve instigations, identifications, and whisper campaign, are characteristic prior to the witch hunt. In calculated attacks, all four steps take place. One interesting feature in the steps that are common to both categories of hunts is the awareness or lack of awareness of the accused with respect to the instigation and the whisper campaign against her. In calculated attacks, during both the steps, the accused is aware of the accusations and the whisper campaign.

## The Real Victims of Witch Hunts

The trauma experienced by the victims of witch hunts, the accused women, is extreme; and often the ordeal does not end with the witch hunt. The psychological scars of the horrific incident stays with the living accused women and their relatives long after. Bhutiya, whose mother-in-law was dragged out of the house on accusation of witchcraft recounts the ordeal:

> *Buria* kept on saying—let me go. I do not know anything. I did not do anything . . . but they did not listen to her. You know she had just eaten a fistful of rice... but they hit her . . . hit her a lot.

Bhutiya could not get over the trauma of her mother-in-law's ordeal or how the helpless old woman was dragged from her hut, just when she had started eating her dinner. Speaking in anger, Bhutiya vowed: "I will not leave them [meaning the accusers]. After they get out of jail, *ami kukri diyeh kuchi kuchi korey katbo* [meaning that she will cut them into pieces with a knife]." The accusers, according to Bhutiya, were threatening her and her family from prison. "After we get out we will see you," they told her. Bhutiya was both very scared and angry at the events.

Chandrani, an accused witch who escaped from her attackers, is yet to get over the trauma. "I am staying at a relative's place and scared to go home, since Shibu [accuser] and others are still threatening me," she said. Her daughter expressed unhappiness over alleged police inaction. The reaction of the police to her plight was insensitive, and frustrating. Their replies to the queries were predictable and revealed an attitude of dismissal as well as a lack of interest in pursuing the culprits. To them, *adivasis* and witchcraft accusations are way of life: "We started a case before the second was filed in court. We have also arrested one of the accused persons. The rest are still absconding."

Similarly, Basanti expresses her fear of returning to her husband's village, despite having a job, which is a scare resource in a community where unemployment is high, waiting for her (Chatterjee 2001, 277):

> I am scared about my security. My ordeal is . . . they trapped me. I will give up my life but I will never go back to the village. I am very angry . . . very angry and sad (*amar khub raag acchey. . . . Raaag oh dukh sobh acchey*).

To escape from witchcraft accusations, many living victims of witch hunts convert to Christianity, thinking that conversion will help them shed the wild image and thus escape the accusations. Both Dulari and Basanti's families converted to Christianity to escape the accusations. Interviews with both families reveal the level of commitment towards their new identity, such as attending Sunday mass at the local village church. However, the witchcraft accusations against them continue, despite their new image. The local NGO (NBPDC) has established shelter homes where victims of witch hunts can have temporary accommodations. But, as the name suggests, these are temporary solutions. The victims often return to their villages after their stay, and they encounter the daily accusations and stresses once again. Basanti was provided shelter in such a home after she escaped to Mourighat. Within a few weeks of her stay, Basanti decided to move back to her mother's home. The shelter did not have provision to keep children, and Basanti was separated from her daughter. Unable to adjust to the life of the shelter, Basanti missed her daughter and decided to go back to Mourighat, where the threats continue.

# Notes

1. A number of my participants remarked how Christian *adivasis* were progressive compared with non converted *adivasis*. They commented that their houses were cleaner, their children were better educated, and they had better paying jobs in the plantations. However, I did not come across evidence in my study that confirmed their statements. I did find the social and economic conditions of all *adivasi* migrant workers in the plantations very similar.

2. Since Alfred was a permanent worker in the plantation, his nearest kin, meaning his wife, would get his job on grounds of compensation.

3. This is a common accusation also among the non-*adivasi* population. In Bengali, the term "*swami kheko*" or "one who has devoured her husband" is used against married women by their in-laws.

4. *Kharap* means "bad," and *bath* translates as "talk." It means bad language that consists of curses and abuses.

# Chapter 6

# Tea Plantation Politics, Oppression, and Protest

## Dulari's Story

Mourighat is often referred as the *dainir boshobash*, or the "area where the witches live," by locals. At the time of my fieldwork, there were already 12 cases of witch hunts for that year, according to reports of the NBPDC. My local contact in the area encouraged me to meet Dulari (a female *adivasi* migrant worker in her late twenties or early thirties), who was an accused witch. Dulari came with her husband to meet me on a Sunday, after attending church. Her family had recently converted to Christianity.

Dulari's story of witchcraft accusations had begun more than a decade earlier, when her neighbor, Shankar, accused her of murdering his pregnant wife by using witchcraft. Shankar's wife had complications during her pregnancy, and the local *janguru* was unable to cure her. At the time, the *janguru* suggested that Shankar should conduct a ritual to detect the cause behind the complications. After an entire day of rituals that accompanied offerings of rice, hibiscus flower, *haria*, and animal sacrifice, the *janguru* informed Shankar that a "dark woman" near his house was causing the trouble. Later that evening, when Shankar came back home, he discovered that his wife was already dead.

After a few days following the death of his wife, the distraught man who had been drinking *haria* to forget his misery, came over to the house of Dulari at nine in the evening and threatened to kill her with his kukri. Later that week, Shankar was arrested by the police on charges of assault, and he was quickly released on bail. The village *panchayat* met, and Shankar confessed his assault against Dulari on suspicion of witchcraft. He cited his recent grief of his wife's passing and his recent drinking as factors that had made him threaten Dulari. He promised in front of the villagers never to attack Dulari again.

Six months later, Dulari was again accused of practicing witchcraft. This time the accuser was Otno Oraon, another villager from the same plantation. Otno had an infected wound in his hand that refused to heal. He threatened to kill Dulari and chop her into pieces if his wound did not heal. From this time onwards, all the illnesses in the village were blamed on Dulari, and she slowly came to be known as "*dain* Dulari." The third accusation against Dulari happened a few days later, when another *adivasi* worker had a fever that lasted over a week. By this time, all illnesses and daily misfortunes were being blamed on Dulari's witchcraft. Growing increasingly tired and being threatened by the constant accusations, Dulari offered to "to take an oath before the goddess Kali" to prove her innocence. However, Dulari's offer was met with resistance by the rest of village, because the Goddess Kali,[1] the source of power for the dark forces and witches, was a "natural" ally of the *dain* Dulari. When the *adivasi* worker got well after a few days, the accusations against Dulari died out, and she was able to get back into her normal life as a worker in the plantation.

For a few years, after the third accusation against her, Dulari did lead a normal life. She made a few friends in the village, and among those was the family of Jaggu Oraon. Jaggu Oraon and his family became so close to Dulari that she was beginning to contemplate moving closer to their family. Dulari's husband had purchased a small piece of land very near Jaggu's house, and Dulari wanted to build a house on that plot. However, when they decided to go ahead with the plans, Dulari and her husband discovered that Jaggu had taken over the land illegally. Because neither Dulari nor her husband was able to read or write, Jaggu convinced them to put their thumbprints on papers they thought were for some other cause. In this way, Jaggu transferred the ownership of the land to himself. Troubles started between the two families.

Soon after, Dulari found out that two of her banana trees were cut into pieces. When she confronted Jaggu and his wife, they did not deny they had done it, and the couple threatened Dulari with the same fate. The families, which had once been friends, were now enemies. The former friends fought at any pretext, and relations became very bitter.

One evening, Jaggu had organized a feast at his house, where there was plenty of goat meat to eat and *haria* to drink for everyone. Dulari, who was returning to her home after fetching water, met Jaggu's wife at the village well. A heated argument between the women followed, and Jaggu's wife hit Dulari and fled home. Later that evening, a group of five men, including Jaggu, attacked Dulari at her home and raped her continuously for the next hour. Dulari's husband was not at home at the time, and Jaggu's wife accompanied the men.

Dulari and her husband filed a complaint with the *panchayat*, and a meeting was held. The *panchayat* asked Dulari to forget the incident and advised them to continue to live peacefully in the village. A few days following her complaint, Dulari was again gang-raped by the same group of men, as revenge against her complaints to the *panchayat*. Dulari went through a lot of trauma, and this time some local activists came to her aid. With their help, Dulari filed a case in the local police station and court. However, to date no legal action has been taken against her rapists due to lack of "sufficient evidence." Dulari's rapists are "friendly" with the local labor union, and the entire village ostracized Dulari and her family. Women refused to talk to her, and Dulari's children were called *dainir baccha*, meaning children of the witch, everywhere they went.

Two months after her second rape, a fifth accusation of witchcraft was made against Dulari. An *adivasi* woman, who was ailing for some time, died in the village. A few days after her death, Dulari, who was coming back home for lunch from the plantation, was stopped by the woman's husband Ramdar. When Dulari came closer to Ramdar, he threw chili power in her eyes and tried to slit her throat. Dulari managed to cry out for help, and a few passersby came to her rescue. Ramdar fled the village, and later the police arrested his father, as Ramdar was on the run. He was let off a few days later after a bail of 300 rupees (five dollars).

Today, Dulari continues to live in the same village and in fear of accusations. Unable to leave her permanent job in the plantation, her husband and she have very few options of finding work elsewhere. Her rapists have joined hands with her accusers and have managed to successfully label her a witch. Not a week passes when Dulari is not accused of witchcraft.

## Comments on Dulari's Accusations and Some Questions

Dulari's case of witchcraft accusations is both typical and unique. Her story is unique in the sense that she is perhaps the only woman I interviewed who had experienced multiple rape and witchcraft accusations. The location of Dulari's village is also unique in the district of Jalpaiguri. This area is located in Jalpaiguri Sadar, a subdistrict where NBPDC had been able to successfully launch an anti-witch-hunt campaign among the *adivasi* migrant workers (see Chakravarty and Chaudhuri 2012 for details on the campaign and strategies for success). Thus, this is also a case where the *panchayat* and the police were involved as an attempt to dissolve the accusations against Dulari. However, despite some initial attempts made by the *panchayat* and the police to prevent the accusations against Dulari and to gather support from the rest of the villagers, her complaints to the *panchayat* made the threats against her worsen; and she was gang-raped multiple times. Here I would like to make two comments: the first, on Dulari's treatment of rape (both by her, the victim, and by others) and the second, on how Jaggu was successful in reinstating the *dain* label on Dulari. Both comments are connected to the politics of patronage in the plantation.

Rape is treated by the *adivasi* migrant workers in Jalpaiguri as a "secret knowledge shared between women . . . shamed into registers of public silence."

Chatterjee (2001) observes a striking contradiction that plays out gender, class, and ethnic inequalities in the plantation villages. She illustrates this contradiction by contrasting the lack of public discourse in a case of a rape of a lone *adivasi* woman by a stranger or a manager with a case in which the same *adivasi* community publicly whipped a rapist as punishment. Because the alleged rapist was not fired from his job, despite complaining to his superiors at the plantation, the community took justice into its own hands. In one case Chatterjee (2001) observes social silence, while in another she observes public shaming; both are enacted by the same *adivasi* community against the rape of an *adivasi* woman (235–37). In the first case, the perpetrator was a manager (a clear representative of power); in the second case, a fellow *adivasi* was merely rebuked by his superiors and allowed to continue his work as a watchman in the plantation. In both cases, the rape of the *adivasi* woman is trivialized. The community's reaction to the rape is a re-creation of the politics of patronage (by the management over the *adivasi* migrant workers) within the power and authority of the *adivasi* migrant worker villagers (236). Dulari was ashamed of her experience of rape, and she did not want to go to the police to register a complaint against her rapists. Recounting the ordeal of rape before strange policemen is traumatic for women, because most of these police stations do not have female constables. Further, stereotypes of *adivasi* women as having "less sexual morals" compared with mainstream Hindu women would have placed the burden of substantiating rape on her. In a culture where political officials react to the rape of urban educated women with intimations that the victims' provocations had some part to play in the rape,[2] Dulari's pursuit of justice through the police and the law would have been utopian. "To forget and move on" was the practical advice that the *panchayat* gave Dulari.

The descriptions of the accused women, both by themselves and by the accusers, as being dark (for example, Dulari, Bhagawan's description of why Vishnu accused his neighbor, and Ramani's own reflection as to why her neighbors targeted her as a *dain*) reveal the civilized versus *jungli* duality that is at the heart of the tea plantation social order and that is crucial to its sustenance. Dark skin color is also used to describe the *adivasis* as a contrast to the anglicized perception of upper castes bodies of the managers and planters as white. These images have roots in their colonial heritage. The management's and owners' self-images of superiority serve to rationalize their ruling over and civilizing of the inferior *jungli adivasi* bodies. The gendered nature of the politics of patronage is reflected in the image of the *adivasi* woman, whose thoughts are inferior to the planters, managers, and other *adivasi* men, and who is trapped within the "cycles of her dark body" (Chatterjee 2001, 169–71).

My second comment about how Jaggu was able to mobilize support against Dulari reveals the complex nature of the politics of patronage within the plantation. The plantation owners and management are the invisible forces of authority in the daily life of the labor lines. They operate through social distance and strict social hierarchy. Union leaders, the postcolonial replacement for the garden *sardars* in the tea plantations, serve as a powerful group of subpatronage (143–

46). For the *adivasi* migrant workers, the union leaders are the life source who decide the distribution of the permanent and temporary jobs within the plantation and negotiate with the owners for wage raises. Union leaders are the *adivasis*' only link to the plantation owners, and Jaggu's proximity to this group helped in establishing the *dain* label on Dulari and in alienating her from the rest of the village.

## Alienation, Ostracism, and Witchcraft Accusations: A Story of Two Classes

The story of witch hunts is one of oppression and conflict. It is a story of conflict between men and women, workers and management, and the dominant mainstream non-*adivasi* community and the *adivasis*. In this chapter, I present the overall context of the politics of witchcraft accusations and witch hunts. In seeking to explain why the witch hunts were prevalent among the migrant *adivasi* workers of the plantation, I take a detailed look at the complex labor-management relationship within the plantation and the class-based divisions that exist within the industry and beyond. I trace how the local-level conflicts that result in witchcraft accusations leading to a witch hunt have their roots in the complex network of relationships between the workers and the planters.

I argue that witch hunts among the *adivasi* migrant workers of Jalpaiguri are the products of alienation experienced by the workers within a capitalist mode of production. They are not a result of the *adivasis*' superstitious primitive thinking, as is often mistakenly believed by others, but a result of the oppression protest discourse against the alienation experienced as wage laborers within the plantation economy. In other words, I argue that witchcraft accusations and the resulting witch hunts are reactions of this community to an economy that is as alien to them as the resulting impacts (of wage economy) on the workers' daily lives. I devote this chapter to explaining how the alienation results in a witch hunt.

Karl Marx, in reference to the alienation experienced by the workers in the capitalist system, wrote that the increase in the worker's alienation is directly related to the increase in wealth for the capitalists. This alienation is necessary in a system where all human relationships are reduced to their profit utility, and this makes them less than men. In other words, the alienation of the worker is not just an outcome of the capitalist system; it is a necessary condition for increasing capital and profit. In this system of production, the worker is not just isolated from the product that he produces; he is isolated from the very process of production, from his relationships to others in the community, and from his species being (Giddens 1971; Marx 2005). So, how does this alienation work through witchcraft accusations among the *adivasi* migrant workers? I use Michael Taussig's (1980) work to explain the connections between *dain*, worker alienation, and plantation politics.

In a seminal work on the significance of the Devil in folklores among the plantation workers in South America, Michael Taussig (1980) argues that the Devil is a fitting symbol of alienation experienced by the local peasants as they enter the ranks of proletariat. The Devil came to represent the tensions in the conquest and history of imperialism, a system that caused men to barter their souls for the Devil's commodities, which are represented as the evils of wealth. This observation of wealth being in alliance with evil has also been observed by Parish (2005) writing about the African immigrants living in United Kingdom. There, a gambler (who was originally from central Africa) who is feeling guilty about his earnings and new fortune is terrified that the witch and his other relatives might feel that they have been cheated. Here, witches are described as greedy women who are envious of people's wealth (Taussig 1980, 105, 107). Human souls cannot be bought or sold, yet Taussig argues that certain historical conditions (meaning market economies) create conditions where, alongside poverty and ethical laws, wealth and economic laws prevail. "Production, not man, is the aim of the economy, and commodities rule their creators" (xi–xii). Further describing folk societies, Taussig writes that such societies have an organic interconnection with the mind and hand, where the world of magic and enchantment is as intensely human as the other relations that they enter into. With the entrance of commodity production through capitalism, this organic interconnection is challenged. As a result, the soul either becomes a commodity or becomes a deeply alienated and disenchanted spirit. Until the complete assimilation of the capitalist spirit takes place in these communities, capitalism will be interpreted with "pre-capitalist" (devil) meanings (11). Taussig suggests that devil beliefs emerge during sensitive periods in human history to mediate "two radically distinct ways of apprehending or evaluating the world of persons and the world of things" (17–18). The Devil represents not only the misery that the new plantations and mines symbolize but also the deliberation of the peasant turned wage workers in these new plantations and mines. These workers view the market economy to be a distortion of the principles of reciprocity that were enforced in their own peasant communities by supernatural beings' mystical sanctions. The Devil in these mines and sugarcane plantations reflects a self-conscious allegiance to the worker precapitalist peasant background that views the wage economy as exploitative, destructive, and unnatural (37–38). It represents a class struggle in the classic Marxian sense.

The structure of the Jalpaiguri tea plantation very much resembles the capitalist system of production that Marx described and that Taussig used to describe the production at the South American mines and sugar plantations. Additionally, the Jalpaiguri tea plantations have the culture of patronage that places the management class at the top of the pyramid of social stratification and the *adivasi* migrant workers at the bottom of this hierarchy. This pyramidal structure serves two functions. One, it helps keep the working class in place by forming this boundary of seclusion around the workers, hidden through coercion that was initially administered through the *sardars*, and by the union leaders of the gardens today. The union leaders have been correctly described by Chatterjee (2001) as the postcolonial version of the *sardars*. She describes the union leaders as descendents, both metaphorically and in reality, of the notorious garden *sardars*, who were instrumental in keeping the *adivasi* migrant workers isolated in the colonial times. The *sardar* controlled the workers for the planters, initially by bringing them from the *adivasi* homelands to the plantations. They later on took on a subpatronage role within the plantation economy. The workers paid a commission to the *sardar* to ensure their safety of work and security within the plantations. The patronage later changed to "payoffs" for union leaders for acquiring a job in the plantations, in which constant unemployment by an ailing industry is a reality. The trade union leaders thrive on a black market economy in which bribing is almost necessary to get any work done (Chatterjee 2001, 6, 144–49). I will explain how the alienation and exploitation of the *adivasi* worker operates by looking at the terms of employment, wages, and the control of management through the union leaders.

The plantation system further continues the exploitation of workers by employing temporary or casual (*bigha* or *faltu*) workers instead of permanent workers to do the bulk of the work during peak seasons in the plantations. Here, the exploitation operates in two ways. First, these temporary workers are employed on a 60-day basis only, because employing them beyond that period of time would require the owners to pay benefits. The *bigha* workers are further contracted for a 10-day cycle when the peak seasons are at its best. This practice results in the mass employment of temporary workers compared with permanent workers, and it serves to keep wages down and employment scarce in the plantations. This is most beneficial for the plantation management. Second, the employment of the *bigha* workers is further conditional on a family employment situation for *adivasi* migrant workers (how many permanent workers are employed within the family), benevolence of the union leader, and the assessment of need (implying appropriation of maximum profit) by the managers (Chatterjee 2001, 191–92). The employment of one-third temporary workers in the plantations, and the employment of this casual labor force from the households of permanent workers, has resulted in the availability of a large pool of unemployed labor and created an advantageous situation for the plantation owners (Bhowmik 2011, 246–47).

Chatterjee and Bhowmik's arguments on the use of temporary workers in the tea plantations for profit maximization is also observed in the Cauca Valley sugar plantations, where contractual labor consists of one-third of the total workforce. The motivations for employing contractual labor are similar: lower than average wages are required to hire permanent workers, and the payment of benefits can be avoided. Further, this contractual system brings in a time-work system of payment, intensifies labor, and creates competition between workers for employment. This leads to a vicious cycle in which the contracting system appears to be appealing to the workers (Taussig 1980, 84). The debates and conflict over daily wages continue even today in the Jalpaiguri plantations, and the strategic manipulation of such demands by the plantation management class towards low-wage but casual labor versus higher-wage labor lowers the chances of employment arguments and ensures that the exploitation of the workers continues (see Bhowmik 2011 for details on the wage negotiation conflicts and outcomes in the current times in Jalpaiguri).

The isolation and marginalization of the plantations *adivasi* workers, a necessary condition for their alienation, was strategized by the very foundations on which the tea plantations in Jalpaiguri operate. Limited access to education and restrictions on alternative occupations as a result of lack of access to education were deliberate on the part of the plantation owners. For instance, most plantations have a school up to the fourth grade. However, the lack of school supplies and teachers, and the permanent lack of resources that have existed for decades (both from the Government and from the plantations) towards education for worker's children have had an effect. Second, in the initial years following the set-up of the plantations, the forest departments in Jalpaiguri tried to recruit the *adivasi* workers for forestry jobs. However, efforts to employ *adivasis* in places other than the tea plantations of Jalpaiguri were met with strong resistance by the planters' associations. The planters' associations claimed that these migrant workers should only work in the plantations because their migration had cost the planters substantial money (Bhowmik 2011, 245–46). Third, today within the plantation workforce culture, even among the workers, other groups (such as the *Nepalis*, *Totos*, and *Bhumiputras*) demonstrate a culture of superiority over the *adivasi* migrant workers. These groups are employed as watchmen, guards, and machine operators in the tea-processing factories; and they are also the ones who end up being union leaders. As Chatterjee (2011) argues, because patriarchies rest within patriarchies, the culture of patronage and isolation, together with continuing stereotypes of *adivasis* as "wild," along with their migrant status (in a land that has its own indigenous "tribes"), contributes to the marginalization and isolation of the migrant workers.

Thus, in a system in which isolation is the biggest weapon, the trade union leaders use their powers to further isolate the workers from the planters. In most cases, wage negotiations, conflict arbitration, and jobs are fiercely controlled by the union leaders, and the workers almost always have to come to these leaders if there are problems in wages and employment. This is a powerful nexus of patronage and subpatronage, both of which are necessary in maintaining the pyramid of authority over the *adivasi* migrant workers. Within this nexus, the position of the worker is merely that of a cog in the wheels of production. Workers have almost no rights, because trade unions in the region are mostly ineffective (and wage negotiations through the trade unions have historically been largely ineffective; see Bhowmik 2011 and Talwar, Chakraborty, and Biswas 2005), Thus, all avenues of protest against work conditions are closed off to the *adivasi* workers.

The pyramidal structure of the plantations also alienates the *adivasi* migrant worker, according to Marx's definition of the term "alienation." The migrant workers are not only alienated from the community and fellow workers; they are also alienated from the product (tea) and the process of production. This alienation is accomplished through the plantation owners' careful wage employment strategies, which are implemented by the union leaders. The migrant workers have only one identity: that of workers who can easily be displaced and replenished. Coercion, patronage, and exploitation exist hand in hand in the plantation, where the wages are controlled by the patrons and the subpatrons. In a system where social mobility of these *adivasi* migrant workers is almost nonexistent and where geographical mobility is not encouraged, the job at the plantation almost represents a fetish. It is a fetish that is both hopeless and perhaps the only hope the workers have in attempting to make ends meet. Added to the misery of these workers is the crisis in the Indian tea industry that began 10 years ago. Wrangling over the control of the commodity chain in the tea industry has led to the closure of many plantations in the region and subsequent unemployment for the *adivasi* migrant workers. Starvation deaths are common in closed plantations, and reports of these incidents are mostly ignored in the media (Chatterjee 2008, 499). The story of these workers is one of alienation, neglect, and dismissal. It's a story that is echoed in the witchcraft accusations and witch hunts. I now turn to the significance of the *dain* in the *adivasis*' everyday life in the plantation.

The *dain* has always existed in the spiritual life of the *adivasis*. It can be traced back to well before *adivasis*' migration to the plantations of Jalpaiguri and the change of their status from peasant agricultural workers to landless wage earners. Within the confines of the plantation, the familiar symbol of all things associated with misfortune, the *dain*, took on a new role. The Devil in the sugar plantations of South America was in direct confrontation with the capitalism that was responsible for the alienation of the workers. In Jalpaiguri, the tight hold of the trade unions, along with the dependency of the *adivasi* laborers to the plantations, prevents the group from direct conflict with the management. Trapped in a system in which the exploitation is hidden behind benevolence and patronage, the *adivasi* turns to the old enemy closer to home: the *dain*. The *dain* has always represented malevolent powers, and the constant lack of resources in the *adivasis*' lives, the persistent unemployment, lower wages, illness, and anything that was opposite of prosperity began to be attributed to the work of the *dain*. *Adivasi* women and the *dain* have an old bond. Much has been written about the alliance of women and witches in the *adivasi* community (see chapters three and five) and the further devaluation of the *adivasi* women in the plantation economy that was accomplished by the planters through lower wages, fetishization of their bodies, and violence against the women. This made them the natural icon of the *dain* in real life. *Adivasi* women are in competition with *adivasi* men over work in the plantations (Bhowmik 2011; Chatterjee 2001), and one hears of the constant arguments over the ownership of the women's wages by the men in the family. The conflicts over the control of women's wages are not unique to the *adivasi*; they are a reality in all cultures, tied to gender-based social rules and often demonstrated through violence against women. For the *adivasi* migrant workers, the misery of their life conditions takes on a new meaning through the *dain*, because they take control over their lives only through the *dain's* demise.

Scholars in the past have made connections between witch hunts and communities that are witnessing tremendous impoverishment. For instance, Federici (2010) writes that regions in India that have encountered some of the more intense witchcraft accusations (such as Bihar, Jharkhand, Chattisgarh, Andhra Pradesh) are areas that have suffered.

> [These regions] have witnessed a tremendous impoverishment of the peasantry during the past decades, with thousands of farmers committing suicide, mostly as a consequence of the fall in the price of cotton and other agricultural products triggered by the liberalization of imports in the region. They are also sites of conflict between the government troops and the Naxalites . . . . For the moment, we can only speculate about the economic interests and deals that may be hiding behind many murders now attributed to tribalism (Federici 2010, 18).

Going back to Dulari's case, there were two pressing observations in the entire episode of witchcraft accusations: first, the apparent ease by which Dulari's rapists could mobilize support against her and second, the lack of any justice for Dulari. Both of these observations could be tied to the alienation experienced by the *adivasi* migration worker community in the tea plantation. Also related to these observations is the conflict over resources during witch hunts.[3] In the following subsections, I will elaborate on the connections between alienation and witchcraft accusations (through the use of data from this study), and I will present the implications of these connections for the oppression-protest discourse.

## Mobilizing Support During a Witch Hunt

In almost all incidents of witch hunts in Jalpaiguri, gathering support against the witch was often both partially planned and partially voluntary. While some of the villagers were persuaded to participate in the witch hunt through alcohol or by being paid small sums of money (as little as 50 rupees or one dollar), the bulk of the villagers joined without needing much persuasion and with almost no transaction. In all cases, gossip played a crucial role. Stories of the *dain* in the community exist through gossip that forms networks through which the fears and challenges are transmitted. As Stewart and Strathern (2003) have argued, rumors about the *dain* enter at the very early stages of social stress in the plantation through networks of gossip, and rumors become instrumental in identifying the witch who is responsible for the evil. Conflict is thus produced and spread through gossip, resulting in witchcraft accusations. This mobilization of public support is an important step during witch hunts. Dulari describes the gossip against her: "The women in the village were all a part of the conspiracy behind my continued accusations. They supported their men." She continues, referring to her rape:

> They wanted it to happen. They gave their *shai* [consent] . . . . We all work together in the tea garden. But they did not walk with me to work. They did not talk to me . . . . They did not let my son and daughter play with their children. They drive my children away. They say—*jao jao, dainir baccha. dainir baccha khelbi nah.*[4] They said that my children will eat and chew their children, and warned their children not to play with my children as they will fall ill. I am so sad . . . they are children after all [*amar monner khub kosto. Ora to baccha*].

Dulari was portrayed as the blood-thirsty *dain* who feasted on men, women, and children in the village, responsible for all the illness and deaths. Her rape was seen as a fitting punishment to achieve control over a *dain* who was perceived to have loose morals. The plantation in Mourighat was not closed, although the wages were not paid regularly. The labor union holds a lot of clout in this region, and Dulari's attackers were able to tap into this network to label her as a witch. The transfer of the blame for the misery in the plantation onto Dulari the *dain* was not difficult to comprehend for the rest of the villagers, because unemployment and infrequency of payment of wages, along with illness and misery, made life in this region very difficult. For the rest of the villagers, Dulari's victimization was necessary to soothe their brewing anger over the conditions in the plantations.

The transaction that takes place to attract the core group of supporters in the initial stages of the hunt is typically negotiated among relatives and friends of the accusers. For instance, Nepul, Benglu, and Sushil, in the Central Dooars case, served *haria* during a meeting at their home. The purpose of the meeting was to explain to their relatives why they were experiencing bad luck. Similarly the feast at Jaggu's house and the rape of Dulari that followed were not separate incidents. Though feast and the alcohol were used to buy consent to punish Dulari for witchcraft, support for the witch hunt was not hard to obtain in the community. This also explains why Dulai's rape was justified as necessary punishment.

Explaining how the support and consent to punish the *dain* was given, Hari, a friend of Benglu who was present at the meeting and who later participated in the witch hunt, narrates:

> We were all drinking. Benglu and all of us were very drunk. The drink made us very angry. When Benglu said that the two women were witches, we decided that we would have to do something . . . today Benglu's family is ill tomorrow the entire village will be ill because of these witches. From every household in the village the men joined us. Soon we became a group of thirty men. We went to Benglu's house where the rest were waiting. We went to the witch's houses to kill.

The plantations in Central Dooars were closed for more than six months at the time of the hunt. Additionally, this region is located in one of the most isolated areas in Jalpaiguri. During the monsoon, for three months, the region is virtually closed off from the rest of the district because of flash floods. Hari's comments here, and Sushil's comments in the previous chapter, expose the deep resentment and anger that is inside every *adivasi* migrant worker in the plantations: anger against the misery, and the frustrations of not being able to do something about it. Sushil's comments "we would have to do something" and his comment on the "*shaali*" (see chapter 5) reveal the urge of the community to take matters under their control.

Money, too, played a role in enticing some villagers to join. Gundur Oraon, a relative of one of accused women in the Central Dooars incident provided some details about how the village organized against the women and their families and convinced people who were initially reluctant to join the witch hunt:

> Sushil and his friends went around the village telling us that they had found out that Savitri and Padma were witches. Some of us tried to reason with the group and told him that they were very old ladies . . . they cannot do any harm. But they would not listen. We saw that the villagers were joining their group and their group was becoming larger. Some of these people initially were going along with the group to watch the fun . . . later those same people would throw stones at the old women. Others joined in because Sushil was promising them money that Benglu will pay. . . . They did not end up paying the money but there was a lot of alcohol. . . . The group met at Benglu's house, and by this time we had got the news that they were going to kill Savitri and Padma. I rushed to inform them but a large group of people were blocking my way. They all had Kukri and sticks. . . . I stayed in my house. . . . These men were all Sushil's friends.

A few points become evident from the above narratives. Even though alcohol and promises of money were made, most villagers joined in the witch hunt initially out of curiosity or to "watch the fun." Some (mainly relatives of victims) expressed discontent over the accusations, but their protests were dismissed by the others with threats. In the end, the entire village (barring a few who are related to the victims) participated in the hunt. While one can understand the support of those villagers who joined in with the promise of rewards, how does one explain the actions of the supporters who joined without any promise of rewards? After all, the threat of repercussions of homicide leading to imprisonment was a very high economic cost for the villagers. In previous incidents of witch hunts, the police, who often appeared long after the murder of the witch, would arrest everyone (irrespective of their involvement) in the village (see Chandmoni tea estate case details). Because the legal process works very slowly, innocent people would often be locked up for days and sometimes months before making bail. This would complicate life further for the villagers, because they could lose jobs on the plantations, their only source of income.

Yet, both men and women were willing to ignore the high risk of being involved in witch hunts. Perhaps their rationale for joining goes beyond the "joining in for fun" explanations. For instance, in an interview with Duli, the daughter of Nepul from the Central Dooars case, Duli explained how the witches worked:

> Incidents started happening in our house that made us suspicious of witchcraft. There was someone who was doing *ban-mantra* on our house. There was illness in our family. Everyone was sick. [She asks me.] How does illness happen? Do you know? Do you understand *ban*? That was in our house. Our chickens kept dying. My sister-in-law could not conceive for years . . . now her leg is swollen for months. . . . My niece became ill. Who was doing this [the illness]. There were two *buri* in our *para* [community] who was doing the mischief. [I asked her whether the family members became well after the witch was killed.] The illness went away. Our chickens were okay. We did *jaar-puch* [the rituals conducted by the *janguru*]. But some of our chickens died.

At the time of the interview, Nepul and his son were still in prison. His family was going through economic hardships because the two primary wage-earning members were behind bars. His house had a deserted look. He said:

> They [the police] have everyone. They are all in Alipurduar Jail . . . they [the accusers] could not give bail. They are still in jail. . . . There is no one in our house now except for me. No one wants to stay here. How will they stay? The police have arrested everyone.

It is poverty and not strict laws that often lead to longer prison (jail) time for the accusers. Because the *adivasis* are very poor, the bail money is often too high for them to pay. Duli explains, "My father and brothers should have got bail within a week of their arrest. But where is the money? How will they get bail?"

The threat of being under the spell of witchcraft was perhaps a bigger threat than the threat of being arrested by the police or the threat of losing a job. Sometimes it is the fear of *dain*, along with the need to take control over their lives, which leads the *adivasi* migrant workers to join in the witch hunt. For some, witch hunts are a good opportunity to settle scores. In the following narrative, Sunil, a villager who was at the meeting when the causes behind Anil's death were revealed to the villagers in the Chandmoni tea estate incident, mentions individuals who joined in the hunt with other motives (creating trouble).

> They [Anil's brother and family] were very upset . . . came to the meeting drunk . . . started telling the village that there was witchcraft involvement in the issue. And then what, other people in the village joined in . . . some of them were just looking for an opportunity to create trouble in the village. They started supporting Suresh . . . there was a lot of people . . . they all looked like they wanted to do some harm.

Frustration over the epidemics, anger, encouragements of alcohol, and miscreants are some of the reasons behind the support for the hunts. In another interview, I asked some of the villagers in Chandmoni about the rationale behind the selection of these five women as witches. Srabani, my interpreter and also a local activist explained: "There was no logic. In that entire day of rituals, everyone in the village was drunk. The *janguru* himself was intoxicated too. It was good business for him. . . . Suresh had spent around thousand ($20) rupees. The villagers were happy too. There was plenty of *haria*."

Joining for fun, to create trouble, or because rewards were offered, are perhaps, only on-the-surface rationales for why people joined the accusers. The very fact that the accusers did not use threats to convince most of villagers to join reveals the real reason for the support. The only threats that were used were applied against the relatives of the accused women. In a community where diseases and illness are everyday occurrences that can lead to deaths, the power of the *dain* to cause harm is very real threat. This can explain why individuals were ready to believe that the witch was responsible for the misery in their lives or why the entire village stood vigil during witch hunts and prevented relatives of witches from asking for help from the outside. This gave them the necessary legitimacy required to punish the witch by rape, torture, and death.

## Alienation and Fetish of the *Adivasi* Migrant Worker

Similar to observations among communities in Africa and South America (see Comaroff and Comaroff 1993, Taussig 1980), among the *adivasi* migrant workers' seemingly natural (natural to most of us in "commodity-based" societies, borrowing the term from Taussig, 1980) occurrences in everyday lives that can be deemed either good or bad, are deemed unnatural. Both failures and successes in activities, illness, and health have reasons and purposes. While the good is credited to that of the powers of the *janguru*, the bad is always due to witchcraft. Thus when children die, they do not die because of lack of medications or nutrition. They die because the witch cast a spell. Similarly, when an individual falls ill, he falls ill because his spurned lover does not want him to lead a normal life, or because a *dain* has given him *buri nazar*.

The witch takes the shape of all anxiety in the plantations. The workers have no opportunity to better their lives, because they are in a social class where the fate of the *adivasi* migrant workers is decided from the day that they are born, where there is no opportunity of mobility, where ordinary curable ailments go untreated, and where they are nothing but workers required to keep the plantation running. Ignored by political leaders, the government, and the plantation owners, the *adivasi* workers are constantly at the mercy of the *janguru* and the union leader.

The plantation, that was supposed to have given the *adivasis* some respite from the economic troubles in their homeland, turned into a promise that was never delivered. The migrant *adivasi* worker is alienated from the local people, both because of the taboos against *adivasis* and the strict rules of hierarchy within the plantation economy that discourage the workers from interacting with people outside their community. He faces a new economic structure, where everything is controlled by wages. To make sense of this new world, the migrant *adivasi* worker transferred the belief in witches. In this new world, everything is represented by wages, which are both a source of hope and despair. Wages, plantation jobs, promises of rewards, and good health become their fetish. The fetish represents happiness, and the *dain* becomes the only hurdle that stands between the *adivasis* and happiness.

How did wages, jobs, and other material objects become fetishized in this community that had no conception of private property? Explaining how objects are fetishized, Taussig (1980) argues that in traditional peasant communities in Bolivia the fetishism that existed was the result of the organic unity between individuals and their products. Land, social wealth, and environment were all owned by the community, in which everyone, humans and nature alike, had a stake. With the coming of the capitalist mode of production, individuals became subordinate to the products that they produced. In this new distorted economy, commodities are fetishized; and the goal is the accumulation of endless profit. As a result, the Devil becomes the mediator of the two different systems of production (old organic versus the commodity production). Thus the Devil was not only a symbol of the pain and havoc that the new system caused in the lives of the workers, for the peasants, the new economy was exploitative, nonreciprocal and destructive of all relationships between men (37–38).

For the *adivasi* migrant workers, the witch represents all that is wrong in their lives, and wages are fetishized. The witch hunts in Jalpaiguri can be seen logically as functional responses to situations in which the fetish is threatened. The accused women become credible scapegoats for the alienation of workers. The functional explanation of witch hunts from a sociological theoretical perspective can be best explained by Jensen (2007, 39–44), who applies Stinchcombe's logic of functional explanations (1968).[5] Jensen explains:

> Some type of threat either to society or to some members of a society or to some members of a society (e.g., plague), leads to a decline in security. The minus sign between the threat and the homeostatic variable means as the threat increases, security decreases. People do not like such a state and begin to search for a response (e.g., scapegoating). The minus sign between security and the response means that as security declines, the search for response increases. Finally for the response to function as expected, it has to reestablish security (the homeostatic condition)—hence, the positive sign between the response and the homeostatic variable. In the example, scapegoating increases and security increases (i.e., a positive relationship). A variety of different threats, homeostatic variables, and responses can be found in the witch hunt literature (40).

Applying Stinchcombe's model and Jensen's adaptation to the hunts among the *adivasi* migrant workers, one can explain why the hunts continue to occur. Among the *adivasi* workers, a threat to society or some of its members can occur in the form of diseases or illnesses. This threat is deep-seated in insecurities about wages, employment, and politics in the plantations. This undermines security in the society and elicits a response in the form of the hunt for a scapegoat that would take the blame for undermining the stability in the community. The scapegoat takes the form of a witch, and the fear-displacing response takes the form of witch hunts. In scapegoating, the target takes the blame for the crisis that is threatening the group either "as an intentional diversionary tactic or as a cathartic displacement of anger and frustration" (53).

## The Other Class: Failure of the Police

What does the attitude of the state (through police involvement) tell us about the perception of witchcraft accusations?[6] What does it tell us about the larger policy of the state of West Bengal towards its *adivasi* migrant worker citizens? To answer this question, I first introduce a case of violence that erupted at a soccer match in Palestine some years ago. In April 1981, two neighboring Palestinian Arab towns competed in a soccer match. Kafr Yassif was a predominantly Christian town, and Julis was a predominantly Druze town. The match took place in Kafr Yassif, and a fight broke out between fans of both teams, during which a fan from Julis was stabbed. The match continued despite the violence, and the team from Julis won the match. As soon as the game was over, violence erupted from both sides causing a fan (later that day) from each side to die (Shihade 2011). Because the state is the sole body endowed with the legitimate use of violence against its citizens, the response of the state, through the police who were present during the attack and who did not do anything to stop the attack, reflected the attitude of the state towards the citizens: here the state is Israel, and the citizens are Palestinians. The state claims that such violence is part of the Palestinian Arab culture of violence. In contrast, Shihade argues that the claims of the state and the noninterference of the police encouraged the violence between the towns as a part of their strategy to rule (139, 143–45, 147).

Shihade's arguments about how the noninterference of the police during acts of violence is a strategic ploy to maintain power and control can also be applied in the context of the witchcraft accusations and the incidents of witch hunts in the tea plantations of Jalpaiguri, particularly through the repercussions on the way the hunts are "handled" by the police. I argue that the attitude of the police, especially in the district of Jalpaiguri, reflects the attitude of the state and plantation management towards the *adivasi* migrant workers, who are treated as wild, savage, and incorrigible tribals. This attitude reflects the construction of wildness as argued by Skaria (1997b). Skaria argues that the roots of the construction of the category "tribes" in colonial India has continued in institutional structures of the state even today. As a result of its continuation, the question that begs to be asked is: how does the institutionalization of the category of tribes have a role in the way the Government (primarily through the police and the senior bureaucrats) neglects the situation of witchcraft accusations in the plantations of Jalpaiguri?

Perhaps the most problematic feature of the reports of the witch hunt incidents in Jalpaiguri is the neglect of the police in serving justice to the victims of witchcraft accusations and their families. Typical reactions of the police towards local incidents of witch hunts range from reluctance in getting involved in the lives of the *adivasis* to treating the victims of witch hunts with distrust. I explain how the local police react to reports on an impending witch hunt by using a narrative. When Padma's (victim in the Central Dooar's case) son Viral managed to escape from the village and ran towards to nearest BSF post to ask for help, his complaints were dismissed by the security guards.

> I managed to give the mob a slip and escaped through the back door of the hut and ran to the nearest security post of the plantation [Special Security Bureau or paramilitary]. I pleaded with the guards—my mother is going to get murdered by the village. They are calling her a witch. Please do something. The guards dismissed my claims and said—Go away. You are drunk. If you are serious, go back to the village and get us a written complaint approved by the *panchayat*. Only then we will do something. . . . This is a domestic issue. Every day you guys drink, get drunk and start fights between mother and son, husband and wife . . . *sobh din halla hoi*.

Viral's narrative brings out the attitude of cultural superiority towards the treatment of the *adivasis* by the BSF. As reported in Viral's narratives, the BSF guards dismissed his urgent cries for help in rescuing his mother as being almost childlike—he was a drunk who did not know what he was talking about—and it was fitting behavior for *adivasis*, who are always drunk (*matal*). This image of a drunk unruly worker who is up to no good and who constantly lies has been constructed as a part of the politics of patronage by the planters so that they can exert control and discipline over the workers (Chatterjee 2001, 282). The worker is almost reduced to the status of a child who must be constantly dismissed, disciplined, and put in his place. This treatment of the worker ties in to the paternalistic need for the government, the police, and the planters to civilize the *adivasi* migrant workers (Skaria 1997b, 737, 739).

Almost one-third of the cases of witchcraft accusations do not make it to the police reports; and in about half of the cases, there is often no action from the part of the police after complaints are lodged. In the remaining cases where police intervene, they often arrive on the scene long after the hunt has taken place. In such cases of "intervention," the most that the police do against the accusers is to randomly arrest people in the village. These arrests are conduct much like raids, where the police arrest anyone who is present in the village. As a result, both guilty and innocent people are arrested. (For example, in the Chandmoni incident, the entire adult population of the village was arrested.) Tippo, a 43-year-old *adivasi* male plantation worker, whose wife, Arati, was arrested in Chandmoni, explains:

> I do not know [meaning why his wife was arrested]. She did not do anything. She was not involved [in the witch hunt] . . . they [the police] came and they arrested her. She was alone at home. They did not get the culprits. So they arrested whoever was available in the village at that time. My wife was innocent. . . . I had to give bail to free her. The case is still going on. There has been no justice so far.

When I asked Tippo why he thought that the police did not believe his wife's statement, he replied: "We are tribals. They hate us. They think that we are *jangli* [uncivilized] . . . *boka-shoka manush* [limited intelligence] . . . *amader kothar dam nei* [our words have no value]."

Tippo's and Viral's comments as to why the police refused to take their complaints seriously are not unique. The attitudes of the police towards the *adivasis* are neglectful and rest on an assumption that because the *adivasis* are not "civilized," their problems are characteristic of their lower status. Thus, witch hunts, drunken brawls, and the homicides that follow are normal and should not be taken seriously. Their attitude reflects simplistic constructions of causes behind witchcraft accusations. Skaria (1997b) calls this "selective blindness" when he describes two incidents in which a British judge let off a Dang man accused of killing a witch on the argument that the poor man was innocent because he was only practicing his religion. The argument, perhaps from the point of the Colonial officials, viewed the Dangs as a group that believed that they were not doing anything wrong by killing the witch (726–27). But Skaria writes: "[S]urely there was more to the ambivalence of colonial officials than this." Skaria traces the reluctance on the part of the colonial administrators to the colonial distinction between caste and tribes and the colonial construction of wildness. She explains how the difference between these two is based on different forms of wildness, each with its distinctive politics of gender and time. Thus, because *adivasis*' are at the lowest end of the wildness scale, they are expected to conduct witch hunts. This is a rationale that has continued in the institutional responses to witchcraft accusations among the *adivasi* migrant workers in the tea plantations of Jalpaiguri.

For example, one of the common responses to my research topic by district administrators was surprise to what they thought was "an incurable disease." "It is a simple case of economics. Witch hunts always have an economic motive." This was the reaction of a senior administrator who denied that there was more to witch hunts than conflict over material goods or a primitive practice of a primitive community. The solution was simple, too, from their point of view: "[A]void getting involved too much in their lives. After all what good will it do to them? They will never change their [superstitious ways]." Isolation (through not getting involved in *adivasis*' lives) is perhaps the biggest strategy of control that the plantation owners and the state have administered over the workers, and the comment above is an expression of the ideology.

The attitude of the plantation management towards the witchcraft accusations and witch hunts among migrant *adivasi* workers was similar to that of the police. Most planters did not have a clue what happened in the labor lines, and witch hunt accusations were treated with irritation. Others ignored the accusations or sent the junior managers, trade union leaders, or *panchayat* to intervene if it caused "too much trouble," i.e., disrupted daily work in the plantations. In most instances, the management came to know of witch hunt incidents after the hunt took place (Central Dooars and Chandmoni tea estate incidents). For the planters, witch hunts are practices that are indigenous to the *adivasis*, and getting involved would cause unnecessary trouble. Their tactic was one that maintains aloofness from the daily lives of the workers. As long as the *adivasi* migrant workers showed up for work and contributed towards production and profit, all was good in the plantations. Similar to Tippo's and Viral's complaints to the police, Dulari and Basanti's complaints of the witchcraft accusations against them were dismissed by the plantation management. For example, referring to accusations against Dulari, one of the managers in the tea plantation where she worked remarked that her accusations against her were "all false," thereby implying that she was speaking the untruth. "Yes there is someone by that name and we know her. But she is to blame . . . *kharap meyeh* . . . [bad woman] . . . *beshi joraben nah* . . . [don't get involved]." The manager's remarks about Dulari are symbolic of the image of the *adivasi* woman as a low moral character who is promiscuous and thus not fit company for civilized people like me and him.

Dulari's trauma, like that of Viral and Tippo, was dismissed. They were dismissed as individuals who had no claim to their lives or dignity. Their characters were already judged before they had made their complaints: they were considered drunk, superstitious, and loose individuals who did not have a right to justice. For the plantation management, they represented workers who were necessary for the production in the plantation but who were not indispensable. As one plantation owner told me: "[*A*]*pni ki bujben? Ora ohrokom ee.*" [Implying that I should not waste my time on these workers as they deserve the misery].

## Witch Hunts as Protest

What is particularly intriguing about the tea plantation community is the lack of any outward show of protest (such as through public demonstrations, activism, or strikes) by the alienated and oppressed *adivasi* migrant workers against their conditions of life and work. The strikes that have happened in the region were mostly union-led strikes that were motivated by mainstream political parties (see

Bhowmik 2011 for details) and in which the *adivasi* workers did not play a dominant role. Previously in this book, I have mentioned how the very avenues of protest in this community, which is much marginalized and alienated, are nonexistent. By avenues I imply activism and the organization of *adivasi* workers by political groups that only portray the interests of *adivasis*. For instance, while there may be sporadic protests against the unfair dismissal of a worker, the *adivasi* migrant worker has remained mostly silent to the oppressive existence in the plantations. Perhaps the reasons for their supposed nonreactions against their conditions are tied to their alienation; the workers are controlled by a strict class hierarchy mediated through union leaders. Coercion and control are tools in an economy that treats them as disposable.

How can the *adivasi* migrant worker who has no opportunity of getting away from the plantation in search of a different livelihood react against the plantation that is the only source of livelihood? In response to my question, as to why there is a lack of protest against the plantation management, an *adivasi* village elder, Shamlal, explained the "foolishness" behind the very thought of protesting against the owners. "If we say anything against the Babu we will lose our jobs the next day. Why do we want to kick our rice? We earn enough to make ends meet. . . . If we lose that then we have nothing left."

It is out of feelings of helplessness, in a culture of oppression and tyranny, that witch hunts emerge as a normalcy/balancing factor in stressful times. The link between illness and instigations of witchcraft accusations best illustrates the above connection. Because health conditions, like most other social goods such as education and the right to drinking water, are dismal in the plantations, diseases that can be easily cured through medications become fatal. It is in this context that the role of the *janguru* becomes important: he represents the only hope that the community has towards getting some control. After the *janguru* fails in his role, the community turns to the witchcraft as the source of the misfortune and the failure of the *janguru* to provide a cure. The *janguru* can never be blamed for the misfortune or for his failure in finding a cure. He is, after all, the symbol of hope, just like the plantation management, which can never be blamed for the poor wages and lack of health care or educational facilities. In this context, blaming the accused *adivasi* woman as a witch is the easier solution.

So how does an act that is prompted by extreme oppression become a protest against the very alienation that caused it? I argue that the act of a witch hunt becomes a protest when it attracts the attention of the outside world to the conditions of the *adivasi* migrant workers. For the workers, witch hunts are the only way to shake the outside world's conscience on their plight. Ramlal explains it best: "They have to do something [against stress] . . . otherwise they will lose their sanity. They have to live."

## Notes

1. It is certainly interesting that Dulari, an *adivasi* woman, would make a reference to Kali, a Hindu goddess. It is, however, common for Hindu gods and goddesses to be worshiped along with *adivasi devta*, as a part of the social and cultural assimilation of the adivasis to the mainstream religions.

2. See "Party's Murmur: It is Mamata's Mess," *The Telegraph* (Kolkata), February 21, 2012.

3. As mentioned in previous chapters, in surprise attack witch hunts, conflicts over resources are never present. It is only in some calculated attacks that resources play a role in instigating conflicts.

4. Translated from Bengali as: "Go away, children of the witch. Children of the witch do not play with our children."

5. Functionalism has come under harsh criticism since the 1970s. Stinchcombe's model seems to answer most of the criticisms leveled at functionalism. "Nothing is assumed about the nature of homeostatic variables—except, of course, that they must be of certain practical value to a group of people. . . . Change, while provoked by extraneous factors, is inherent to the system. . . . Moreover the model is not alien to a notion of revolution. And since the environment of a system can never be controlled, there is also no need to assume an end-state involving total equilibrium" (Arditi 1988, 284). Arditi extends Stinchcombe's model to show how equilibrium structures, structural conditions, and social conflicts are variations of the extended functional model.

6. Some states in India, like Jharkhand and Chhattisgarh, have very active police forces that are more involved with *adivasi* problems than the West Bengal police is. For instance, the Free Legal Aid group (FLA) in Jharkhand and Bihar works closely with the police in that state to provide justice to victims of witchcraft accusations. Also, see Macdonald 2009 for how the police intervene and provide justice in witchcraft accusations cases in Chhattisgarh.

# Chapter 7

# Towards a New Direction: Activism and Protests

Oh hear all . . . hear all . . . hear all . . . hear all
Oh come here oh brother
Oh come here oh sister
Put an end to the tradition of *dain pratha*
Put an end to the tradition of *dain pratha*

Oh hear all . . . hear all . . . hear all . . . hear all
*Dain . . . dain . . . dain . . .*
She takes all our lives
That's what you think!
But there are no *dain* in this world
Just a creation of your mind!
So put an end to the *dain pratha*
Put an end to this tradition.

Oh come here oh brother
Oh come here oh sister
Put an end to the tradition of *dain pratha*
Put an end to the tradition of *dain pratha*
Superstition and "bad" education
Superstition and "bad" education
The *dain* pleads you to grant her life
Drive out this madness
Drive out this madness
Put an end to this tradition of *dain pratha*

After my first interview with Basanti ended, Balwant sang the above song at Basanti's house. He had composed the song as a part of the anti-witch-hunt campaign for the region. The song was originally sung in Sadri.

How does one organize protests in a community that has apparently no avenues of protest? The literature on social movements has commented on the role of political and historical opportunities that create prospects for the emergence of social protests in a community (see Kriesi 2007; Tilly 1995). However, given the social, political, and historical background of the *adivasi* migrant workers in the tea plantations of Jalpaiguri, a social protest led by the *adivasi* workers against the foundations on which the plantation economy rests is perhaps up against enormous practical challenges. In this context, how does a community organize itself against witchcraft accusations? What are the outcomes of these organizations on the status of *adivasi* women and on the relationship between *adivasi* workers and management in the plantations? Before I explore these questions in this final chapter, I will first discuss the status of campaigns against witchcraft accusations in other parts of India. This discussion will give a comparative perspective to the readers and provide insight into the unique situation and challenges for conducting an anti-witch-hunt campaign among the *adivasi* migrant workers in Jalpaiguri. Later in this chapter, I demonstrate how a local NGO organized campaigns against witch hunts among the tea plantation *adivasi* worker community by targeting the *adivasi* women (the ones who are most likely to be focus of witchcraft accusation) to participate in the campaign. I end the final chapter in this book with a reflection on the repercussions of the campaigns on *adivasi* migrant worker life in the plantations and their impact on future witch hunts.

## Anti-Witch-Hunt Campaigns in Other Parts of India

In 1999, Bihar was one of the first states in India to pass an anti-witch-hunt law. The state of Jharkhand followed soon after, in 2001,[1] Chhattisgarh passed an anti-witch-hunt law in 2005. Other states in India, along with West Bengal, such as Assam, Madhya Pradesh, Gujarat, Rajasthan, Andhra Pradesh, and Maharashtra are facing the problem of witchcraft accusations mainly among the *adivasi* sections of their populations. However, as in West Bengal, these states do not have anti-witch-hunt laws or acts that can perhaps legally protect the victims of witchcraft accusations. In this section, I focus on the work of anti-witch-hunt campaigns in Jharkhand, Bihar, and Chhattisgarh in order to provide a comparative context for the campaigns in Jalpaiguri.

In Bihar and Jharkhand, the name Free Legal Aid Committee (FLAC) comes up frequently on the topic of anti-witch-hunt campaigns. The FLAC, an NGO originally based in Bihar (before the creation of the state of Jharkhand), originally operates from Jharkhand. It runs a campaign against witchcraft accusations in the state by providing social and legal support to the accused women, organizing street plays, producing films, and running awareness campaigns. It has been very successful at promoting the problem of witchcraft accusations in Bihar and Jharkhand at various national legal and human rights forum. It was widely due to the efforts of the FLAC (initially though a proposed Identification of Witch (prevention) Act in 1995 that later served as a guideline for the Witchcraft Prohibition Act in 1999 in Bihar) that laws against witch hunts were passed in the two states (Macdonald 2009, 299).

The efforts of FLAC in the two states did not end with the passage of laws. Its awareness campaigns and messages about the evils of witchcraft accusations in the states have encouraged other NGOs to join. One of them is Human Rights Law Network (HRLN), which works solely to provide legal aid to the victims and represent their cases in the state's high courts. FLAC has also inspired the victims of witchcraft accusations and their relatives to create their own awareness campaigns in Jharkhand. One of these is the campaign in Jharkhand titled: "If I do not speak, then who will?" This campaign was created by former victims of witchcraft accusations. The campaign revolves around street plays (*nukkad natak*), awareness campaigns, and similar programs directed at *adivasis* in Jharkhand and Bihar (Kiro 2008; Sukhla undated).

Similarly, in Chhattisgarh, another NGO, the Andh Shraddha Nirmulan Samiti (ASNS or Blind Faith Eradication Committee) played an important role in the passage of the anti-witch-hunt law in that state in 2005. The ASNS works in close association with the police and legal aid in the state, and at present it conducts the "*Koi nari tonhi nahi*" (woman is not a witch) campaign. This campaign is widely circulated through the media, not only in the areas where witchcraft accusations in Chhattisgarh are predominant, but also on the Web, through blogs, and on YouTube videos. The president of ASNS (Dr. Dinesh Mishra) had published books and newspaper articles in which he writes about "exposing fraudulent tricks," and he stresses a "scientific awakening" of society (see http://drdineshmishra.blogspot.com/). In 2001, with the help of the National Human Rights Commission (NHRC) and ASNS, a seven-member committee, led by the Communist Party of India, the All India Women's Committee, and a women's organization in Chhattisgarh (Mahila Jagrati Sangathan), investigated a *tonhi* (witch) accusation. The three accused women were encouraged to publicly address a large gathering of women from ten neighboring villages. The public address was broadcast on national television, and each victim was given a compensation of 5,000 rupees from the Chhattisgarh government. This was a remarkable event in the history of anti-witchcraft-accusation in the state because it was the first time that there was involvement of the state government both through investigation of the witchcraft accusations as well as in providing compensations for the victims. Following similar examples in the state, the need for a Chhattisgarh state law against *tonhi* accusations was raised in the state legislative level in 2004. In November 2004, a local NGO filed a Public Interest Litigation (PIL) petitioning the ban on the *tonhi* accusations, and public pressure demanding a law continued. Finally, the Chhattisgarh government passed the Witchcraft Atrocities (Prevention) Act in 2005 (Macdonald 2009, 299–300).

## Anti-Witch-Hunt Campaign in Jalpaiguri Tea Plantations

Federici (2010, 24–25) has called for a feminist intervention to develop an alternative strategy to understand witchcraft accusations in Asia and Africa that would lead to building collaborations between human rights activists and social justice groups, which would then work together to end the practice. In Chhattisgarh and Jharkhand, we have seen how collaborations between women's organizations, human rights watch, social justice forums (such as ASNS or FLAC), and the government have worked to effect the passage of acts that criminalize witchcraft accusations and give compensations to the victims. In these states, the audience towards whom the campaigns were directed was broad, extending not just to the *adivasi* groups but also to the non-*adivasi* population. Perhaps the realization and the appeal of a broader audience were tied to the very nature of these states: these states were created on powerful emotions of *adivasi* identity. In contrast, in West Bengal, the issues of *adivasis* play a minor role in state politics, and as a result the audience for similar kinds of campaigns (the *dains* in Purulia or Malda districts in West Bengal), which are mostly misrepresented as "*adivasi* problems," are difficult to appeal to (Singh 1990). This ties in to my argument in the first chapter of this book that the study of witchcraft accusations in the tea plantations of Jalpaiguri fell off the radar of both academics and activist groups. Perhaps the neglect is because the *adivasi* workers in the tea plantation of Jalpaiguri are a migrant community and their role as workers became prominent in the wage economy of plantation politics. It is their worker identity that has taken precedence over their *adivasi*/tribal identity.

When I first started studying NGOs in the Dooars area that worked on anti-witch-hunt campaigns in the fall of 2003, one name emerged, North Bengal's Peoples Development Center (NBPDC) or JEU as it was known then.[2] There are approximately 52 NGOs that work in this area, but only one, NBPDC, actively worked on anti-witch-hunt campaigns (Chakravarty and Chaudhuri 2012, 494–95). In this chapter, I trace the anti-witch-hunt campaigns of the NBPDC over two years. I focus on the audience of the campaigns, the frames that they use, and their aims. In this context, I also focus on the involvement (or lack of) of the administration and the role that the plantations workers (women) play in the anti-witch-hunt campaigns. A discussion about the anti-witch-hunt campaign in the plantation is useful for understanding and perhaps working out a possible solution of eradicating witch hunts in the plantations. Anti-witch-hunt campaigns and activism provide clues about the issues affecting the lives of the *adivasi* migrant workers and the areas where the witch hunts figure. As the previous chapters point out, social stress (mainly caused by a plantation wage economy) that is triggered by incidents of diseases, illness, and deaths within the *adivasi* migrant worker communities plays a huge role in instigating witch hunts. How do the activists of NBPDC use these factors of instigating the witch hunts in their campaign to prevent future hunts? How do the two categories of hunts (calculated and surprise) play a role in the activism? In other words, do the activists promote different strategies for preventing hunts based on the two categories? To whom are these campaigns addressed to? What are the goals of the campaigns? These are some of the questions that I will address in the following sections of this chapter. I begin with a brief background of the NBPDC.

## North Bengal's People's Development Center

> Sundari Munda a member of our *Sudata* self-help group, was called a witch . . . and was to be put to *janguru's* scrutiny and killed. . . . Suddenly, we got the news. . . . Our Secretary met Sundari . . . and we started holding group meetings there every day . . . and informed the authorities. . . . Our volunteers and activists composed and wrote songs and enacted a drama . . . in Sadri and Sadri-Nepali-Bengali-Rajbongshi dialect. . . . Mobilization among the women of Sukhpuri, against witch hunting reached its peak. . . . And Sundari speaks out to the general gathering of all women of that locality. . . . This is one example of all those daily core, for which we say: NBPDC symbolizes empowerment. . . . Peoples' awakening on witch hunting reached its peak.

The excerpt above is taken from the anti-witch-hunt pamphlet of the NBPDC, "A Pictorial Story of Dhamiranpur, JEU pamphlet, 2005." NBPDC was established in the early 1980s in the courtyard of a private home. In its initial years, the organization worked against various forms of social violence against women (such as dowry, domestic violence, and girl illiteracy) in poor urban neighborhoods of Jalpaiguri city. Gradually, the organization launched campaigns in the rural and poor urban neighborhoods of Jalpaiguri in the following areas: mother and child care, hygiene, providing drinking water in villages through tube wells, banking, adult literacy, vocational training for women (such as tailoring, handicrafts, making of jams, jellies, and squashes), family planning, and child education. As a part of its campaign, NBPDC provided counseling, especially on legal aid to settle disputes between families. It also organized various health camps (polio vaccination camps), eye camps, and blood donation camps in various parts of Jalpaiguri, Darjeeling, and Cooch Behar districts.

Over the years, NBPDC grew from a local community-based organization to a representative of the Dooars area and its people. The primary focus of the NBPDC expanded from women's problems to encompass the marginalized population in the tea plantation areas. Its website describes the organizational goals as follows: "[NBPDC] aims towards the empowerment of women, tribals and other marginal groups at the grass root level in North Bengal, through economic independence, education and campaign against various forms of abuses against them." (www.jeumvs.northbengal.net). As a result, it changed its name from being a "*mahila sangstha*" to a "people's development center." In the last four years, NBPDC has included witch hunts as one of the major social problems in this area and it is working towards "sustainable development to eradicate the problem."[3] It is important to note that that NBPDC is the only NGO in the Dooars area that is working against witch hunts.

## Anti-Witch-Hunt Protest and Activism on Sundays

As mentioned above, anti-witch-hunt protests became one of the primary foci of the NBPDC over the last four years (2003 onwards). The decision to work against witch hunts was a gradual one for the activists and volunteers of NBPDC. Suchetana, an activist who works with the NBPDC explains:

> We have been observing and working against witch hunts (in this region) for the last nineteen years . . . well we are trying . . . so that it can be stopped. For the last nineteen years we have been unable to do something. For the last three four years we have been able to get the support from police, administration, media and money that helped in launching the campaign.

Typically regular campaigns/meetings against witch hunts are held on Sunday afternoons at tea plantation villages. These campaigns are not explicitly named as "witch hunt campaigns" but are tagged along with meetings of "self-help groups" in which participants in the programs meet to discuss their progress. Self-help groups are usually a group of eight women including the group leader. These groups are microcredit groups organized under the Government of India Schemes,[4] and NGOs are typically assigned the task of administering these programs at the grassroots level.

Each woman in the group is loaned a small amount of money at no interest to start her own business to supplement the family income. Scholars studying microcredit argue that because women are thought to successfully repay loans more often than men, the lending bodies direct these programs to target women. Every month, the managing NGO holds a meeting at the village with the members of the self-help groups. Economic incentives are generally found to be successful in ensuring that every woman in the village participates in meetings. Over the years, the NBPDC found that attendance at anti-witch-hunt campaigns is poor, mainly because of suspicion and fear among the villagers. Instead they realized that if the anti-witch-hunt campaign is aligned with something else (in this case an economic program that already had success in ensuring attendance at meetings), it brings together a larger group for potential audience. For instance, an entry in my field notes reports an observation that I made when I accompanied NBPDC to attend one of their "regular" self-help group meetings:

> [B]arely weeks after the Sundari Munda case where the villagers reacted against a witch hunt incident and rescued the alleged witch, a microcredit meeting was held so that the women could come out of their homes on the pretext of credit loans. Towards the second half of the meeting, the discussion turned into a campaign for anti-witch-hunt (Field notes June 2005).

During the same meeting, Balaram, an *adivasi* social activist who is a volunteer with NBPDC, addressed the group.

> All of you [addressing the women] are members of our micro credit groups. All of you are aware about a witch hunt incident in this village. In that incident you have together as a unit protested the incident and transformed it into a unified campaign. We [meaning the members of the microcredit group] have been successful in our *andolan* [movement]. The people, who have been torturing women in the name of witches, because of our *andolan*, have been forced to confess their guilt and wrong doings in front of the entire community . . . and had to beg for forgiveness.

During one of my travels with the NBPDC, I was invited to accompany the NGO to a meeting organized in Mourighat. The purpose of the meeting, as it was announced weeks, was to discuss the progress of the self-help Group (*Chetana*) and the launching of Below Poverty Line (BPL) schemes of the Government.[5] The meeting was held in the courtyard of the village high school. The school was a single-story three-room structure furnished with broken furniture. The school needed a fresh coat of paint and repairs. However, as this was one of the "better" schools in the area with two brick structured latrines and a big playground, it provided the perfect spot for the meeting.

The meeting started around three in the afternoon. About 70 percent of the audience was women who were participants in the self-help programs conducted by NBPDC, and they came accompanied by their children. Sundays are the day off for the plantation workers, thereby making it a perfect day for a meeting. The discussion turned into an anti-witch-hunt protest after BPL logistics were discussed. Suchetana, speaking about the benefits of participation in programs that promote both individual and social benefits, addressed the audience:

> We did not form this group just to give and take loans. We, the organizers and you [addressing the women] want, through Chetana, that within this community, may there be peace. The *Ku-shangaskar* [superstition] that is within us, within our society, especially within our *adivashi* community regarding *daini pratha* . . . we want to get rid of it. *Daini pratha* is in existence for a long time. This is not just today's problem. Why did this [meaning belief in witches and witch hunts] come to happen, what are the real reasons behind witch hunts, which areas are it most prevalent . . . we have to bring these forward in front of you.

In other words, because of the fear among the *adivasi* community towards *dain* and their previous experience with the police and their legal reaction after a witch hunt, meetings solely organized against witch hunts have little participation. *Adivasi* migrant workers are sensitive to any conversations against witchcraft accusations, especially if it comes from outside institutional representatives (the police and activists in this case). As it was seen in the discussions on the police and administration in the plantations, the police make large-scale arrests after witch hunt incidents. Innocent people, who had no role to play during the witchcraft accusations, often get arrested. In Jalpaiguri, the police, along with the administration, are often insensitive to the sentiments of the *adivasis*, and as a result, the *adivasis* are often suspicious about campaigns that attack their traditions. Thus, for any movement to succeed, it is important that the audience targeted (meaning the participants) resonates with the theme of the protest or movement. It is particularly difficult to organize movements for sensitive topics such as witch hunts, particularly in Jalpaiguri, and the discussion in the next few subsection will focus on how the NBPDC is organizing the movement in the face of institutional challenges.

## Composition and Character of the Campaign Against Witch Hunts by NBPDC

There has been considerable research in the field of social movements focusing on the composition of movements. Movement actors, who constitute the movement, are viewed as signifying agents actively engaged in the production and maintenance of meaning for constituents, bystanders, antagonists, or observers (Snow and Benford 1988; Benford and Snow 2000). The actors or the activists are the active participants of the movement. Further, no discussion about movements can be complete without a discussion of the movement's sup-porters–individuals who might not be directly involved in the movement. Likewise, the audience targeted is an important part in a discussion of a movement. A social movement is made up and influenced by each of these components: actors, audience, supporters, and counter-actors who react to the movement and its supporters. Each of these components is linked to the other: the actors are the active participants who help in targeting the audience and the supporters; the actors react to the counter-actors, who in turn create counter-movements; the actors react again and the process continues.

In the anti-witch-hunt campaign in Jalpaiguri, the actors are primarily the social activists associated with the NBPDC and its networking partners. They are the active participants of the movement. In addition, the audiences of the campaign, in this context, the *adivasi* women who are participating in the self-help program, are also an important part of the movement against witch hunts in Jalpaiguri. The supporters of the anti-witch-hunt campaign consist of other villagers and some legal and police administrators,[6] who act as secondary supporters or passive actors.

The character of the anti-witch-hunt movement in the Dooars area consists of a single movement organized by a single organization. The lack of diversity of other actors (meaning involvement of other NGOs and similar organizations) for the campaign at this initial stage can be attributed to its "new" status. The movement is four years old and lacks financial support from the government. The sensitive nature of the issue has been a factor in the lack of interest among other agencies in taking up the cause. For example, a central government-funded NGO, Arohi, stated in an interview that it is "too much trouble" to get involved in anti-witch-hunt campaigns. Subir, a social activist associated with Arohi, explained:

> "Firstly it is a tribal issue. Tribals are very superstitions and they believe in witches. You cannot get this mentality away from them. It is impossible. All these campaigns [meaning the ones organized by NBPDC] are good . . . but they can never solve the problem. Can you cure the tribals from the superstitions?" Referring to the lack of interest from the administration and government on the issue of witch hunt, he continues, "The government does not want to get involved. It is very complicated. Tribals have their own rules. As long as they do it within their own [people] the government is not bothered."

Every movement has counter-actors, and in the anti-witch-hunt campaign of Jalpaiguri, the counter-actors are the accusers and the conspirators of the hunt. It is interesting to note that though the *janguru* is mentioned during the interviews as a conspirator, he is not overtly mentioned as a counter-actor during the speeches in the campaigns.

## Audience

The *adivasi* women are the main audience for the anti-witch-hunt campaigns in Jalpaiguri, and the frames that the campaign uses are all directed towards them. Suchetana explains the rationale for targeting the *adivasi* women as audience for the campaigns: "Targeting the women is important. They are the ones that start the witch hunt initially. If they stop calling each other *daini* then at least sixty percent of the accusations would stop." Suchetana's comments are reflective of *ghorelu jogra* argument of Balwant that is behind the witchcraft accusations in the region. It is interesting to note that these campaigns are not directed towards the *adivasi* men but at the *adivasi* women who play a huge role in witchcraft accusations either by lending support to the men or by starting the initial conflict against the accused woman.

Meera, another activist with NBPDC, explains Suchetana's rationale for directing the campaign towards *adivasi* women: "Men come later. The accusations come from the women. Today if all the women are united against the witch accusations then witch hunt would not have taken place." She continues, "Look at dowry cases. It is the mother-in-law and the sister-in-law that harasses the bride. So if you manage to make these women understand that what they are doing is not right, the problem can be solved." But there are incidents of witch hunts in which the men instigate the conflict, especially in surprise cases. For Meera this does not seem to be a real problem for witchcraft accusations in the region. She argues:

> There are two things. One the women have to realize that there are no witches. The troubles and the mischief that witches cause are not caused by witches. It is the men, their alcohol and their lust . . . the women have to realize that. And second the superstition is a big issue.

In other words, for Meera, even though there are cases (cases in Chandmoni and Central Dooars) in which men instigate the witchcraft accusation throughout, the support that the women give to the accusers is crucial. According to Meera, if the women supporters realize that there are no real witches and that the belief in witchcraft is based on superstition, then they would perhaps refrain from lending support to their men. She strengthens her argument for targeting women by blaming alcoholism and not witches as bigger threats for the *adivasi* migrant workers. Meera's comments provide clues as to why the activists target the women as the audience in the campaign. In both categories of witch hunts, if the support from the women is taken away, then the accusations would lose much of their credibility. In Basanti's and in Dulari's cases, if the women did not come forwards with accusations of witchcraft, then the cases against the accused women would not have been strong. In other words, the women accusers and supporters are seen as important elements of the instigators of witch hunts during calculated attacks. Their role is vital during the initial stage and during the stage of the whispering campaign that leads to the social isolation of the accused. As seen in Basanti's case, her social isolation resulted in her forced confession during the trial. In cases of surprise attacks, the role of the women accusers is mainly in the form of lending support to the accusers and justifying their act. For Duli, whose father and brother are in prison serving a sentence, the murder of the two old women was necessary to get rid of the witchcraft in her household. She did not see the murders as an act against law, despite the fact that the main waged-earning members of the family were in prison, and the family was facing financial hardships.

Because the *adivasi* women are the primary audiences of the anti-witch-hunt campaign, activists have formulated the frames used in these campaigns directed towards them. However, while targeting the female audience, the activists face the big challenge of making the *adivasi* women speak about witch hunts. For instance, I note my observations on the challenges of engaging the *adivasi* women in a dialogue with the NBPDC activists at a Sunday meeting.

> [S]peaking at a meeting after a witch hunt incident, Suchetana wanted to know details about the event. She addressed the crowd asking for details. The women murmured among themselves. Suchetana picked out a woman in the crowd and asked her, "Why don't you give us the details of the incident?" The woman replies, "We do not know what happened." (Field notes 2006)

As discussed in the previous chapters, making the *adivasi* women respond to witch hunts was a challenge for the researcher. In this context, the activists face the dual challenges of not only making the *adivasi* women attend the campaigns but also of engaging them in a dialogue that encourages them to speak about witchcraft accusations and the threat it poses for *adivasi* women in the plantations. In this context, I next discuss the frames that the activists of the NBPDC use to address the dual challenges of attendance and resonation of the campaign with the *adivasi* women.

## The Frames Used in the Anti-Witch-Hunt Campaigns

The study of framing is useful in understanding the social and political dynamics of a movement (Coy, 1996), and the literature on social movements has mentioned that the composition of a movement and other aspects of the movement (audience, supporters, and counter-actors) has some influence on frames (Benford and Snow 2000; McCammon et al. 2004; Ryan 1996; Valocchi 1992). The concepts of frame and the framing process have been popularized in sociology through Goffman's (1974) book on the topic (Benford and Snow 2000). The Goffmanian definition of frames as "schemata of interpretation" that enable individuals "to locate, perceive, identify, and label" occurrences within their life space and the world at large is widely accepted today by most frame scholars in social movements. For the purpose of this chapter, I will refer to "frames" as a holistic concept that includes both the dynamic action-oriented element and the interpretive function.

The framing perspective views movements as signifying agents engaged in the production and maintenance of meaning for protagonists, antagonists, and bystanders. The frames assign meaning to and interpret relevant events and conditions in ways that are intended to mobilize political adherents and constituents, to gather bystander support, and to demobilize antagonists (Snow and Benford 1988; Snow 2004). The framing process has come to be regarded as a central dynamic in understanding the character and course of social movements. There has been considerable scholarship on collective action frames and framing processes in relation to social movements in the past one and half decades (Benford and Snow, 2000). Moreover, there are a number of studies on the frame as the dependent variable (Snow 2004) and on the dynamic character of the frame. The anti-witch-hunt campaign by NBPDC uses a number of frames directed towards the audience, the counter-actors and the supporters of the movement. There are three categories of frames used by the activists in the campaign: a superstition frame, women's development and development of a community of women frame, and a justice frame.

## The Belief in Witches and Witch Hunts as "Superstition" Frame

In most if not all the meetings in the campaign against witch hunts, NBPDC activists made a direct reference to witchcraft accusation and witch hunts as being a part of the "backward" mindset of the *adivasi* community. The belief in witches and witchcraft was attacked as being a part of the *ku-shangaskar* (superstition) and thus needed to be done away with. The song composed by Balwant, quoted at the beginning of this chapter, sums up what the activists think about witch hunts by calling it a form of "madness" and "superstition" and a result of "bad education." In other words, the activists are rigid in their agenda that there are no real witches. For instance, an activist speaking at a group meeting in one of the plantation villages makes a direct reference to *daini pratha* as a *ku-shangaskar*:

> [W]e have seen that no matter how many times we have fought against this *ku-shangaskar*, we have been victorious. We have to understand that this *daini pratha* (witch tradition) is *ku-shangaskar*. Not *Shu* but *ku-shangaskar*.[7]

Similarly, another activist speaking at a meeting explains:

> We have to understand that this [witch hunt] has done us no good. It cannot do any good. Look at you. You fight to eat barely two meals a day . . . nothings fancy just rice and salt . . . you have to survive and being buried in superstitions does not help. We have to get rid of these beliefs.

The above quotes are typical illustrations of the frame of superstition in the speeches of the activists. The superstition frame is used to "enlighten" the audience that witch hunts cannot be beneficial to a community that fights for the basic needs to survive. Along with the stress on superstitions, the activists often refer to how some people in the community manipulate the beliefs in witches to serve some other purpose through witch hunts. The activists refer to a "conspiracy theory" in their speeches, by which they reason that *adivasi* beliefs and superstitions about *dain* are exploited to serve the interest of some people in the village. Suchetana, addressing the village crowd at a Sunday meeting explains how the conspiracy works by manipulating superstitions:

> *Opobadh, opoprochar*, makes men divided . . . brings in division and animosity between families, just to serve an individual's personal interest. . .We have to understand that this [witch hunt] has done us no good. It cannot do any good...

> you have to survive, and being buried in superstitions does not help. We have to get rid of these beliefs. . . . Witches are mere creations of some evil conspirators . . . who do not want to see you developed. They do not want to see you debt free. They do not want your children to go to school. Because if they did [really want your children to go to school], then it would not serve their interest.[8]

The activists identify illiteracy as the main problem that makes the *adivasis* so vulnerable to the conspirators. In other words, the superstition frame is an important and continuing reference in all meetings about the anti-witch-hunt campaigns. One can see that the activists make reference, without being explicit, to both categories of witch hunts in the speeches. While referring to superstition as the cause of witch hunts, one can see the link to the surprise attack category of hunts. When they link superstition to the conspiracy theory, the activists make a reference to the calculated attack category of hunts.

In all of the speeches addressed to the audience, the activists stressed the connection between beliefs in witches and *adivasi* superstitions. The common phrase that the activists use to summarize the development of the witch hunts is "*ek dui tin*" (translated as one-two-three). "The accusations start on day one; Wednesday-Thursday the *janguru* intervenes and three is on Friday when the witch is killed." As the above quotes illustrate, the activists, through their speeches, stressed how the "simple, uneducated" *adivasis* were manipulated because of their superstitions by individuals who used witch hunts to serve their own purposes. The message in the superstition frame was direct: there are no real witches and thus there is no need to hunt for witches.

## Women's Development Frame

Along with the stress on witchcraft beliefs as superstitious, the activists of the anti-witch-hunt campaign applied a parallel frame when addressing the *adivasi* women during the meetings. As discussed in the section under "Anti-witch-hunt protest and activism on Sundays," the meetings of anti-witch-hunt campaigns are typically "concealed" under microcredit meetings under the self-help programs the *adivasi* women workers in the tea plantations are encouraged to attend. The activists directly target the women as the audience for the campaigns during these meetings. The focus is on issues of development for *adivasi* women and encouraging bonds and a network of community-building among the women participants. Frames such as "We want every woman in this village to be enlightened" and "We are a single community . . . we can fight all these evils and bring up empowerment" are used to attract the women. These frames are combined with anti-witch-hunt and anti-witchcraft accusations messages. The combination of these frames results in a stronger message, in which the NBPDC activists argue that beliefs in witches cannot go hand in hand with women's development. This point is well illustrated by Suchetana in one of her speeches: "We are a group whose interest does not end with loans. We want to uplift our lives. You [the women] cannot continue to believe in witches and talk about *unnati* [development]."

Suchetana, the main speaker in these meetings, often makes the connection between the two very explicit in her speeches.

> Sisters, you have formed this community. . . Because of this community you all have benefited some things. What are these benefits? I do not think that I have to explain because you know these [benefits] very well. In every para [community] in this village we have formed a "group" . . . there is good relations between everyone because of these groups . . . you are there in sorrow and happiness for everyone in this group. Previously you had to think to borrow a mere fifty rupees. Now you do not have to think about these any more...this has given all of you dignity. Your children go to schools . . .You have realized that there are no witches. Witches are mere creations of some evil conspirators . . . who do not want to see you developed. They do not want to see you debt free. They do not want your children to go to school. Because if they did [really want the children to go to school], then it would not serve their interest.

At a meeting addressed to the women after a witch hunt was "attempted" in the village, Suchetana talks about how the campaigns have served their purpose in preventing the hunt.

> After the big incident [of witch hunting where two women were murdered] a few years ago, you have participated in meetings at the primary school, at the village ground, at the village *sansadh*. There was only one purpose in these meetings: to stop the tradition of witch hunt in this village.

Speaking of how the women's microcredit groups came together, she continues:

> There were five hundred women from our micro credit groups who participated . . . not one or two. The *panchayat* became tired at our persuasion and agreed to join us. . . . Soon after this we thought that there will be no future witch hunts in this area. But what did we see? We saw that the hunts began again . . . within our micro credit groups. But we, the women have been again successful in preventing it. This is because we have come together as a group . . . we take development of our women seriously.

Within the women's development frame, alcoholism is addressed by the activists as a barrier. Alcoholism is a severe problem among the tea plantation villagers (Chatterjee 2001). As discussed in previous sections, Fridays are typically pay days and the beginning of the weekend. On Friday afternoons, visitors to the villages can smell the odor of fermented rice that would be used in the preparation of *haria*. Some of the local people that I interviewed talked about the link between alcohol consumption and witch accusations. According to these locals, Friday nights are "nights of mischief." In other words, on Fridays typically the entire village gets drunk, and fights break out between people, leading to an exchange of verbal insults. One of the common verbal insults used is the term *daini*, which often leads to witch accusations between the conflicting groups in the fight. In some cases, Friday night accusations lead to surprise witchcraft accusations. In cases of calculated categories of witchcraft accusations, the accusers and their supporters often consume a large quantity of alcohol before the actual witch hunt starts. Participants in this study, during their narration of events, have repeatedly described the smell of *haria* and the "red eyes" of the accusers.

For the activists in the anti-witch-hunt struggle, alcoholism is a major culprit for instigating witch hunts and accusations. In meetings, the activists address the issue of alcoholism along with women's development frame. The main argument was that unless alcohol consumption in the villages ended, the witch hunts would continue. Lipi, a 34-year-old female activist, addressed a meeting shortly after a woman was rescued by the villagers from a witch hunt. The villagers managed to drive away the accusers and the *janguru*, and informed the NGO. "Even though we have managed to stop this [witch hunt], the foundations for the complete eradication of the witch hunts is still shaky. The *peena* [alcohol consumption] is still on. As long as the *peena* continues you cannot do anything." The audience members often murmur and shake their heads in response. To them, alcoholism is a part of their life, something that is hard to fight against. Dhani, an *adivasi* woman responds, "[W]hat do I say? Things [meaning alcohol] are like this here. What happens after the *penna* who knows? We all know the reality, but this is a tribal area. What do we do?"

Addressing the women, Lipi continues, raising the issue of public humiliations if the witch hunts start again after the success story:

> [Y]ou will have to tread very carefully in the plantation area. Your success story, our anti-witch-hunt meetings, the songs that you have composed, the plays have been broadcast on television. The outside world now knows your story. The outside world knows that the women of Bhirpur have fought and protested against the tradition of witch hunts. They [the women] have come out in the streets and the world thinks that the tradition of *daini* has been eradicated from this area. But if the witch hunts start again, and they will if the *peena* continues among your men, you will be ashamed to show your faces to the outside world. I am saying this, this will happen.

The women's development frame addresses the day-to-day problems of the women in the plantation, like finances, schools for children, alcoholism, and women's empowerment to make the women of the plantation feel responsible for the eradication of witch hunts. Making the women feel responsible for witch hunts is a useful strategy from the standpoint of the NBPDC activists to prevent future witch hunts. In addition to responsibility, the *adivasi* women now have a real reason in preventing hunts: the benefits of the credit groups have resulted in significant changes in their lives. Thus, the activists have successfully employed these strategies to make the *adivasi* women workers become involved in the campaign and raise their voices against witch hunts (see Chakravarty and Chaudhuri 2012).

## Justice Frame

At the heart of the anti-witch-hunt campaign is the focus on healing and a sense of justice towards the victims and their families. The justice frame is used in meetings that are held in villages that may have had a recent incident of a witch hunt. Because of the lack of police involvement or, in some cases, a delayed response of the police in cases where the administration decides to intervene, the justice frames are used to encourage the women in the microcredit group to stand up for their members. The justice frames use slogans like "victory for the women of Chetana," "anti-witch-hunt mobilization reaching its peak under NBPDC" and "confession of guilt" to make its case. Speaking of the Chandmoni incident where five women were murdered, activists from the NBPDC talk about justice towards the family members of the victims. At a village meeting, Shova addressing their families' promises: "We will make sure that every guilty person in this incident is locked up. We will not let the guilty get away."

In Mourighat area of Jalpaiguri, some of the anti-witch-hunt campaigns have been successful. The case of Lalitha Oraon, a married *adivasi* woman, illustrates how microcredit self-help groups mobilized to rescue an accused witch. Lalitha had been accused on two prior occasions by her neighbor, Ravi, an Oraon man whom fellow villagers described as a powerful individual with close connections to *panchayat* (elected village-level governing body) members. In both instances, Lalitha produced a false confession and paid a fine in order to stave off a possible attack. It was not long before her neighbor renewed his accusations. He alleged that her witchcraft had produced disease in his livestock. A lower-level police inquiry, in which a constable was sent to the village to investigate, did nothing to stop the accuser from conspiring to kill the intended victim. By this time, however, Lalitha was a member of a microcredit self-help group. When one of the women in this network happened to pick up on information that the Ravi and his friends had planned to attack their target that same night, she immediately informed the local NBPDC activist and spread the word among the remaining women in the group. Within a few hours, all of the twenty-six self-help groups in the plantation had been alerted. Some of the women gathered in a vigil around Lalitha's home while others surrounded the accuser's home and called out to his wife, Golap, who happened to be a member of Lalitha's particular group. Recalling the events of that night, Rajani, one of the women participants in the Lalitha's self-help group, narrated:

> [W]e sort of outsmarted [*chalaki korey*] them [the accusers], by holding a meeting at their place. Seeing our numbers . . . and we had the local activist as well . . . Golap was frightened . . . and of course there was Ravi who kept on saying that Lalitha was a bad influence and wanted to get some of us to support him. All the self-help group members started to persuade Golap to withdraw the accusations. We told her that Lalitha was our self-help group sister. She [Lalitha] needed our support. We reminded Golap how Lalitha had looked after her children when she was ill, and how much she [Golap] had benefited from our support financially. We reminded her that it was us who came to her rescue every time her husband got drunk and beat her. . . . Golap became persuaded, and she joined our group against her husband and his friends. Seeing this we got a huge support . . . emotionally [*monner dik thekey joor elo*].

The vigil lasted all night. It turned into a meeting in which many of the women were joined by their families and other villagers (including men and women), who collectively insisted on the withdrawal of the accusations.

> We were united . . . it was remarkable how the self-help groups came together. Everyone was speaking and talking about how there are no real witches. We kept the pressure on Ravi all the time. We spoke about the superstitions and how some people [Ravi] took advantage of our simple minds. In the end it worked.

Cowed by the unyielding social pressure and the arrival in the morning of a senior NBPDC activist from the city, the accuser and his accomplices capitulated.

> Ravi and his friends became very quiet. He started saying that he made a mistake. . . . As soon as he said that, we dragged him to Lalitha's house. . . . Golap was the one who insisted that Ravi should beg for Lalitha's forgiveness. She said, "You should be taught a lesson." They begged for forgiveness [*Lalithar paa dhorey khoma chailo*]. . . . From that day onwards Lalitha was never harassed anymore.

## Difficulties and Challenges in the Campaign: The "Other" Actors

Despite the enormous challenges that NBPDC faced while conducting the anti-witch-hunt campaigns in Jalpaiguri, the organization was successfully able to tap into the networks of microcredit groups among the *adivasi* women. This was crucial for cases of successful interventions of witchcraft accusations. Through the strategic use of frames that resonated with the audience of women *adivasi* migrant workers, the activists were able to connect to the self-help groups' potential for collective action (Chakravarty and Chaudhuri 2012, 490). There is a body of scholarship that focuses on the unintended beneficial consequences of microcredit and similar lending groups' capacity for collective actions (see Sanyal 2009), and the NBPDC did achieve some success using the networks for the campaigns. However, some challenges remain for the organization as they work towards further consolidation of the campaign in the region.

Perhaps the biggest challenge for the NBPDC and its campaigns arises from the fact that it is perhaps a lone institutional actor in the intervention of witch hunts in Jalpaiguri. The examples of successful anti-witch-hunt campaigns that led to the passage of laws in the states of Bihar, Jharkhand, and Chhattisgarh point out that the police, the state government, and other NGOs did play an active instrumental role in collectively tackling the challenges posed by witch-craft accusations in the state. But in Jalpaiguri, I observed that the state government administration and the police were often passive actors and sometime "selective actors" in the anti-witch-hunt campaigns, unlike in the other states where they played a visible active role. For example, in the initial years before the NBPDC got involved in the campaign, the local police were either reluctant to interfere in witchcraft accusations or they arrived typically after the witch hunt was over. Their role with respect to witchcraft accusations either ended with arrests or in some cases an FIR (First Information Report). Even though in the last couple of years (particularly in the years 2003 and 2004) the police have been working with NBPDC to eradicate witch hunts in Jalpaiguri, the interest has mostly come from senior-level police administrators (the IPS-level officers). However, such interests are sporadic and are often dependent on the support of individual police officers and their relations with NBPDC. For example, the campaign in Dhanirampur region (2003–2005) in Jalpaiguri took off on a strong note with the support of the police, as the then Superintendent of the Police was a supporter of the campaign, and he often addressed the campaigns in civilian clothes. However, with his official transfer in 2005, which coincided with my entry in the field, the police department of Jalpaiguri withdrew its support for NBPDC campaigns in the region. Much of the lack of interest from police and other similar institutions lies in their attitude towards the witch hunts and the *adivasi* workers in the plantations. For example, during one of the interviews with a senior police official, the officer dismissed any idea that witchcraft accusations among the *adivasi* migrant workers have to do with the exploitation of their labor at the tea plantations. According to him, witch hunts incidents occur solely because of economic reasons and that the deprivation of education and health facilities plays a role in stimulating an attack against an alleged witch. He justifies:

> Currently poor pay in the tea gardens are [sic] one of the causes for their poor economic conditions. Don't you think it is interesting that in a community that goes to attend polio drop health camps would have witch hunts? The health condition, as these NGOs shout . . . is not a factor. It is pure economics.

The officer, though correctly identified wages as one of the factors that prompts the witchcraft accusations, shifted the responsibility of the hunts to a generalized "economics" and politics within the *adivasi* community.

Similarly, a common response when I approached some government officials for interviews was an expression of surprise at the topic: "[W]itch hunts do not occur in Jalpaiguri." Upon further discussions, some administrators commented that witchcraft accusations in West Bengal took place in the *adivasi* districts of Purulia or Malda, but they did not know that Jalpaiguri has one of the highest rates of witchcraft accusations in West Bengal in the last five years. Perhaps their comments of disbeliefs are a reflection of the lack of government interest in the topic and are tied to the poor support for requests for governmental grants made by the NBPDC for the campaigns. The frustrations of the activists of NBPDC are expressed in a letter to the Jalpaiguri district magistrate, in which they narrate how both the local and the district police ignored the complaints of NBPDC of an impending witch hunt in Chandmoni. Articulating the need to create a formalized campaign against witch hunts in the region and requesting a modest grant of 100,000 rupees from the West Bengal government, the activists wrote in the letter dated in 2003:

> Our organization got the news on the second day when not all of the victims were even killed. Despite our request to the highest administrative authority of the district, no immediate measures were taken. Our report on the missing women who were taken on suspicion of witchcraft was received with a pinch of disbelief . . . our report . . . was not believed till dead bodies started appearing.

The dependency on the occasional support of few sympathetic senior police officers and the lack of funds from the government to support the campaign made the NBPDC rely on the microcredit programs. Suchetana explains:

> Our hands are tied without the help of police in the area. . . . If we do not have the resources [through microcredit] then how will we stop witch hunts? Why would the women [of the village] pay attention to our lectures? The other NGOs who operate in the area are not interested in collaborating with us against witch hunts . . . and why would they? The government does not have programs to stop witch hunts! No programs means no money.

During the times when the police and the NBPDC have collaborated together on the campaigns, fundamental differences have emerged between the two institutions. The biggest criticism coming from the activists about the police operations in the areas is over the issue of police reports on witchcraft accusations. Most accusations of witchcraft, the activists argue, do not make it to the reports. Perhaps this calls for a stronger demand for the passage of a law that would criminalize witchcraft accusations. Second, while the activists want a legal change to prevent future hunts in the region, the police and administrators prefer counseling centers to deal with the victims. To the activists, while counseling centers are useful for the victims and their families, they do not necessarily prevent future hunts. Shipra, a NBPDC activist explains the conflict between the two strategies:

> The police wants NBPDC to organize a family counseling centre as part of the anti witch hunts campaign. What will a family counseling center do? We want total eradication of witch hunts that can only be possible if we are able to involve the community, particularly the women, as a whole. There are differences in the way we and the police want to operate. We have grievances against the police for their neglect of the problem and for not realizing the importance of the problem of witch hunts.

To prevent future witchcraft accusations, NBPDC argues that anti-witch-hunt laws are essential, an opinion that local politicians and administrators do not want to take seriously. They are more interested in concentrating on issues of health and education rather than on witch hunts, because government aid for health and education projects is readily available. Suchetana summarizes the attitude: "We requested one lakh rupees ($2,000) as aid for the anti-witch-hunt project. This is not a huge amount . . . but they will not fund us. Witch hunts are just not important enough."

Perhaps the other big challenge facing the NBPDC after they rescue accused women, are the rehabilitation services for the victims. Unlike the examples in Chhattisgarh (Macdonald 2009), there are no governmental compensations for the victims. NBPDC houses the rescued accused woman in its "short stay home," a woman's shelter that does not have the necessary counseling facilities needed to rehabilitate and counsel victims of witchcraft accusations. Also, as the name suggests, the shelter is temporary, and activists are confused as to how to rehabilitate the women. Most often rescued women either leave on their own (Basanti) or are "returned" to the village by the police. The following is an excerpt from a local newspaper that described the return of an accused woman, Purnima, to her village:

> On our way (to Malbazar), we tailed two sleek vehicles. The first carried a posse of policemen, while the sub divisional police officer and the officer-in-charge of Matelli occupied the other. It was a strange spectacle: civil and State institutions—the police, the media and an NGO— had colluded to force a reluctant community to take back an innocent woman. On reaching (Malbazar), a quaking Bishwanath (the accuser) was produced in the *mukhia's* [elected local leader] office and then instructed to give a written undertaking guaranteeing Purnima's safety. The man promised all that and more. It was arranged that Purnima would live with Bishwanath's family till she got her job back. Before parting, the two were made to stand together and their photographs taken to symbolize Bishwanath's (and hence the community's) acceptance of Purnima. By late evening, the policemen had left and I could hear the activists talking excitedly about another successful rehabilitation. But I could not forget Purnima's face as she stood near her attacker. What I saw on it was unspeakable fear: the fear of being abandoned once again (Mukherjee 2010).

The excerpt demonstrates how NBPDC is dependent on the police for rehabilitation and how the responsibility of Purnima's safety was left to her accuser (Chakravarty and Chaudhuri 2012, 502–503), raising concerns about whether the anti-witch-hunt campaigns are sustainable in the long run as a successful strategy to combat the witchcraft accusations.

## Concluding Thoughts

I as near the end of this chapter and comment on the final subsection of this book, I begin by reflecting on what is going on in the states where there has been successful passage of anti-witch-hunt laws. In Chhattisgarh, where it has been seven years since witchcraft accusations came to be criminalized in the states, concerns are being raised as to whether the passage of the law is preventing witchcraft associations in reality. For some, passage of the law was a "hollow victory" (Women's News Network 2012). For others, the passage of a law in Jharkhand did not ensure severe punishments for the perpetrators (Saxena 2007). At present, the punishment for accusations can range from 1,000–2,000 rupees and jail time of three to six months for the most serious cases (Kiro 2008).

Perhaps criminalization of witchcraft accusations will not lead to eradication of witch hunts in Jalpaiguri. After all, the evidence from Africa has shown us that witchcraft has reemerged in modern times and that witchcraft is as much a modern rational phenomenon in global times (Comaroff and Comaroff 1993). Thus, claims of "scientific and rational" realization of minds (ASKS in Chhattisgarh) as an argument to end witchcraft accusations will not prevent hunts in reality. Instead, what might work is the realization of the causes from which witchcraft accusations emerge among the *adivasi* migrant workers in the tea plantations of Jalpaiguri: as manifestations of the labor-management conflict in the plantations. The avenues of protest for the *adivasi* migrant workers need to come within their own communities and not through external nongovernmental or governmental organizations that claim to articulate the interests of the *adivasi* workers. Over the last year (2010), there have been reports of the growing popularity of *Adivasi Vikas Parishad* (AVP or Tribal Development Council), an *adivasi* organization of migrant workers in the plantations. The popularity of this organization has started to raise concerns among the local trade unions and non-*adivasi* political leaders in the region, because AVP has registered a trade union (Progressive Plantation Workers Union), and it is formulating separate negotiation proposals (from the other trade unions in the plantations) with the state government for *adivasi* migrant workers wages in the plantations (Bhowmik 2011, 251). Perhaps it is the development of organizations like the AVP, which are created by, composed of, and representative of *adivasi* migrant workers, that will promote empowerment among the plantation laborers. In addition, programs (such as the self-help groups) that promote opportunities for earning livelihoods separate from that of the wage economy of the plantations create a social community that stresses the importance of women's development and the education of children. This produces the seeds of success in the development and political empowerment of this group of workers and provides alternatives that could end their oppression within the wage economy of the plantations.

## Notes

1. The state of Jharkhand was created out of the state of Bihar in 2000. At the time of the passage of the anti-witch-hunt law in Bihar, in 1999, Jharkhand (a region in the south of Bihar) was a part of Bihar. Later the state passed its own anti-witch-hunt law in 2001.
2. North Bengal's People's Development Center was known as JEU *Mahila Vikas Sangstha* till fall 2005. After that it changed its name to NBPDC. The change was the result of the NBPDC's broadening its focus from women-oriented problems to a focus on the problems of the people in North Bengal.
3. By the last four years, I mean from 2003 onwards to 2007, the year that I made my final visit to the field.
4. Indian Government, at all levels, announces Welfare Schemes for a cross-section of the society from time to time. These Schemes could be either Central, State specific, or a joint collaboration between the Centre and the States. The NGOs are often assigned the task of administering the schemes. The schemes could be of a variety of topics from agricultural, educational, health, and hygiene and so on. See http://india.gov.in/govt/schemes.php.
5. BPL schemes are a major crowd-puller in villages. Under this scheme, families are classified on the basis of whether they fall "below" or "above" the poverty line. Falling below the poverty line brings in some benefits from the Government in the form of interest-free loans and special economic schemes.
6. Some high-level police administrators had given support to the campaign against witch hunts by NBPDC, especially in the early years. Their involvement was mainly at the personal level, (for example, addressing the crowd in civilian uniform), and, following the routine transfer of these officers, the support from the police for the campaign has weakened over the years.
7. The word *Shu* means "good," and the word *Ku* means "bad." *Shuu-shangaskar* thus refers to good traditions, and *ku-shangaskar* refers to bad traditions or superstitions.
8. The word *opobadh* means derisions or false accusations, and the term *opoprochar* means bad publicity or spreading of false allegations.

# Appendix A

# Outline of Interview Guides

*I. Guides for police officers, administrators, management and activists*

**General demographics and Involvement in the witch hunts:**

1. What is your occupation?
2. About how many incidents of witch hunts have you dealt with or are acquainted with within the last 4 years?
3. Did you provide any aid to the victims? What kind of aid (legal, investigative or social support) did you provide for the victims?

**Intensity of the hunts:**

1. To the best of your knowledge, how many incidents of witch hunts occur in India per year? How many of them occur in West Bengal? What are the major districts in West Bengal where the hunts occur?
2. Where does Jalpaiguri figure in the overall picture of witch hunts in India?
3. What do you think is the percentage of the incidents that gets re-ported to the police?
4. Do you think there are incidents that don't get reported to the police? About what percentage gets reported and what percentage do not?
5. Why are there some incidents that do not get reported?
6. Do you know if anyone tried to make an estimate of unreported incidents? (Get details if yes).

**Community:**

1. Are witch hunts a feature of tribal/*adivasi* communities in India?
2. How common are witch hunt incidents among the *adivasi* migrant tea workers?

**Ecological and demographic characteristics of the labor lines:**

1. What is the level of literacy among the labor line community to the best of your knowledge? What is the literacy rate among men? What is the literacy rate among women?
2. How far is the nearest state run hospital or health center from the labor lines?
3. How far is the nearest police post from the labor lines?
4. How far is a local newspaper office from the labor lines?

**Reference on witch hunts:**

1. What do you think are the major causes of witch hunts in the plantations?
2. Why do the tribals/*adivasis* belief in witches?
3. Who gets identified as a witch in the village?
4. Does disease seem to be a major cause leading to a witch hunt?
5. What role does prior conflict between the instigator and accused parties of witch hunts play?
6. Does internal village politics have a role in instigating an attack?
7. What is the role of the *janguru* in the village? Does he have a role in instigating an attack?
8. Do you think gender is involved in the conflicts, meaning, does the conflict take place between a man (instigator) and a woman (accused), between two women or men? Is it common for men to accuse women of practicing witch craft?

**Witch:**

1. Who/what is a witch? Describe the witch? What is the idea of a witch among the *adivasis*? Does the witch always cause harm or good?
2. Who is considered to be a witch in the village?
3. How do villagers identify a witch? Are there any tell tale signs?
4. What happens after a witch is identified?

**Witch hunts:**

1. How old are the witches typically? Can you give me a range?

2. Are the accused witches typically single women (unmarried, separated, divorced or widowed? Or are they married?
3. Do they typically have children?
4. What happens during an attack?
5. Do all the villagers get involved in the attack?
6. What is the reaction of the village authorities and management when there is an accusation of witchcraft?
7. Does the village authority try to mediate between conflicting par-ties? How do they mediate? How often are impositions of fines a form of mediation?
8. What happens if the accused refuses to pay a fine?
9. What happens if she does?
10. What instigates the witchcraft accusation to turn into a full-fledged attack?
11. Does the attack involve lynching, killing, banishment or ostracism of the accused witch?
12. What is the reaction of the village authorities after the attack? What happens to the accusers?
13. What happens to the accused witch (if she survives the attack)? Does she leave the village?

**Diseases:**

1. What do you think are some of the common diseases that have been attributed to have been caused by a witch?
2. Because some people think that witches are responsible for causing illness in people, what percentage of attacks is caused due to the prior occurrence of disease in the village?
3. What do you think are the common diseases that occur in rural India, particularly West Bengal?
4. What do you think are the major years (last 25 years) in which epidemics, such as of tuberculosis and polio, have occurred in West Bengal?
5. Could you say something about the witch hunt statistics in those years?

**Land:**

1. Who owns the land in the plantations?
2. Can the *adivasis* own land in the plantations?
3. Is there a scarcity of land holdings among *adivasis*?
4. Can women own land among the *adivasis*? Do they inherit land?
5. What do you think is the rate of witch hunts that have been caused by a property (meaning land) dispute?

**Gender:**

1. What do you think is the gender of the individual who gets accused of practicing witchcraft? It is always female?
2. What do you think is the percentage of the attacks towards male witches?
3. What percentage of the attacks, do men compared to women, instigate?
4. Is there possibility of multiple instigations (example mixed gender coalitions: man and woman)?

**Status of women:**

1. What can you tell us about the status of women in the *adivasi* society? Are they economically independent? Do they inherit property (land, house, money etc)?
2. Do you know if there is a traditional system of inheritance among the *adivasi* women, or is this a new development? After the death of a father or husband, who has the first claim on the property: wife/daughter or son/other male relatives?

**Government reaction:**

1. What is the reaction of the state and central government towards witch hunts?
2. Apart from registering these cases under murder or physical assault case, what are some of the other legal actions against the accused?
3. What policies are the government thinking to combat witch hunts?

**Legal aid and social support:**

1. What kind of legal aid does victims of witch hunts receive?
2. Who provides it?
3. Are there any provisions of shelter for the victims?
4. Who runs the shelters?
5. What kind of social support, counseling do the victims get?
6. Who funds the shelters?
7. Are there any local bodies (in the villages) that work against witch hunts?
8. What are they doing to prevent such attacks?

**Police:**

1. What role does local police play in areas where witch hunts occur?
2. Do they intervene when there is a complaint of a witch accusation by the victim?

3. What action do the police take against the instigators of the witch hunt?
4. Among the total number of cases registered as witch hunts, what is the percentage of cases that had the instigators punished?

**Other general questions:**

1. Why do witch hunts take place primarily in rural areas?
2. What are the causes behind it?
3. What do you think are the social reasons that instigate such hunts?
4. What is the state and central government doing to prevent further hunts?
5. How do you think that a central law against witchcraft (India currently does not have a law) would affect witchcraft accusations?
6. Will there be a rise or decline in incidences of witchcraft accusations as a result of stronger laws? Why?

*II. Interview guide for villagers (accusers, accused, relatives and other villagers)*

This particular interview guide is going to be very open-ended. The level of comfort experienced by the interviewee, during the interview, will determine the direction of the interview. The interviewer's aim will be to get a clear picture of witch hunt cases that have occurred, using their narratives. Sometimes certain questions will be dropped, while at other times a lot of additional questions will be asked during an interview, depending upon the cooperation of the interviewee. I have tried to make this interview guide as broad based as possible.

**General questions:**

1. Has there ever been a witch hunt in this village?
2. When did the last incident of witch hunt occur?
3. How often do these incidents occur in your village?
4. What was the age, gender of the accuser and relationship to the accused in the last incident of witch hunt?
5. What was the age and gender of the accused? Is she single, married, or widowed? If married, does her husband stay with her? Does she have kids?
6. Can you recall any other incidents of witch hunts? If yes then de-scribe those incidents.

**On the incident of witch hunt:**

1. So tell me why the incident of witch hunt occurred in this village? In other words, what instigated the accusation of witchcraft against the accused?
2. Was there some conflict between the two conflicting parties?
3. Did the parties (instigator and accused) know each other?

**Accusation of witchcraft:**

1. What did the instigator accuse the witch of doing?
2. Did someone from the instigator's family fall sick?
3. When did the accuser and his/her family realize that witchcraft was taking place?
4. Did they consult a *janguru*?
5. How did the *janguru* know that a witch is behind the illness?
6. How did the accuser and his family identify the witch?
7. What did the accuser and his/her family do after the witch was identified?
8. What role do other villagers play in the identification of the witch?
9. What happens to the accused witch?
10. Is the witch punished?
11. How is the witch punished?
12. What happened during the witch hunt?
13. Who decided the punishment for the witch?
14. Who administered the punishment to the witch?
15. How was the punishment administered?
16. Was it necessary to kill the witch?
17. Does the punishment of the witch result in the eradication of witchcraft from the accuser's family?
18. What happened to the family member who was sick after the accusation/attack? Did s/he recover?

**Characteristic of the witch:**

1. Have you seen a witch?
2. Do you believe in witches and do witches really exist?
3. How do you know that the particular person is a witch?
4. How does a witch look? Describe some of her physical characteristics.
5. How does a witch operate? In other words what are her tools?
6. How does a witch harm individuals?
7. How do you get rid of the witch's spell?

**Questions for the accused and her relatives:**

1. Why do you think you/or your relative was accused?
2. Do you believe in witches?
3. Did you have any conflict with the accuser and his/her family?
4. Describe the accusation?
5. Did you try to defend yourself/your relative who was accused?
6. How did other villagers react to the accusations against you?
7. Was there a trial involved?
8. How conducted the trial?
9. Did you go to the police for help?
10. How did they react?
11. Describe what happened during the hunt?
12. Who led the hunt?
13. What do you think was the real motive behind the hunt?
14. What happened after the hunt?

**Additional questions for the accusers and their relatives:**

1. How did you know that the accused was a witch?
2. What did the accused do?
3. Did you go to the *janguru*?
4. Did the punishment help?
5. What is your reaction to the way the police reacted on the witch hunt?

# Appendix B

# Selected List of Participants for Interviews (Out of 80 Participants)

| NAME | SEX | AGE |
|---|---|---|
| *Accused witch* (Total interviewed 8) | | |
| Basanti | F | 27 |
| Chaili | F | 60s |
| Chandrani | F | 45 |
| Dulari | F | Early 30s |
| Mita | F | 27 |
| Ramani | F | 60 |
| *Relatives of accused witch* (Total interviewed 16) | | |
| Alfred | M | 28 |
| Bhutiya | F | 40 |
| Bila | F | 33 |
| Chandrima | F | 23 |
| Gundur Oraon | M | 44 |
| Lali Oraon | F | 40 |
| Lata | F | 29 |
| Lattu | M | 18 |
| Monohar | M | 45 |
| Pokua | F | 45 |
| Seema | F | 35 |
| Shilpi | F | 45 |

| | | |
|---|---|---|
| Smita | F | 50 |
| Sumitra | F | 50 |
| Viral | M | 35 |

*Accuser* (Total interviewed 9)

| | | |
|---|---|---|
| Dipti | F | 28 |
| Duli | F | 18 |
| Hari | M | 30 |
| Pukhani | F | 18 |
| Radha | F | 30s |
| Rimi | F | 40 |
| Sukhni | F | 40 |
| Sumi | F | 30s |
| Sushil | M | 38 |

*Villagers* (Total interviewed 12)

| | | |
|---|---|---|
| Bhagawan | M | 60 |
| Rajani | F | 34 |
| Ramdev | M | 40 |
| Ramlal | M | 40 |
| Shamlal | M | 50 |
| Shanti Devi | F | 42 |
| Sunil | M | 30 |
| Tippo | M | 43 |

*Janguru* (Interviewed 1)

| | | |
|---|---|---|
| Hariram | M | 60 |

*Plantation management, police and administrators* (Total interviewed 9)

| | | |
|---|---|---|
| Champa Devi | F | 50 |
| Minoti | F | 45 |
| Ranajit Jha | M | 42 |
| Salil | M | 38 |

*Activists* (Total interviewed 25)

| | | |
|---|---|---|
| Balaram | M | 40s |
| Balwant | M | Mid 40s |
| Chanda | F | 40 |
| Lipi | F | 34 |
| Meera | F | 38 |

| | | |
|---|---|---|
| Rani | F | 38 |
| Shamita | F | 42 |
| Shipra | F | 35 |
| Shrabani | F | 45 |
| Suchetona | F | 46 |
| Subir | M | 45 |

# Appendix C

## List of Abbreviations

| | |
|---|---|
| ASKS | Andh Shraddha Nirmulan Samiti |
| BFEC | Blind Faith Erradication Committee |
| BSF | Border Security Force |
| FLAC | Free Legal Aid Committee |
| HRLN | Human Rights Law Networks |
| JEU | Jalpaiguri East Ukilpara Mahila Sanghstha |
| NBMR | North Bengal Mountain Rifles |
| NBPDC | North Bengal People's Development Center |
| NHRC | National Human Rights Commission |
| MPLA | Movimento Popular de Libertacao de Angola |

# Appendix D

# Glossary

*Adivasi/ adivashi:* tribals; indigenous community
*amader kothar dam nei:* there is no value to our words
*andha-bishash:* blind faith
*andolan:* protest
*arkatis: recruiting agents for Assam plantations*
*ban:* arrow
*ban mara:* shooting of arrows
*bari*: house; home
*bhath*: boiled rice
bhumiputras: sons of the soil
*bigha* or *faltu* worker: temporary worker
*boka-shoka manush:* simple-minded folks
*buri*: old woman
*buria*: old woman
*buri nazar*: evil eye
*chowki*: low-rise wooden stool
*churi:* young girl
*dal*: lentils
*dai:* midwife
*dain/ daini/dains:* witch
*dainir boshobash:* where the witches live
*Jangijati: wild caste*
*Janguru/ ojha*: medicine man
*jid dhorey thakkey*: express stubbornness
*karon*: reason
*ki jani*: who knows
*kala jaadu*: black magic
*kala nazar*: evil eye
*kharap bath*: talking ill about someone
*kharap*: bad
*kukri*: local small knife
*ku-shangaskar*: superstition
*kya malum*: who knows
*laathi*: stick
*madesia:* another name for *Oraons*
*mai-baap:* parents (mother-father)
*matabar*: headman
*mathar thekey*: creation of the mind
*meye- cheley*: reference to woman
*nazar:* eye
*opobadh*: spreading false accusations
*opoprochar*: spreading false accusations
*pahalwan*: wrestler
*panchayat*: village headman
*pati parameshwar*: husband is God
*peena*: drinking

*dainir baccha*: children of the witch
*daini Protha:* the tradition of believing in witches
*daini vidya:* the knowledge of witch-craft
*dal-roti:* lentils and bread
daru: liquor
*devta*: God
*didi*: older sister
*fagun mash*: the month of February
*gala gali:* curses
*gharelu jogra*: household quarrels
*haria/handia*: the name of the local rice brew
*jaar-puch*: the chanting of mantra used to get rid of the witch's spells
*jadu mantra*: magic
*jangli/jungli*: uncivilized or uncultured
*pichla-rog*: complications during pregnancy
*puja*: rituals
*purnima*: full moon
*raj:* rule
*sahib:* master (planter)
*sansadh*: forum
*sardars*: middle men
*shaali:* sister-in-law, also used as a derogatory slur
*shai:* consent
*shustho*: healthy
*sindoor*: vermilion
*thika:* incentive wage
*tuktak*: hocus pocus
*vidya*: knowledge
*vyayu*: wind

# Bibliography

Arditi, George. "Equilibrium, Structural Contradictions, and Social Conflicts: Revisiting Stinchcombe." *Sociological Forum* 3, no. 2 (Spring 1988): 282-292.

Ashforth, Adam. *Witchcraft, Violence, and Democracy in South Africa.* Chicago: University of Chicago Press, 2005.

Bailey, F. G. *The Witch Hunt or the Triumph of Morality.* Ithaca, NY: Cornell University Press, 1992.

Baker, Therese L. *Doing Social Research*, 2nd Edition. New York: McGraw Hill Inc., 1994.

Bandyopadhyay, Tarashankar. "The Witch." In *Of Women, Outcastes, Peasants and Rebels,* edited by Kalpana Bardhan (translated with an introduction), 110-123. Berkeley: University of California Press, Berkeley, 1990.

Barman, Mita. *Persecution of Women: Widows and Witches.* Calcutta, India: Indian Anthropological Society, 2002.

Barstow, Anne Llewellyn. *Witchcraze. A New History of European Witch Hunts.* San Francisco: Pandora. A division of Harper Collins Publishers, 1995.

Baruya, Ananya. *Belief in Witch. Witch Killing in Dooars.* New Delhi: Northern Book Center, 2005.

Bates, Crispin. "Coerced and Migrant Laborers in India: The Colonial Experience." *Edinburg Papers in South Asian Studies* 13 (2000): 2-33.

Becker, Howard S. *Tricks of the Trade. How to Think About Your Research While Doing It.* Chicago: University of Chicago Press, 1998.

———. *Outsiders: Studies in the Sociology of Deviance.* New York: Free Press, 1963.

Behringer, Wolfgang. *Witches and Witch Hunts: A Global History.* Cambridge, UK: Polity Press, 2004.

Benford, Robert D., and David A. Snow. "Framing Processes and Social Movement: An Overview and Assessment." *Annual Review of Sociology* 26 (August 2000): 611-639.

Ben-Yehuda, Nachman. "The European Witch Craze of the 14th to 17th Centuries. A Sociologist's Perspective." *American Journal of Sociology* 86 no, 1 (July 1980): 1-31.

———. "Problems Inherent in Socio-Historical Approaches to the European Witch Craze." *Journal for the Scientific Study of Religion* 20, no. 6 (December 1981): 326-338.

———. *Deviance and Moral Boundaries. Witchcraft, the Occult, Science Fiction, Deviance Sciences and the Scientists*. Chicago: University of Chicago Press, 1987.

———. *The Politics and Morality of Deviance: Moral Panics, Drug Abuse, Deviant Science, and Reversed Stigmatization*. Albany, NY: State University of New York Press, 1990.

Bever, Edward. "Witchcraft, Female Aggression, and Power in the Early Modern Community." *Journal of Social History* 35, no.4 (Summer 2002): 955–988.

Bhadra, Gautam. *From an Imperial Product to a National Drink: The Culture of Tea Consumption in Modern India*. Calcutta: The Center for Studies in Social Sciences (in association with Tea Board India), 2005.

Bhadra, Mita. *Women Workers of Tea Plantations in India*. New Delhi: Heritage Publishers, 1992.

Bhadra, Ranajit K. *Social Dimension of Health of Tea Plantation Workers in India*. Dibrugarg, Assam: NL Publishers, 1997.

Bhadra, Ranajit K., and Mita Bhadra, eds. *Plantation Laborers of North-East India*. Dibrugarg, Assam: NL Publishers, 1997.

Bhowmik, Sharit, *Class Formation in the Plantation System*. New Delhi: People's Publishing House, 1981.

——."Ethnicity and Isolation: Marginalization of Tea Plantation Workers." *Race/Ethnicity* 4, no. 2 (Winter 2011): 235–253.

Bhowmik, Sharit K., Virginius Xaxa, and M. A. Kalam. *Tea Plantation Labor in India*. New Delhi: Friedrich Ebert Stiftung, 1996.

Black, Donald. *The Behavior of Law*. New York: Academic Press, 1976.

Bodding, P. O., *Studies in Santhal Medicine and Connected Folklore*. Reprint, Calcutta: Asiatic Society of Calcutta (1925), 1986.

Bosu Mullick, Samar. "Gender Relations and Witches among the Indigenous Communities of Jharkhand, India." *Gender Technology and Development* 4, no. 3 (November 2000): 333–358.

Bradman, Norman, Seymour Sudman, and Brian Wansink. *Asking Questions: The Definitive Guide to Questionnaire Design for Market Research, Political Polls, and Social and Health Questionnaires*. San Francisco: Jossey-Bass, 2004.

Breslaw, Elaine G., *Tituba Reluctant Witch of Salem: Devilish Indians and the Puritan Fantasies*. New York: New York University Press, 1996.

Briggs, Robin, *Witches and Neighbors: The Social and Cultural Context of European Witchcraft*. New York: Penguin, 1996.

Brinkman, Inge."War, Witches and Traitors: Cases from the MPLA's Eastern Front in Angola (1966–1975)." *Journal of African History* 44, no. 2 (2003): 303–325.

Carstairs, G. Morris. *The Death of a Witch: A Village in North India 1950–1981*. London: Hutchinson, 1983.

Chakraverti, Ipsita Roy. *Beloved Witch: An Autobiography*. Noida, India: Harper Collins India, 2000.

Chakravarty, Anuradha, and Soma Chaudhuri. "Strategic Framing Work(s): How Microcredit Loans Facilitate Anti Witch Hunt Movements." *Mobilization: An International Journal* 17, no. 12 (June 2012): 489–508.

Charmaz, Kathy. "The Grounded Theory Method: An Explication and Interpretation." In *Contemporary Field Research: A Collection of Readings*, edited by Robert M. Emerson, 109-126. Boston: Little Brown, 1983.

———. "Grounded Theory." In *Contemporary Field Research*, edited by R. M. Emerson, 335-352. 2d ed. Prospect Heights, IL: Waveland, 2001.

Chatterjee, Partha. *The Nation and Its Fragments*. Princeton: Princeton University Press, 1993.

Chatterjee, Piya. *A Time for Tea: Women, Labor, and Post/Colonial Politics on an Indian Plantation*. Durham: Duke University Press, 2001.

———. "Hungering for Power: Borders and Contradictions in Indian Tea Plantation Women's Organizing." In "Comparative Perspectives Symposium: Women's Labor Activism." *Signs: Journal of Women in Culture and Society* 33, no. 8 (Spring 2008): 497–505.

Chatterjee, Suranjan, and Ratan Dasgupta. "Tea-Labor in Assam: Recruitment and Government Policy, 1840–80." *Economic and Political Weekly* 16, no.44–46 (November 1981: 1861–1864.

Chaudhuri, A. B., *Witch Killings Amongst Santals*. New Delhi: Ashish Publishing House, 1987.

Chaudhuri, Soma, Merry Morash, and Julie Yingling. "Marriage Migration, Patriarchal Bargains and Wife Abuse: A Study of South Asian Women." *Violence Against Women*, Forthcoming.

Chaudhuri, Soma. "Women as Easy Scapegoats: Witchcraft Accusations and Women as Targets in Tea Plantations of India." *Violence Against Women* 18, no. 10 (October 2012): 1213–1234.

Chaudhury, Samrat, and Nitin Varma. "BetweenGods/Goddesses/Demons and 'Science': Perceptions of Heath and Medicine among Plantation Laborers in Jalpaiguri District, Bengal." *Social Scientist* 30, no. 5-6 (May-June 2002): 18–38.

Chauhan, Abha. *Tribal Women and Social Change in India*. Etawah, India: A. C. Brothers, 1990.

Chong, Kelly. H. "Negotiating Patriarchy: South Korean Evangelical Women and the Politics of Gender." *Gender & Society* 20, no. 6 (December 2006): 697–724.

Comaroff, Jea, and John Comaroff. *Modernity and its Malcontents. Ritual and Power in Post Colonial Africa.* Chicago: University of Chicago Press, 1993.

Cohen, Stanley, *Folk Devils and Moral Panics: The Creation of the Mods and Rockers.* 3rd ed. London: Routledge, 2002.

Coy, Patrick G., and Lynne M. Woehrle. "Constructing Identity and Oppositional Knowledge: The Framing Practices of Peace Movement Organizations During the Persian Gulf War." *Sociological Spectrum* 16 (July-September 1996): 287–327.

Critcher, Chas. "Moral Panic Analysis: Past, Present and Future." *Sociology Compass* 2, no. 4 (July 2008): 1127–1144.

Curries, Elliot P. "Crimes Without Criminals: Witchcraft and its Control in Renaissance Europe." *Law and Society Review* 3, no. 1 (August 1968): 7–32.

Daily News and Analysis, "Woman Branded Witch, Beheaded." *Daily News and Analysis* [Mumbai], April 21, 2008.

Dalton, Edward Tuite. *Descriptive Ethnology of Bengal.* Calcutta: Firma KL Mukhopadhyaya, 1960.

Das Dasgupta, Shamita. *Body Evidence: Intimate Violence Against South Asian Women in America.* New Brunswick, NJ: Rutgers University Press, 2007.

Dasgupta, Pranab Kumar, and Iar Ali Khan. *Impact of Tea Plantation Industry on the Life of Tribal Laborers.* Calcutta: Anthropological Survey of India, 1983.

Das Gupta, Ranajit. "Oraon Labour Agitation: Duars in Jalpaiguri District, 1915–1916." *Economic and Political Weekly* 24, no. 39 (September 1989): 2197–2201.

de Blecourt, Willem. "The Making of the Female Witch: Reflections on Witchcraft and Gender in the Early Modern Period." *Gender and History* 12, no 2 (July 2000): 287–309.

Delius, Peter. "Witches and Missionaries in Nineteenth Century Transvaal." *Journal of Southern African Studies* 27, no. 3 (September 2001): 429–443.

Desai, Amit. "Subaltern Vegetarianism: Witchcraft, Embodiment, and Sociality in Central India." *South Asia: Journal of South Asian Studies* 31, no. 1 (June 2008): 96–117.

Devi, Mahasweta. "The Witch Hunt." In *Of Women, Outcastes, Peasants and Rebels: A Selection of Bengali Short Stories*, edited and translated by Kalpana Bardhan, 242-271. Berkeley: University of California Press, 1990.

DeWindt, Anne Reiber. "Witchcraft and Conflicting Visions of the Ideal Village Community." *Journal of British Studies* 34, no. 4 (October 1995): 427–63.

De Young, Mary. *The Day Care Ritual Abuse Moral Panic.* Jefferson, NC: McFarland, 2004.

Douglas, Mary, eds. *Witchcraft: Confessions and Accusations.* London: Tavistock, 1970.

Ehrenreich, Barbara, and Deirdre English. *Witches, Midwives and Nurses.* New York: Feminist Press, 1973.

Elwin, Verrier. *Nagaland.* Shillong, India: The Research Department Adviser's Secretariat, 1961.

———. *Baigas*. Delhi: Gyan Publications, 1986.

Emerson, Robert M. *Contemporary Field Research. Perspectives and Formulations*. 2nd ed. Long Grove, IL: Waveland, 2001.

Erickson, Kai T. "Notes on the Sociology of Deviance." *Social Problems* 9, no.4 (Spring 1962): 307–314.

———. *Wayward Puritans: A Study in the Sociology of Deviance*. New York: Macmillan, 1966.

Errington, Frederick, and Deborah Gewertz. *Yali's Question: Sugar, Culture and History*. Chicago: University of Chicago Press, 2004.

Estes, Lehland L. "The Medical Origins of the European Witch Craze: A Hypothesis." *Journal of Social History* 16, no. 2 (Spring1983): 271–284.

Evans-Pritchard, E. E. *Witchcraft, Oracles and Magic Among the Azande*. Oxford: Oxford University Press, 1976.

Farberow, Norman L., ed. *Taboo Topics*. New York: Artherton, 1963.

Federici, Silvia. "Women, Witch Hunting and Enclosures in Africa Today." *Sozial Geschichte Online* 3, (2010): 10–27.

Felson, Marcus. *Crime and Everyday Life*. Thousand Oaks, CA: Pine Forge, 1994.

Fenstermaker, Sarah, and Candace West, eds. *Doing Gender, Doing Difference: Inequality, Power, and Institutional Change*. New York: Routledge, 2002.

Fortune, Reo F. *Sorcerers of Dobu: The Social Anthropology of the Dobu Islanders of the Western Pacific*. New York: Dutton, 1932.

Frankfurter, David. *Evil Incarnate: Rumors of Demonic Conspiracy and Satanic Abuse in History*. Princeton: Princeton University Press, 2006.

Fuji, Lee Ann. *Killing Neighbors. Webs of Violence in Rwanda*. Ithaca: Cornell University Press. 2009.

Garland, David. "On the Concept of Moral Panic." *Crime Media Culture* 4, no. 1 (April 2008): 9–30.

Gerami, Shahin, and Melodye Lehnerer. "Women's Agency and Household Diplomacy: Negotiating Fundamentalism." *Gender & Society* 15, no. 4 (August 2001): 556–573.

Geschiere, Peter. *The Modernity of Witchcraft: Politics and the Occult in Postcolonial Africa*. Charlottesville: University Press of Virginia, 1997.

———. "Globalization and the Power of Indeterminate Meaning: Witchcraft and Spirit Cults in Africa and East Asia." *Development and Change* 29, no. 4 (October 1998): 811–838.

Giddens, Anthony. *Capitalism and Modern Social Theory: An Analysis of the Writings of Marx, Durkheim and Max Weber*. Cambridge: Cambridge University Press, 1971.

Glaser, Barney, and Anselm Strauss. *The Discovery of Grounded Theory: Strategies for Qualitative Research*. Chicago: Aldine, 1967.

Gluckman, Max. "Psychological, Sociological and Anthropological Explanations of Witchcraft and Gossip: A Clarification." *Man, (New Series)*. 3, no. 1 (March 1968): 20–34.

Godbeer, Richard. *The Devil's Dominion: Magic and Religion in Early New England.* Reprint, Cambridge: Cambridge University Press, 1994.

Goode, Erich, and Nachman Ben-Yehuda. "Moral Panics: Culture, Politics, and Social Construction." *Annual Review of Sociology* 20, (August 1994): 149–171.

———. *Moral Panics: The Social Construction of Deviance.* Oxford, UK: Cambridge, 1994.

Goffman, Erving. *Frame Analysis: An Essay on the Organization of Experience.* New York: Harper & Row, 1974.

Goode, Erich. *Deviant Behavior.* Englewood Cliffs, NJ: Prentice Hall, 1994.

Gottfredson, Michael R., and Travis Hirschi. *A General Theory of Crime.* Stanford, CA: Stanford University Press, 1990.

Gupta, R. K. "Witchcraft Murders in the *Duars.*" In *The Santhals: Readings in Tribal Life, Volume 1: Religion and Magic,* edited by J. Troisi, 265–275. Delhi: Indian Social Institute, 1979.

Harley, David. "Historians as Demonologists: The Myth of the Midwife Witch." *Social History of Medicine* 3, no. 1 (April 1990): 1–26.

Harris, Marvin. *Cows, Pigs, Wars and Witches: The Riddles of Culture.* New York: Vintage Books, 1989.

Hill, Frances. *A Delusion of Satan: The Full Story of Salem Witch Trials.* Boston: Da Capo Press, 1997.

Hoak, Dale. "The Great European Witch-Hunts: A Historical Perspective." *American Journal of Sociology* 88, no. 6 (May 1983): 1270–1274.

Hondagneu-Sotelo, Pierette. *Gendered Transitions: Mexican Experiences of Immigration.* Berkeley: University of California Press, 1994.

Hutton, Ronald. "The Global Context of the Scottish Witch Hunt. In *The Scottish Witch Hunt in Context,* edited by Julian Goodare, 16-32. Manchester: Manchester University Press.

The Indian Express. "Tea Workers Union Threaten Fresh Strikes." *Indian Express* (Kolkata), August 12, 2011.

Indian Institute of Management. "Public Systems Report on Study of Labor Conditions in Tea Gardens of New Jalpaiguri." Kolkata: Indian Institute of Management, Undated.

Jacobs, Bruce A. *Investigating Deviance: An Anthology.* Los Angeles: Roxbury, 2002.

Jenkins, Philip. *Moral Panic: Changing Concepts of the Child Molester in Modern America.* New Haven: Yale University Press, 1998.

Jensen, Gary F. *The Path of the Devil: Early Modern Witch Hunts.* New York: Rowman & Littlefield, 2007.

JEU. *A Pictorial Story of Dhanirampur.* [Jalpaiguri]: Jalpaiguri East Ukilpara Mahila Samiti, 2005.

Jha, J. C. *Aspects of Indentured Inland Emigration to North-east India 1859–1918.* New Delhi: Indus Publishing Company, 1996.

Kandiyoti, Deniz. "Bargaining With Patriarchy." *Gender & Society* 2, no. 3 (September 1988): 274–290.

Karlsen, Carol F. *The Devil in the Shape of a Woman: Witchcraft in Colonial New England.* New York: Norton, 1988.

Kelkar, Govind, and Dev Nathan. "Women, Witches and Land Rights." In *Gender & Tribe: Women, Land and Forests in Jharkhand,* 88–109. New Delhi: Kali for Women, 1991.

———. "Women's Land Rights and Witches." In *Continuity and Change in Tribal Society,* edited by Mrinal Miri, 109–118. Shimla: Indian Institute of Advanced Study Rastrapati Nivas, 1993.

Kelkar, Govind, and Meera Warrier. "Indigenous Asia; Knowledge, Technology and Gender Relations." *Gender Technology and Development* 3, no. 2 (July 1999): 313–319.

Kennedy, G. John. "Psychological and Social Explanations of Witchcraft." *Man, New Series* 2, no. 2 (June 1967): 216–225.

Kivelson, Valerie A. "Male Witches and Gendered Categories in Seventeenth-Century Russia." *Comparative Studies in Society and History* 45, no. 3 (July, 2003): 606–631.

Kiernan, James, ed. *The Power of the Occult in Modern Africa: Continuity and Innovation in the Renewal of African Cosmologies.* Berlin: Lit Verlag, 2006.

Kiro, Santosh. "Legal Eagles Join Government Fight against Witchcraft." *Telegraph* (Kolkata), April 19, 2008

Kohnert, Dirk. "Magic and Witchcraft: Implications for Democratization and Poverty-Alleviating Aid in Africa." *World Development* 24, no. 8 (August1996): 1347–1355.

Kramer, Heinrich and James Sprenger. *The Malleus Maleficarum.* New York: Dover, 1971.

Kriesi, Hanspeter. "Political Context and Opportunity." In *The Blackwell Companion to Social Movements,* edited by David A. Snow, Sarah A. Soule, and Hanspeter Kriesi, 67–90. Hoboken, NJ: Wiley-Blackwell, 2007.

Larner, Christina. "Witchcraft Past and Present." In *Witchcraft and Religion. The Politics of Popular Beliefs.* edited by Christina Larner, 79–92. Oxford: Blackwell, 1984.

Latner, Richard. "The Long and Short of Salem Witchcraft: Chronology and Collective Violence in 1692." *Journal of Social History* 42, no. 1 (Fall 2008): 137–156.

Lee, Raymond. *Doing Research on Sensitive Topics.* Thousand Oaks, CA: Sage, 1993.

Lemert, Edwin M. *The Trouble with Evil: Social Control at the Edge of Morality.* Albany, NY: State University of New York Press, 1997.

Levack, Brian P. *The Witch Hunt in Early Modern Europe.* 3rd edition. London: Pearson Longman, 2006.

Liu, Andrew B. "The Birth of a Noble Tea Country: On the Geography of Colonial Capital and the Origins of Indian Tea." *Journal of Historical Sociology* 23, no. 1 (March 2010): 73–100.

Lofland, John, David Snow, Leon Anderson, and Lyn H. Lofland. *Analyzing Social Settings: A Guide to Qualitative Observation and Analysis.* 4th ed. Independence, KY: Thomson and Wadsworth, 2006.

Macdonald, Helen M. "Handled with Discretion: Shaping Policing Practices through Witchcraft Accusations." *Contributions to Indian Sociology* 43, no. 2 (May-August 2009): 285–315.

Macleod, Arlene Elowe. *Accomodating Protests: Working Women, the New Veiling and Change in Cairo.* New York: Columbia University Press, 1991

Mair, Lucy. *Witchcraft.* New York: McGraw-Hill, 1969.

Man, Edward Garnet. *Sonthalia and the Santhals.* Reprint, New Delhi: Mittal Publications, (1867), 1983.

Mann, K. *Tribal Women in a Changing Society.* Delhi: Mittal Publications, 1987

Marx, Karl. "Economic and Philosophical Manuscripts." In *Karl Marx Selected Writings,* edited by David McLellan, 83–121 . Oxford: Oxford University Press, 2005.

———. "Capital." In *Karl Marx Selected Writings,* edited by David McLellan, 452–546. Oxford: Oxford University Press, 2005.

Masquelier, Adeline. "Vectors of Witchcraft: Object Transactions and the Materialization of Memory in Niger." *Anthropological Quarterly* 70, no. 4 (October 1997): 187–198.

Mazumdar, Rinita. "Marital Rape: Some Ethical and Cultural Considerations." In *A Patchwork Shawl: Chronicles of South Asian Women in America,* edited by Shamita Das Dasgupta, 129–144. New Brunswick, NJ: Rutgers University Press, 1998.

Melchior, Florence. "Feminist Approaches to Nursing History." *Western Journal of Nursing Research* 26, no. 3 (April 2004): 340–355.

Meyer, Birgit, and Peter Pels, eds. *Magic and Modernity: Interfaces of Revelation and Concealment.* Stanford, CA: Stanford University Press, 2003.

McCammon, Holly J., Lyndi Hewitt, and Sandy Smith. "'No Weapon Save Argument': Strategic Frame Amplification in the US Woman Suffrage Movements." *Sociological Quarterly* 45, no. 3 (Summer 2004): 529–526.

Miguel, Edward. "Poverty and Witch Killing." *Review of Economic Studies* 72, no.4 (February2005): 1153–1172.

Mishra, Archana. *Casting the Evil Eye.* New Delhi. India: Roli Books, 2003.

Mixon, Franklin G., and Len J. Trevino. "The Allocation of Death in the Salem Witch Trials: A Public Choice Perspective." *International Journal of Social Economics* 30, no. 9 (August 2003): 934–941.

Moore, Henrietta, and Todd Sanders, eds. *Magical Interpretations, and Magical Realities. Modernity, Witchcraft and the Occult in Postcolonial Africa.* London: Routledge, 2001.

Mui, Vai-Lam. "Information, Civil Liberties, and the Political Economy of Witch Hunts." *Journal of Law, Economics and Organization* 15, no. 2 (Summer 1999): 503–525.

Mukherjee, Uddalak. "Victims of a Cruel Spell." *TheTelegraph* (Calcutta), August 19, 2010.

Munshi, Indra. "Women and Forest: A Study of the Warlis of Western India." *Gender, Technology and Development* 5, no. 2 (July 2001): 177–198.

Murray, Margaret. *The Witch-Cult in Western Europe*. Oxford: Claredon, 1921

Nag, Dipak Kumar. *Political Culture of the Tea Garden Workers*. Calcutta: Minerva Associates, 2000.

Nathan, Debbie. "Satanism and Child Molestation: Constructing the Ritual Abuse Scare." In *The Satanism Scare*, edited by J. T. Richardson, J. Best, and D. G. Bromley, 75–94. New York: A. de Gruyter, 1991.

Nathan, Dev, Govind Kelkar, and Xu Xiaogang. "Women as Witches and Keepers of Demons. Cross-Cultural Analysis of Struggles to Change Gender Relations." *Economic and Political Weekly* 33, no. 44 (October 1998): WS58–WS69.

Nathanson, Constance A., and Robert Schoen. *A Bargaining Theory of Sexual Behavior in Women's Adolescence*. Montreal, Canada: Proceedings of the 1993 IUSSP. (Hopkins Population Center Papers on Population WP92-13, *available at* https://jscholarship.library.jhu.edu/handle/1774.2/923.)

Niehaus, Isak A. "Witch-Hunting and Political Legitimacy: Continuity and Change in Green Valley, Lebowa, 1930–91." *Africa: Journal of the International African Institute* 63, no. 4 (October 1993): 498–530.

———.Witchcraft, Power and Politics. Exploring the Occult in the South African Lowveld. Sterling, VA: Pluto Books, 2001.

Nongbri, Tiplut. "Gender Issues and Tribal Development." RGICS Paper No. 47: Problems in Tribal Society-Some Aspects, 1998.

Ong, Aihwa. *Spirits of Resistance and Capitalist Discipline: Factory Women in Malaysia.* Albany, NY: State University of New York Press, 1987.

———. "On the Edge of Empires: Flexible Citizenship among Chinese in Diaspora." *Positions* 1, no.3 (Winter 1993): 745–778.

Orion, Loretta. *Never Again the Burning Times: Paganism Revived.* Long Grove, IL: Waveland, 1995.

Pangsapa, Piya. *Textures of Struggle: The Emergence of Resistance among Garment Workers in Thailand.* Ithaca, NY: Cornell University Press, 2007.

Parish, Jane. "Witchcraft, Riches and Roulette: An Ethnography of West Indian Gambling in the UK." *Ethnography* 6, no. 1 (March 2005): 105–122.

Quaife, G. R. *Godly Zeal and Furious Rage: The Witch in Early Modern Europe.* London: Croom Helm, 1987.

Redding, Sean. *Sorcery and Sovereignty. Taxation, Power, and Rebellion in South Africa, 1880-1963.* Athens, OH: Ohio University Press, 2006.

Reed, Isaac. "Why Salem Made Sense: Culture, Gender, and the Puritan Persecution of Witchcraft." *Cultural Sociology* 1, no. 2 (July 2007): 209–234.

Reis, Elizabeth. *Damned Women: Sinners and Witches in Puritan New England.* Ithaca: Cornell University Press, 1997.

Robben, Antonius C. G. M., and Jeffrey A. Sluka. *Ethnographic Fieldwork: An Anthropological Reader.* London: Blackwell, 2007.

Robinson, Enders A. *The Devil Discovered: Salem Witchcraft 1962*. Long Grove, IL: Waveland, 2001.

Rowlands, Michael, and Jean-Pierre Warnier. "Sorcery, Power, and the Modern State in Cameroon." *Man, New Series* 23, no.1 (March 1988): 118–132.

Roy, Puja. "Sanctioned Violence: Development and the Persecution of Women as Witches in South Bihar." *Development in Practice* 8, no. 2 (July 1998): 136–147.

Russell, Jeffrey B., and Brooks Alexander. *A History of Witchcraft: Sorcerers, Heretics and Pagans*. 2d ed. London: Thames and Hudson, 2007.

Ryan, Barbara. *Feminism and the Women's Movement: Dynamics of Change in Social Movement, Ideology and Activism*. New York: Routledge, 1992.

Rycroft, Daniel, and Sangeeta Dasgupta, eds. *The Politics of Belonging in India: Becoming Adivasi.* New York: Routledge, 2011.

Sanders, Andrew. *A Deed Without a Name: The Witch in Society and History*. Oxford: Berg, 1995.

Sanyal, Paromita. "From Credit to Collective Action: The Role of Microfinance in Promoting Women's Social Capital and Normative Influence." *American Sociological Review* 74, no. 4 (August 2009): 529–550.

Sarkar, R. L., and Maherndra P. Lama, eds. *Tea Plantation Workers in the Eastern Himalayas: A Study on Wages, Employment and Living Standards*. Delhi: Atma Ram & Sons, 1986.

Sarkar, Kanchan, and Sharit Bhowmick. "Trade Unions and Women Workers in Tea Plantations." *Economic and Political Weekly* 33, no. 52 (September 1998): 50–52.

Saxena, Swati. "Recourse Rage for Witch Hunt Victims in India." Womensenews.org. July 16, 2007 http://womensenews.org/story/the-world/070716/recourse-rare-witch-hunt-victims-in-india, accessed Feb. 17, 2013.

Scarre, Geoffrey. *Witchcraft and Magic in Sixteenth and Seventeenth Century Europe*. London: Macmillan Education, 1987.

Schultz, Pamela D. "Naming, Blaming, and Framing: Moral Panic over Child Molesters and Its Implications for Public Policy." In *Moral Panics over Contemporary Children and Youth*, edited by C. Krinsky, 95–110. Farnham, England: Ashgate, 2008.

Shankar, Irene, and Herbert Northcott. "Through My Son: Immigrant Women Bargain with Patriarchy." *Women's Studies International Forum* 32, no. 6 (November-December 2009): 424–434.

Shihade, Magid. *Not Just a Soccer Game: Colonialism and Conflict among Palestines in Israel*. Syracuse, NY: Syracuse University Press, 2011.

Shukla, Ranjana. "Former Witches and their Next Generations in Awareness Programs." *Jharkhand News (Ranchi), Undated.*

Shuy, R. W. "In-Person Versus Telephone Interviewing." In *Inside Interviewing: New Lenses, New Concerns*, edited by J. A. Holstein and J. F. Gubrium, 175–193. Thousand Oaks, CA: Sage, 2003.

Sieber, Joan E. and Barbara Stanley. "Ethical and Professional Dimensions of Socially Sensitive Research." *American Psychologist* 43, no.1 (January 1988): 49–55.

Singh, Sehjo. *The Woman Betrayed: A Documentary Film, 1990.*

Sinha, Shashank. "In Search of Alternative Histories of 1857: Witch-hunts, Adivasis, and the Uprising in Chotanagpur." In *1857: Essays from the Economic & Political Weekly*. Edited by S. Bandyopadhyay, B. Pati, and D. Chakravarty, 213–225. Hyderabad: Orient Longman and Sameeksha Trust, 2008.

Skaria, Ajay. "Women, Witchcraft and Gratuitous Violence in Colonial Western India." *Past and Present* 155, no. 1 (May 1997a): 109–141.

———. "Shades of Wildness: Tribe, Caste and Gender in Western India." *Journal of Asian Studies* 56, no. 3 (August 1997b): 726–745.

———. *Hybrid Histories: Forests, Frontiers and Wildness in Western India.* New Delhi: Oxford University Press, 1999.

Snow, David. "Framing Processes, Ideology and Discursive Fields." In *The Blackwell Companion to Social Movements*, edited by David A. Snow, Sarah A. Soule and Hanspeter Kriesi, 380–412. Boston: Blackwell, 2005.

Snow, David, and Robert Benford. "Ideology, Frame Resonance, and Participant Mobilization." *International Social Movement Research* 1, no 1. (January 1988): 197–217.

The Statesman. "Family Killed for Witchcraft." *The Statesman* (Kolkata), March 19, 2006.

Stewart, Pamela. J., and Andrew. Strathern. *Witchcraft, Sorcery, Rumors and Gossip*. Cambridge: Cambridge University Press, 2003.

Stinchcombe, Arthur L. *Constructing Social Theories*. New York: Harcourt, Brace and World, 1968.

Straus, Scott. *The Order of Genocide: Race, Power, and War in Rwanda.* Ithaca: Cornell University Press, 2006.

Sudman, Seymour, and Norman M. Bradburn. *Asking Questions: A Practical Guide to Questionnaire Design.* San Francisco: Jossey-Bass, 1982.

Summers, Reverend Montague, trans. *The Malleus Maleficarum of Heinrich Kramer and James Sprenger*. Reprint, New York: Dover, (1486) 1971.

Sundar, Nandini. "Divining Evil: The State and Witchcraft in Bastar." *Gender, Technology and Development* 5, no. 3 (November 2001): 425–448.

Talwar, Anuradha, Debasish Chakraborty, and Sharmishtha Biswas. "Study on Closed and Re-opened Tea Gardens in North Bengal." Paschim Banga Khet Majoor Samity and the International Union of Food, Agriculture, Hotel, Restaurant, Catering, Tobacco, Plantation and Allied Workers' Association (IUF), 2005.

Taussig, Michael T. *The Devil and Commodity Fetishism in South America.* Chapel Hill: University of North Carolina Press, 1980.

*The Telegraph.* "Witch Tag on Neighbor." *The Telegraph* (Kolkata), July18, 2005.

———. "Witch Widow Punished." *The Telegraph* (Kolkata), December 7, 2005.

———. "Arrest over Witch Hunt." *The Telegraph* (Kolkata), April 13, 2006.

———. "Six Land in Net for Killing Family." *The Telegraph* (Kolkata), March 19, 2006.

Thrasher, Frederic M. "The Comics and Delinquency: Cause or Scapegoat." *Journal of Educational Sociology* 23, no. 4 (December 1949): 195–205.

Thompson, Ashley B. "Southern Identity: The Meaning, Practice and Importance of a Regional Identity." PhD Dissertation, Vanderbilt University, 2007.

Tikari, Jeff. *Aroma of Orange Pekoe*. London: Lulu Enterprises, 2010.

Tilly, Charles. *Popular Contention in Great Britain. 1758–1834*. Cambridge, MA: Harvard University Press, 1995.

The Times of India. "Malaria Claims 61 Lives in West Bengal." *Times of India* (Kolkata), July 3, 2006.

Traub, Stuart H., and Craig Little. *Theories of Deviance*. Itasca, IL: F. E. Peacock, 1999.

Valocchi, Steve. "The Emergence of the Integrationist Ideology in the Civil Rights Movement." *Social Problems* 43, no. 1 (February1996): 116–130.

Vidyarthi, Lalita Prasad. "Research on Tribal Culture of India." In *Sociology in India: Retrospect and Prospect*, edited by P. K. B. Nayar, 351–438. Delhi: B R Publishing, 1982.

Warnier, Jeane-Pierre. "L'Economie Politique De La Sorcellerie en Afrique Centrale." *Revue De L'Institut De Sociologie* 3, no. 4 (1988): 259–271.

West, Candace, and Don H. Zimmerman. "Doing Gender." *Gender and Society* 1, no. 2 (June 1987): 125–151.

Weiss, Robert S. *Learning from Strangers: The Art and Method of Qualitative Interview Studies*. New York: The Free Press, 1994.

Willis, Deborah. *Malevolent Nurture: Witch-Hunting and Maternal Power in Early Modern England.* Ithaca, NY: Cornell University Press, 1995.

Women's News Network. "India Law for Witchcraft Accusation Violence Not Protecting Victims." *Women's News Network*, March 15, 2012. http://womennewsnetwork.net/2012/03/15/india-laws-witchcraft-accusation/, accessed February 13, 2013.

Xaxa, Virginius. *Economic Dualism and Structure of Class: A Study in Plantation and Peasant Settings in North Bengal, India.* New Delhi: Cosmo Publications, 1997.

———. "Women and Gender in the Study of Tribes in India." *Indian Journal of Gender Studies* 11, no. 3 (October 2004): 345–367.

Yin, Robert K. *Case Study Research. Design and Methods. Applied Social Science Research Methods Series*, vol. 5, 3rd ed. Thousand Oaks, CA: Sage Publications, 2003.

———. *Application of Case Study Research. Applied Social Science Research Methods Series*, vol. 34, 2d ed. Thousand Oaks, CA: Sage Publications, 2003.

# Index

# About the Author

Soma Chaudhuri is assistant professor of sociology and School of Criminal Justice, at Michigan State University. Her research focuses on violence (collective forms of violence and domestic violence), social movements, gender and witch hunts. She is currently interested in understanding how women's empowerment works at the grassroots and its manifestation through strategies of intervention in cases of domestic violence in Gujarat, India. Chaudhuri's work has appeared in journals such as *American Journal of Sociology*, *Mobilization, Violence Against Women*, and *Comparative Studies of South Asia, Africa and the Middle East.*